JPMorgan's Fall and Revival

D1570508

Nicholas P. Sargen

JPMorgan's Fall and Revival

How the Wave of Consolidation Changed America's Premier Bank

palgrave
macmillan

30984 7596
R

Nicholas P. Sargen
Nicholas Sargen Advisory LLC
Keswick, VA, USA

ISBN 978-3-030-47057-9   ISBN 978-3-030-47058-6   (eBook)
https://doi.org/10.1007/978-3-030-47058-6

This Palgrave Macmillan imprint is published by the registered company Springer Nature Switzerland AG.
The registered company address is: Gewerbestrasse 11, 6330 Cham, Switzerland

Preface

This book is the untold story of how an iconic firm, JPMorgan, battled market forces to preserve its heritage, lost when it was acquired by a rival and then re-emerged as a financial powerhouse. It picks up where Ron Chernow's classic leaves off with Morgan as the pre-eminent bank of the twentieth century.[1] This book depicts the challenges its leaders—Lew Preston and Dennis Weatherstone—confronted when Morgan's business model was disrupted in the early 1980s by the developing country debt crisis and premier corporate borrowers increasingly accessing capital markets.

As Morgan navigated around Glass-Steagall barriers to enter new lines of business, Preston and Weatherstone sought to ensure Morgan would remain a leading wholesale bank serving multinational corporations. Opportunities to grow through acquisition were presented and considered, including purchasing a stake in Citibank in the early 1990s. However, they were reluctant to integrate areas unfamiliar to Morgan such as retail banking or to assimilate cultures that were disparate from the firm's. In doing so, they defied all odds by developing Morgan's capabilities organically, whereas rival institutions expanded via a series of mega-mergers.

This book explores whether Morgan could have stayed independent had its leaders pursued the strategic plan that called for it to make targeted acquisitions in areas such as global custody, asset management and private banking where it had well-established businesses. The plan was to generate a steady revenue stream to help finance the expansion into securities. However, they passed on every opportunity, which left Morgan's earnings heavily dependent on volatile trading revenues.

---

[1] Ron Chernow, *The House of Morgan*, Simon and Schuster Inc., 1990.

When Sandy Warner became CEO in 1995, the tables had turned, and Morgan went from being the hunter to the hunted. Rival banks that had been burdened by bad loans to developing countries and commercial real estate capitalized on rising share prices during the tech boom and wave of leveraged buyouts (LBOs) to acquire other institutions. Meanwhile, Morgan's profits and share price lagged, which left it vulnerable to being acquired. When senior management unveiled a plan to enter the mass affluent market at a gathering of managing directors (MDs) in January 2000, it turned out to be "too little, too late."

I was motivated to write this book after attending a gathering of Morgan alums from around the world in London in July 2018. Many attendees had not seen one another since Morgan merged with Chase in September 2000. As the conversations invariably turned to reminiscing about the "good old days," some contended Morgan's strategy was flawed and they lamented the loss of the culture they cherished.

As I researched the topic, however, it became evident that all of the leading financial institutions struggled to change their business models. In the end, no US money center bank was able to complete the transition to become a universal bank on its own. What ensued was a growing concentration of assets in a handful of financial institutions that was a precursor to the 2008 financial crisis.

In assessing Morgan's strategy, therefore, I examined the sweeping changes in the US banking system. The seminal study was an article published by Brookings in 1995 that depicted the transformation and "long, strange trip" that had occurred from 1979 to 1994.[2] It called the period the "most turbulent in US banking history since the Great Depression" due to record numbers of bank failures and consolidations.

Ten years later, researchers at the Federal Deposit Insurance Corporation (FDIC) updated the Brookings study to cover thrift institutions and commercial banks for the period from end-1984 through 2003.[3] One of the main findings was that forces driving the wave of mergers had changed over time. During the 1980s banks struggled in a turbulent economic environment, and they sought to expand their geographic footprint in retail banking as regulatory barriers came down. By comparison, the mid- to late 1990s was more profitable for financial institutions, and many used their rising share prices to purchase other institutions including non-banks as Glass-Steagall prohibitions were relaxed.

---

[2] Allen N. Berger, Anil K. Kashyap, Joseph M. Scalise, "The Transformation of the U.S. Banking Industry: What a Long, Strange Trip It's Been," *Brookings Papers on Economic Activity*, 2:1995.
[3] Kenneth D. Jones and Tim Critchfield, "Consolidation in the U.S. Banking Industry: Is the 'Long, Strange Trip' About to End?" FDIC Banking Review, February 2005.

Throughout this period there was an extensive debate among economists and policymakers about whether the growing concentration of assets by the largest institutions was desirable. The prevailing view was the US banking system was too fragmented and inefficient, and that consolidation would lead to a more efficient system. However, the evidence from empirical studies was mixed, and several studies sought to examine the impact on lending to individuals and small businesses. In the aftermath of the 2008 financial crisis, the debate has centered on whether the largest institutions have become "Too Big to Fail" and whether they should be broken up.

So, where does Morgan fit into this picture?

My answer is that Morgan stood out as the only financial institution to become a universal bank entirely on its own. In doing so, it sought to maintain its culture and to serve its corporate customers as a fiduciary, rather than become a financial super-market that was bigger and more complex.

While Morgan ultimately fell short of the goal of remaining independent, it did not require federal assistance at any point. The reasons: It had a solid balance sheet, was adept at handling market volatility and was prudently managed. These characteristics would serve the merged bank well during and after the 2008 crisis, when it attracted massive deposits and assets from individuals and corporations seeking a safe haven.

In the end, the foundation was laid for JPMorgan Chase to emerge as the world's pre-eminent financial institution under Jamie Dimon, who successfully integrated wholesale, retail and investment banking. In this regard, Dimon and his team have been able to accomplish what others in the banking industry strived for but fell short. Still, while Morgan alums today are proud of the firm's revival, many cling to the days when "Morgan was Morgan" and had a unique culture they cherished.

This book is organized in four parts. The first part, "Glory Days," presents a first-hand account of what Morgan was like in the late 1970s, as well as the developing country debt crisis in 1982 that disrupted Morgan's business model. The second, "Formulating the Plan," depicts the strategy that was developed in the second half of the 1980s to transform Morgan into a universal bank with investment banking and securities capabilities. The third, "Executing the Plan," describes the successes and challenges implementing the strategic plan in the first half of the 1990s. The fourth, "Playing Defense," depicts the events leading to Morgan being acquired by Chase. The final chapter focuses on the issue of "Why Morgan Matters" and Morgan's revival under Jamie Dimon.

This book is a personal account of what occurred while I worked at Morgan on two separate occasions: 1978–83 when it became embroiled in the Less

Developed Country debt crisis and 1995–mid-2003 when it merged with Chase. In the interim, I observed Morgan's transformation as a competitor and client at Salomon Brothers and Prudential Insurance. In writing this book I interviewed former colleagues and senior executives at Morgan to gain their perspectives, and I also gained access to materials relating to plans to reorient the bank. While I am grateful for their assistance, they are not responsible for the content or conclusions.

Keswick, VA, USA   Nicholas P. Sargen
March 2020

Acknowledgments

This book is a tribute to a unique institution, JPMorgan, and the people who made it special. While Morgan has been at the forefront of global finance for well over a century, little is known about how it was transformed to become a universal bank in the 1980s–90s and the events leading to it being acquired at the turn of the century. The topic came to mind when I left Morgan in 2003. I sent the initial chapters to Susan Bell and am grateful for her encouragement, but wound up putting this book on hold due to work responsibilities.

Over the years, my interest in Morgan was rekindled at annual gatherings with a group of close friends—Shom Bhattacharya, Scott Nycum, Lee Thistlethwaite and Bill Vogt. During these occasions we reminisced about Morgan and shared tales about our experiences and colleagues. John Olds, who headed Asia-Pacific in the 1980s and went on to oversee the bank's return to the securities business, assembled a strong team in the Private Bank in the mid-1990s while laying the foundation for its revival.

The decision to resume writing the book was made at a London gathering in July 2018 to celebrate Lee Thistlethwaite's seventieth birthday. The attendees included Morgan alums from five continents, many of whom spent their entire careers at the firm. What was particularly striking was the common bond we felt. When I mentioned writing a book to Scott Nycum, he urged me to do so because of my background in economics and finance and prior books I had written.

As I undertook the project, my goal was to present an objective portrayal of what happened to Morgan. In addition to those cited previously, I interviewed other senior executives and colleagues to get their perspectives. Contributions from Frank Arisman, the late Rimmer de Vries, Ramon de Oliveira, Phil DiIorio, John Gent, Owen Harper, Jamie Higgins, David Kelso, David

Lawrence, Zung Ngyuen, Susan Restler and Richard Zimmerman are included in this book. I also received insights about the Chase-Morgan merger from John Lipsky, who served as chief economist for Chase and JPMorgan Chase.

As I researched Morgan's transformation, I soon realized all major financial institutions adapted to changes in the regulatory environment that led to a wave of bank consolidations. I am grateful to Robert Z. Aliber, emeritus professor at the University of Chicago's Booth School of Business, and to my former boss, Dr. Henry Kaufman, for their perspectives. Professors Richard Sylla and Ingo Walter of the New York University's School Stern of Business also provided useful feedback.

I also wish to thank my editors at Palgrave Macmillan, Tula Weis and Lucy Kidwell, for their assistance, and Kathy Louden for preparing the manuscript. Judith Bishop provided careful editing of the manuscript and helpful suggestions even as she was writing a book of her own.

Finally, this book is dedicated to my four sons and their families. Hopefully, one day they will share it with my grandchildren when they ask, "What did grandpa do?"

Contents

List of Figures

List of Tables

Part I

Glory Days

1

23 Wall Street

"There it is. The number 23 engraved in stone. No name. It must be the Morgan Guaranty Trust Company." My first thoughts as I arrived for a job interview in the autumn of 1977, after I was contacted by a recruiter from Russell Reynolds about an opening in Morgan.

Being interested in US history, I was immediately struck by the significance of the setting. The House of Morgan formed the apex of a triangle that was flanked on one side by Federal Hall, where George Washington was inaugurated as president of the United States, and on the other by the New York Stock Exchange. This seemed fitting for a firm that financed governments and corporations and which had been considered the de facto central bank of the United States prior to the creation of the Federal Reserve (the Fed) in 1914. (See Box about 23 Wall Street at the end of this chapter.)

Once the door opened, one left the United States and entered a completely different world, one more European and cosmopolitan. The room was enormous, half a street block in one direction and a quarter in the other. Pristine white marble was everywhere—floors and walls—with rich, green brocade panels on the walls providing contrast. Looking up at the three-story ceiling there was an enormous crystal chandelier that hung in the middle of the lobby. "Must be Old World charm." I certainly hadn't seen anything like it on the West Coast.

The atmosphere was eerie. Rows of bankers sat behind luxurious roll-top desks in three distinct areas that were separated by marble railings. Some were talking with their colleagues; yet you couldn't hear a sound. Even more amazing, there didn't appear to be any customers. "What type of bank is this anyway?"

© The Author(s) 2020
N. P. Sargen, *JPMorgan's Fall and Revival*, https://doi.org/10.1007/978-3-030-47058-6_1

All of this made me apprehensive. Morgan, after all, had the reputation of being the bank for the world's elite and an exclusive club for its employees. Its chairman and CEO Elmore "Pat" Patterson attended the University of Chicago, where he was captain of the football team. He was chosen to head the general banking division following the merger of Morgan with the Guaranty Trust Company in 1959, and he subsequently served as the head of the firm from 1972 to 1977.

Patterson played the dual role of many of his predecessors—first overseeing the bank while also playing a leadership role in ensuring the safety and soundness of the financial system. During the New York City financial troubles of the mid-1970s, he was instrumental in shaping the financial community's response along with David Rockefeller of Chase Manhattan and Walter Wriston of First National City (later Citibank).

Morgan Guaranty's president, Walter Hines Page, came from a prominent family, in which his father served as Ambassador to Great Britain. He also married the grand-daughter of J.P. Morgan and was the last partner to serve with him. Page's background included extensive international experience. During the 1960s he helped set up Morgan's offices in Frankfurt, Rome and Tokyo. Then, following the first oil shock in the early 1970s, he helped devise a plan for the creation of Saudi International Bank, and he maintained close ties with the Saudi Arabia Monetary Authority (SAMA), the country's central bank. By the time of my interview, it was announced that Page would replace Patterson as chairman and CEO and Lewis T. Preston would become president.

Considering the pedigree of Morgan's leaders and senior managers, I wondered whether I would fit into such a prestigious organization given my modest roots. Before accepting the interview I solicited the advice of Robert Aliber, a renowned professor of international finance, who was a visiting scholar at the San Francisco Fed while on leave from the University of Chicago's business school. Bob encouraged me to seek out the opportunity, as he thought very highly of Morgan and its people.

To reach the point of being considered for a position in the International Economics Department, I first had to clear two hurdles—an intelligence test and a personality profile. Taking the tests first thing in the morning was tough, as I had been wined and dined by a headhunter the previous night and was suffering from a bad case of West Coast jet lag. When I had difficulty answering the first five questions on the test, I started to panic. How humiliating—a Stanford Ph.D. who flunked a routine test of math and verbal skills! Oh well, at least I made it through twenty years of school and six years of government experience before being exposed.

I managed to calm myself after answering the next few questions and began to get back into my old test taking rhythm. By the time the psychology test came, I was in full stride and ready to outsmart the evaluators. One question asked how you would react if you found a bird on the ground with a broken wing. I rejected the two extreme answers: (1) put the bird out of its misery and (2) feel melancholy, but don't touch it. I opted to help the bird, which was the safe answer I thought a corporation would want.

After finishing the tests, there was a round of interviews. The first was with Dennis Weatherstone, the treasurer of the company. A short gentleman with a trace of a British accent greeted me in the reception area and escorted me to the treasurer's office. I presumed he was an administrative aide because he was very genial and unassuming. I soon realized my mistake, however, when he sat behind the desk.

I came away from the interview not only taken by Weatherstone's hospitality, but also with his intelligence and market savvy. Bob Aliber had told me Weatherstone was one of the most astute currency traders in the business, and he lived up to those high expectations.

Prior to becoming treasurer, Weatherstone headed the foreign exchange area of the firm, and most of our conversation was spent discussing exchange rate issues. I subsequently learned from others how he was admired as a British version of Horatio Alger. Weatherstone began his career as a clerk in the London office in the late 1940s and became a foreign exchange trader after receiving one of the highest scores in an exam. He subsequently became one of the firm's most successful traders and was appointed to head the area by Lewis T. Preston, who ran the London office in the mid-1960s. Thereafter, Weatherstone's career tracked Preston's closely. This was reassuring to me, as it provided concrete evidence that you did not have to be a blue-blood to be successful at Morgan.

My next interview was with Bruce Brackenridge, who headed the administration division and previously served as the senior credit officer for the bank. Brackenridge, who was a classmate of Bob Aliber at Williams College, asked me about him and we exchanged pleasantries. The conversation then turned to Morgan's involvement in lending to governments of developing countries. He was excited about their prospects and Morgan's role in financing them, and he drew parallels with the role British entities played in financing US railroads in the mid-nineteenth century. He then asked about my work in developing a risk appraisal system for assessing country credits at the US Treasury and the San Francisco Fed. At the end of the conversation he mentioned that I was being considered for a similar role at the bank.

The next stop was with Jack Noyes, Morgan's chief economist. Prior to joining Morgan, Noyes headed the Research Division of the Board of Governors of the Federal Reserve System. It was reassuring that someone with such a prominent position at the Fed would be willing to give it up to head economic research at Morgan. After Noyes compared Morgan and the Fed, I felt more comfortable about the transition I was contemplating.

Noyes oversaw the bank's publication, *The Morgan Guaranty Survey*, which was edited by Milton Hudson and widely followed in the financial community and by policymakers. When I asked about his views on the US economy, he gave a very balanced response: On one hand, the economy was growing at a healthy clip; on the other hand, inflation was showing signs of accelerating, which was a problem. Later, a Morgan employee told me my first Wall Street joke about two-handed economists: Noyes' name really meant NoYes—get it? I got it.

The most memorable part of the interview occurred at the end, when Noyes showed me the chartroom where Morgan's economists conducted briefings for clients. Once he turned on the lights, I was overwhelmed by how ultramodern the room was. My first impression was that it was small movie theater, with plush seats and carpet that were a shade of "bordello purple." The two side walls were filled with lighted panels that displayed charts of US and international economic indicators, and additional slides were displayed on a screen next to the podium. Noyes mentioned that bankers liked to bring clients to the room to impress them about Morgan's state-of-the-art coverage of the global economies and financial markets.

The climax of the day was my meeting with the head of the International Economics Department and my prospective boss, Rimmer de Vries. As the editor of *World Financial Markets* (WFM), Morgan's flagship publication, Rimmer was the best-known international economist on Wall Street. An interview with the *New York Times* about the fallout from the second oil shock described him as follows:

> One of the most knowledgeable analysts of the international financial scene is Rimmer de Vries, senior vice president and chief international economist for the Morgan Guaranty Trust Company. Mr. DeVries, a crusty Dutch-born economist, is frequently sought out by United States Government officials and central bankers around the world. Morgan's monthly World Financial Markets produced under his guidance, is considered one of the most authoritative publications on international finance in the country. Mr. DeVries, like many others, is worried.[1]

---

[1] "Talking Business with Rimmer de Vries of Morgan Guaranty," Nov. 15, 1979.

I read WFM regularly while I was at the Treasury and Fed and was impressed by how informative and influential it was. The idea that I could contribute to a publication that was read by officials, business leaders and academics around the world definitely appealed.

The interview with Rimmer was different from the others. His office was at the end of a long corridor that was flanked by two rows of economists who sat behind elegant desks. No one spoke as I passed by, and it seemed as if I was back in Europe again. Suddenly, a voice from the back boomed, DAVID!!! and one of the economists went scurrying in to the office.

When I arrived at the door, a lanky Dutchman greeted me and introduced me to his colleagues, who were making final edits for the next issue of WFM. Rimmer explained the issue would discuss the worsening US trade situation and its implications for the dollar. He said he was concerned that the dollar was likely to depreciate significantly if US policymakers did not heed warning signs about impending inflation.

When Rimmer asked what my views were, I was unsure if he wanted to know what I really thought, or if he was fishing for information about what the Fed believed. He had a reputation for being able to get information out of officials, even when they did not intend to disclose it. I decided to play it safe and gave him the official party line. I answered that the dollar was not a major risk, because inflation was under control and overseas investors were still eager to provide financing for the US trade deficit. My own personal view was that inflation was beginning to heat up and interest rates were about to rise; hence I had refinanced my mortgage.

Rimmer next asked several questions about my personal background. I mentioned that my father was a Greek immigrant, and he asked if I was raised Greek Orthodox. (That was permissible then.) I told him I resisted learning Greek in my youth, and that my parents sent me to a near-by Lutheran grammar school. Rimmer seemed pleased by this, as the Lutheran Church and Dutch Reformed Church, of which he was an elder, followed similar precepts. The next question caught me off guard, "Were the children being raised Lutheran?" "No, my wife's Episcopalian," I answered. I could see the disappointment on his face.

Just when I thought I failed the final screen, Rimmer burst into spontaneous laughter. He held out his hand and indicated he would make me a formal offer if I was interested. I told him I was definitely interested in the job, but my wife, Susan, and I were both from the West and were nervous about moving to the New York area. The headhunter who contacted me about the position suggested I consider living in northern New Jersey, because of its easy access to Wall Street by train. However, based on jokes I heard about the state, I wasn't sure about raising a family there.

Rimmer seized on this, inviting me to visit his home in Oldwick, New Jersey, before I returned to the West Coast. He explained the town had been established by Dutch settlers 200 years ago and retained its original charm. I took him up on the offer, as I was curious to see what New Jersey was really like.

Upon arriving at his farm the next day, Rimmer was tilling his garden in the rain wearing wooden Dutch shoes. He mentioned that he had enough acreage cultivated to feed his family, as well as to sell produce to his neighbors and Morgan colleagues, for which he charged a reasonable price. After visiting with him, I came away impressed that Wall Street's top international economist could literally be so down to earth.

On my flight back to the West Coast, the fun part of the job search was over—flying to New York, being wined and dined and meeting interesting people. The hard part—deciding what to do—was just beginning. And I would have to give Morgan my answer in just two weeks.

Given my training in economics, I started by listing the pluses and minuses of taking the job and moving my family to New York. However, it was a futile exercise. The decision was really about choosing a career or a lifestyle. If it was simply a matter of picking the best paying job or the one with the best opportunity for advancement, Morgan was the clear choice. But my wife and I were both born and raised in the West, our families and friends were there, and Wall Street was a completely different world from the one we knew and liked.

When I told my colleagues at the San Francisco Fed about the offer, they were happy for me, but also raised another doubt. Was I ready to give up a career in economic research to become a "business economist"? Within the economics profession, the pecking order in terms of prestige was academics first, government second and business last. Was I ready to sink that low within my own profession?

My wife and I decided to visit her family in the Lake Tahoe area on the final weekend. The setting was spectacular—glorious Indian summer weather with cloudless blue skies, turquoise water, green pine trees. What more could anyone want in life?

As we headed off for the Bay Area, my wife's family looked at us sadly, realizing this could be the last time they could be close to us and their grandchildren. While I was driving, my stomach tightened, as I had less than 24 hours to go and still couldn't decide.

When we arrived home, I told my wife the decision was impossible; therefore, we should therefore let fate decide. I would toss a quarter, and we would go east if it came up tails and stay in the west if it was heads. When the toss came up tails, we agreed to make it two out of three. The second toss was heads. On the third throw, the coin spun endlessly on the hardwood floor, before finally settling on its edge in the corner of the room. What now???

Just when the situation seemed hopeless, I realized I needed outside counsel. I decided to contact Bob Aliber for his advice. When I spoke to Bob, I asked him to help me resolve the dilemma of choosing between career and lifestyle. "Easy—Nick, you're too young to retire." Put that way, the decision suddenly seemed obvious, and the knot in my stomach began to go away. The next morning, I called Morgan and accepted the offer.

Box: Background on "The Corner"

Owing to the popularity of Morgan's history, three retired officers-directors who played key roles at the bank from the 1920s assembled their recollections in a manuscript titled *Some Comments About The Morgan Bank* that was originally published in September 1979.[2] The manuscript contains a brief history of Morgan, and it also includes an Epilogue titled "The Corner" about the significance of 23 Wall Street location.

The building was completed in 1914, the year after the bank's founder, the elder J.P. Morgan, died. The cornerstone contains a copper box that includes a copy of the firm's articles of partnership, sample forms used for issuing travelers' letters of credit and a copy of the founder's will, in which he bequeathed one year's salary to each member of its staff. It also includes a copy of J.P. Morgan's testimony in 1912 to the Pujo Committee. It was formed to investigate the so-called money trust, a community of Wall Street bankers and financiers that exerted powerful control over the nation's finances.

What the cornerstone also contains, but is not mentioned in the commentary, is J.P. Morgan's motivation for building its headquarters on the historic corner opposite the New York Stock Exchange and Federal Hall. By constructing an edifice that is much smaller than surrounding buildings, he let clients know in a subtle way that he could afford to do so, and their money was in safe hands.

One of the most memorable events occurred on September 16, 1920. At noon when lunchtime crowds were crowding the streets, a huge bomb exploded in Wall Street next to the bank's headquarters, in which thirty people were killed and hundreds wounded. The police subsequently determined that a massive charge of TNT had been detonated in a horse-drawn wagon. The dents in the blocks of Tennessee marble on the Wall Street side of "The Corner" remains as a testimony to the power of the blast. While it was a premeditated crime that some attributed to "Bolsheviks," the mystery of who committed it and why was never solved.

---

[2] The authors are Longstreet Hinton, who joined the bank in 1923 and who went on to build its Trust Department, John M. Meyer, Jr., who began his career at the bank in 1927 and went on to be a revered chairman in 1969, and Thomas Rudd, who arrived in 1935 and became a senior officer.

2

A Private Club

As I headed for my first day of work on Wall Street at the start of 1978, I had overcome most of my angst about leaving the West Coast for life in the Big Apple. I also was comfortable about joining the House of Morgan. When I told family members and friends about my decision, they assured me that Morgan was the best bank in the world and "a class act."

I knew the history of Julius Pierpont Morgan and his involvement in financing American railroads and shaping the steel industry in the second half of the nineteenth century. What really fascinated me, however, was the role the House of Morgan played as a financial advisor to governments and as a quasi-central bank. In 1907, J.P. Morgan rescued the US financial system when he organized a consortium of US banks to provide financing to halt a run on several prominent trust banks and to provide liquidity to several key brokerage houses.[1] Seventy years later, government officials still sought the firm's counsel: A bank examiner at the San Francisco Fed told me the chairman of Morgan always received the first call from the Federal Reserve when problems arose in the financial system.

Aside from these accounts, I knew relatively little about what it was like to work for Morgan. I later realized this partly stemmed from the bank's aversion to any publicity. J.P. Morgan allegedly decided against putting the firm's name on its headquarters, because he believed anyone who didn't know the location shouldn't be a client. Nor did the firm advertise to gain new clients or business. Employees were allowed to speak to the press if they received prior

---

[1] See Robert F. Bruner, Sean D. Carr, *The Panic of 1907: Lessons Learned from the Market's Perfect Storm*, Wiley, 2007.

© The Author(s) 2020
N. P. Sargen, *JPMorgan's Fall and Revival*, https://doi.org/10.1007/978-3-030-47058-6_2

clearance, but they were discouraged from being quoted. The principal exception was Rimmer de Vries, who was cited extensively in the press on international economic and financial issues.

I was not alone. In his prologue to *The House of Morgan*, Ron Chernow observed:[2]

> While people know the Morgan houses by name, they are often mystified by their businesses. They practice a brand of banking that has little resemblance to standard retail banking. These banks have no teller cages, issue no consumer loans, and grant no mortgages. Rather, they perpetuate an ancient European tradition of wholesale banking, serving governments, large corporations, and rich individuals. As practitioners of high finance they cultivate a discreet style. They avoid branches, seldom hang out signposts, and (until recently) wouldn't advertise. Their strategy was to make their clients feel accepted into a private club, as if a Morgan account were a membership card to the aristocracy.

As I approached the employees' entrance on 15 Broad Street, I wondered what it would really be like to work for such a unique firm. Could Morgan really live up to its reputation or would its image prove to be better than reality?

Over the next six years, I learned that one of the keys to the success of the House of Morgan was the firm's ability to make its employees feel they, too, were members of a special club. This impression was planted on the first day of work, when employees learned about the firm's storied history and the importance it attached to core values such as integrity, respect and teamwork. The firm's motto, "First-class business in a first class way," was engrained in each employee from the very beginning of the tenure. It was actually delivered by J.P. Morgan, Jr., to Congress in 1933, when banks were under attack for contributing to the financial crisis that led to the Great Depression. In defending Morgan, he stated:[3]

> If I may be permitted to speak of the firm of which I have the honor to be the senior partner, I should state that at all times the idea of doing only first-class business, and that in a first-class way, has been before our minds. We have never been satisfied with simply keeping within the law, but have constantly sought to act that we might fully observe the professional code, and to maintain the credit and reputation which has been handed down to us from predecessors in the firm.

---

[2] Chernow, op. cit., p. xiii.
[3] JP Morgan Chase & Co., "The History of JP Morgan Chase & Co.," p. 11.

These core values were reinforced by a code of behavior that was ingrained in college recruits who were assigned to the firm's elite training program. As the trainees rose through the corporate ranks, they invariably identified themselves with their class and bonded with other members of their program. Because most trainees regarded the program as the equivalent of an on-the-job MBA, they had little reason to attend business school or to seek a higher paying job elsewhere.

My own situation was different from the typical college recruit: As a mid-career hire and professional economist I did not participate in the training program. Nonetheless, my colleagues and I still felt a sense of pride as members of the International Economics Department, because the department was highly respected within the firm. My "classmates" were the other international economists in the department. We sat together in two rows, with the seating determined by the economist's title, whether vice president, associate economist (equivalent to an assistant vice president) or assistant economist. Rimmer de Vries, as head of the department, occupied the only office at the end of the room.

It took a while to get used to our bullpen area, which seemed quieter than most libraries. I had to lower my voice when speaking on the telephone or with colleagues. Only Rimmer was exempt from this practice, as he would holler our names from his office when he summoned us. Other customs were easier to observe, even though some were definitely quaint. Officers of the bank, for example, always wore their suit coats whenever they left their work area, even for visits to the restrooms.

One of the most revered traditions was the provision of a free lunch for the employees. This practice allegedly was initiated by J.P. Morgan himself, as a means of discouraging employees from drinking at lunch. (J.P. Morgan favored prohibition and his will stipulated that there be no drinking on the premises.) While every employee received a free lunch, the officers—which included all professionals with the title of assistant vice president or higher—were served a superb meal replete with a selection of cigars at the end. For someone who never belonged to a country club, I couldn't imagine a better way to combine outstanding cuisine with interesting company.

The lunch in the Officer's Dining Room helped foster a high degree of camaraderie. The standard practice in our group was for the economists to congregate by the Reuters ticker, where we would scan the tape to see what was happening in the markets, before heading for lunch. In those days there were no computer screens or monitors. During the meal, we would compare notes on our various assignments and also socialize with one another. The luncheon usually lasted a full hour and consisted of a five-course meal beginning with choice of soup (including vichyssoise) and concluding with a selection of cigars.

The close of the business day for our group was largely dictated by train schedules. Rimmer had the furthest commute and was the first to leave shortly after 5 p.m. Norman Klath, who lived in Princeton and was the second in command in our department, was the next to leave. I could usually leave soon after them and be home in time to have dinner with my family. After all my worries that Wall Street would change my life irreparably, I was pleasantly surprised that my workday was not much longer than when I was in government. I would usually put in several hours of reading or writing at home, but still had time to enjoy my family before my wife and I put the children to bed.

While Morgan's traditions helped instill a bond among the employees, the pride they felt about the firm ultimately reflected a belief that they were contributing to its success. In the late 1970s, the Morgan Guaranty Trust Company had about 8000 employees in total, of which about 10% were officers. It seemed more intimate, however, because most employees were stationed in three locales, the New York headquarters, London and Tokyo. Junior officers also had frequent contact with division heads and occasional interaction with the most senior members of the firm.

While I was initially lured to Morgan by its research publications, I soon realized that our department's ties to the international banking and treasury divisions made it an integral part of Morgan's business. This active involvement also differentiated Morgan from most other banks that primarily used economists in a marketing role.

Our department was also well positioned for serving areas where the firm was expanding. Morgan's international lending operations surged in the wake of the 1973–74 oil shock, when oil exporting countries in the Middle East placed huge deposits with US multinational banks such as Morgan, Citibank, Chase and Bank of America. The international banks, in turn, recycled so-called petro-dollars by extending loans to oil-importing countries, especially those in Latin America and Asia. By the late 1970s, the international area accounted for one half of Morgan's total revenues, and it was expanding much more rapidly than the domestic side.

One of the principal functions in the International Economics Department was to monitor and forecast economic developments in countries where Morgan had exposure. Our group worked closely with the bank's senior credit officers to set limits for borrowing countries' exposures. Within our department two individuals—Norman Klath and Hargreaves, who was a senior editor for WFM—oversaw the analyses of the respective country economists. They were responsible for creating the framework and developing the data systems for assessing country credit risk. We believed the system was among the best of any bank, but it was not full proof if there were unanticipated developments.

One of my responsibilities was to head a team of economists covering countries in Asia and the Pacific Rim. In this capacity, I worked closely with bankers who covered Japanese banks and corporations, as well as those responsible for loans to sovereign entities and companies in other parts of the region. I had followed the Pacific Rim economies in my previous job at the Federal Reserve, but did not speak Japanese or Chinese. Consequently, I hired two very capable Ph.D. economists, Jai-Hoon Yang and Ching-mai Wu, who did. Jai was fluent in Korean and Japanese and focused on North Asia, while Ching-mai concentrated on China and Southeast Asia. I assumed primary responsibility for Australia and New Zealand—both countries where Morgan has long-standing relations.

One of my biggest assignments in the first year was to develop an "early warning system" to detect potential country default situations. This area was one in which the US government actually was ahead of the banks, because until the 1970s most loans that had been extended to sovereign borrowers were from the public sector. During my tenure at the US Treasury and the Federal Reserve, I helped develop a model for assessing country credit risks, which I refined at Morgan.

The model we deployed recognized that most defaults (or debt reschedulings) follow a fairly typical pattern. The risk of default usually increases when a country pursues highly inflationary policies and its currency is fixed to the US dollar or another reserve currency. Such policies often result in large trade and current account deficits that can be sustained only as long as the country is able to borrow from abroad. Once lenders became reluctant to extend new loans, however, the debtor country increasingly must draw upon its foreign exchange reserves to cover the imbalance.

Debt crises typically occur when the country depletes its foreign exchange reserves and is forced to devalue its currency. At that point, the International Monetary Fund (IMF) and World Bank are called in by the creditor governments to stipulate policies the debtor country must follow in return for having its debt restructured.

While banks such as Morgan understood the conditions that gave rise to country defaults, the ability of banks and other creditors to detect potential default situations in advance was hampered by a lack of timely, comprehensive data on external debt. In the 1970s, the main source of data on external debt was from the World Bank, but it only covered borrowings from public sources, and the data were two years out of date. Morgan's international economists helped fill the gaps in information by gathering data on loans to countries from commercial banks and other private sources. Our international economists were also responsible for projecting countries' borrowing requirements and for assessing how easily they could service their interest payments out of export revenues.

During 1978, Morgan's country risk framework did not signal any immediate problems looming for developing countries. Oil-importing counties benefited from falling oil prices, and primary-producing countries enjoyed strong export growth, as the industrial countries were growing rapidly and prices of most commodities were rising. As a result, the external deficits of many developing countries were well below their peak levels in 1974–75, and their ability to service interest payments out of export revenues was improving. This also meant that international banks such as Morgan were eager to lend to the developing countries, and Morgan's international economists gave the bankers the green light to do so.

At the same time, economic conditions in the United States were deteriorating. Many of the concerns Rimmer de Vries expressed in my job interview about the potential for a dollar crisis proved prescient, as the dollar depreciated steadily against the Japanese yen and European currencies in 1978. US inflation accelerated and both the US trade and current account deficits increased steadily.

Amid these developments, Morgan's international economists worked closely with the Treasury Division and Foreign Exchange Advisory Group of the bank to alert our traders and clients about the risks of higher US interest rates and a falling dollar. I participated in the weekly meetings that were run by Frank Arisman. Morgan's head of foreign exchange, Kurt Viermetz, was also a regular attendee. My responsibilities included briefing the group on key international developments and their implications for currency markets. Our department also produced a monthly publication that contained our views on foreign countries and currency forecasts, which was sold to corporate customers that had multinational operations.

In addition, we worked closely with International Financial Management (IFM) that was headed by Roberto Mendoza, who was widely regarded as a whiz kid with a very bright future. His unit advised multinational corporations on highly sophisticated transactions and where they could obtain the cheapest financing worldwide. Normally corporate treasurers would be inclined to borrow in countries such as Switzerland and Germany, where interest rates were the lowest. However, our assessment was that this strategy could backfire, because the appreciation of the Swiss franc and deutsche mark against the dollar was likely to exceed the difference in interest rates with the United States.

Another group I worked closely with was the unit that advised central bankers on economic and market developments. It was run by John Arnold, who had extensive contacts among central banks, and he hosted annual training sessions for representatives from the various institutions. I met several officials who eventually rose to become heads of their central banks or treasuries at these sessions.

In the *World Financial Markets* articles we wrote about the dollar in 1978, however, Rimmer's target audience were US officials. We believed the greatest risk the United States faced was a resurgence of inflation, and we were critical of the expansionary fiscal policy the Carter administration pursued and the very gradualist monetary tightening by the Federal Reserve. We also maintained the US Treasury's policy of favoring a weak dollar to support US exporters was misguided. We advocated that US economic policy should be geared to control inflation through tighter monetary and fiscal policies and that low inflation would enable US businesses to compete internationally.

It was not obvious that US policymakers heeded our advice. However, we felt gratified in November, when the US Treasury shifted its policy stance to support the dollar. To help convince investors of its new commitment, the Treasury issued bonds denominated in foreign currencies, the proceeds of which could be used to intervene in the currency markets. Still, we were not convinced this action would halt the dollar's slide, because the Fed continued to follow a gradualist approach to monetary tightening and fiscal policy remained expansionary.

As my first year drew to a close, I nonetheless was proud of our department's accomplishments and the firm's performance. My colleagues and I celebrated these achievements with our spouses at a gala Christmas party in the main room of 23 Wall Street. The room was decorated to the hilt for the occasion, and for the first time in my Morgan career, wine was served along with a sumptuous buffet. The Chairman, Walter Page, concluded the festivities by announcing he would retire in the coming year, and that Lew Preston would assume the helm in the fall of 1979. Preston's role as president would be filled by Rod Lindsay, a first rate banker who was also the brother of former New York City mayor, John Lindsay. These changes at the top paved the way for Dennis Weatherstone, who was a strong advocate of our department, to become chairman of the Executive Committee. This move put him in position to one day succeed Lew Preston as chairman and CEO.

As my wife and I left the party, we felt like members of a royal family dining in a European palace. We both thought, "It doesn't get much better than this."

Box: The Morgan Creed and Training Program

The Congressional testimony that J.P. Morgan, Jr., the son of the founder, gave in 1933 contained more than the pithy phrase about "doing first-class business in a first class way" that became the bank's code of behavior. It also spelled out Morgan's views about the duties and uses of bankers. His testimony began with the following statement:

> The banker is a member of a profession practiced since the middle ages. There has grown up a code of professional ethics and customs, on the observance of which depend his reputation, his fortune, and his usefulness to the community in which he works.

He then went on to acknowledge that some bankers are not observant of this code as they should be. However, the banker who disregards this code will sacrifice his credit:

> This credit is his most valuable possession; it is the result of years of fair and honorable dealing, and while it may be quickly lost, once lost cannot be restored for a long time.

This code of behavior was adhered to decades before the bank hired compliance officers to ensure employees followed the letter of the law. It was instilled in employees through the bank's training program, which was established shortly after J.P. Morgan, Jr., gave his congressional testimony. The emphasis was placed on training people, including the sharing of experience, to develop "their ability, character and loyalty in that 'juniors' could be elevated to positions of greater authority and responsibility." The over-riding message was "to know your bank and know your customer" and to guard with care the bank's reputation for fair dealing, candor and integrity.

The Morgan pamphlet notes that prior to World War II, trainees attired in the then mandated stiff collar, began their careers working in the mail room as a runner, proofreader and letter press boy. Among the most famous trainees were the Rt. Honorable Earl of Cromer and Thomas Gates, who served as Secretary of Defense in the Eisenhower administration and who returned to Morgan to become chairman and CEO in the mid-1960s.

3

Preston in Charge

As 1979 began, my colleagues and I wondered what Morgan would be like under Lew Preston and what direction he would take the firm. From the outset it was clear he was a strong, decisive leader whose profile mirrored previous Morgan Chairmen and CEOs very well.

Preston was born in New York City on August 5, 1926, the son of a prestigious family that first arrived in America in the seventeenth century. By the time of the Revolutionary War the Prestons were well established in Virginia.[1] Lew grew up in New York and Paris and was raised in part by the Harriman family after his father's untimely death and his mother's subsequent poor health. After graduating from St. Paul's School in Concord, New Hampshire, like many other Morgan men before and during his time. He enlisted as a private in the Marine Corps even though he had been accepted at Harvard. By the time his basic training concluded, the Japanese had surrendered; consequently, Preston was sent to China to protect Gerneralissimo Chiang Kai-Shek's rail lines from Mao Tse-Tung's guerillas.

After leaving the Marines, Preston entered Harvard, where he captained the ice hockey team.[2] Upon graduation in 1951, he joined Morgan, and after an initial period of training, he worked in the National Division covering the oil sector. Coming from a family that had invested in Texas oil drilling, Preston

---

[1] Preston's ancestors settled into their new home at Smithfield plantation in 1774 and had twelve children. Their offspring founded Virginia Military Institute (adjacent to Smithfield) in 1836 and also had ties with the University of Virginia.

[2] The retrospective published by his colleagues at the World Bank after his death indicates he was a member of the US Olympic squad in 1952, but there is no record of this.

© The Author(s) 2020

N. P. Sargen, *JPMorgan's Fall and Revival*, https://doi.org/10.1007/978-3-030-47058-6_3

had always been interested in commodities and markets, traits that were evident from his earliest days as a banker.

In certain respects, Preston's background was similar to Morgan's former chairman and CEO, Pat Patterson, a University of Chicago alum who played football. However, Preston was considered to be less genteel, and as a former Marine, he could be blunt and tough at times. Some reportedly called him a drill-sergeant in a pin-stripe suit, and he was the only person in the firm who ever intimidated my boss, Rimmer de Vries.

It was readily apparent to Morgan's rank and file employees that Preston had excellent credentials for running the bank: He had an extensive background in both domestic lending and international banking and finance. Following the sudden death of Don Atkin from brain cancer in 1966, Preston was assigned as a vice president to succeed him as head of Morgan's London office, a traditional stepping stone to higher levels at the bank. A roster of London Office heads before and after Preston's time there included Danny Davison (son of a JPMorgan partner), Rod Lindsay (who went on to serve as president of Morgan Guaranty), Bob Engel (who became treasurer and executive vice president (EVP) and Douglas "Sandy" Warner (who became chairman and CEO in 1995)).

Beginning in the late 1950s, when European currency convertibility was re-established, leading US companies began to expand their overseas operations in Europe. The outflux created increasing demands for banking and other services from the financial institutions that had served them. Foremost among them were the large money center banks headquartered in New York City.

By the early 1960s, US banks found added impetus to expand operations in London and other financial centers in Europe owing to US balance-of-payments problems. In 1963 the US government imposed a federal tax of 15% on interest received from foreign borrowers. The interest equalization tax (IET) was intended to diminish capital outflows by making it more expensive for foreign borrowers to raise funds in the United States. However, its actual effect was to stimulate development of the Eurodollar market by driving dollar-based financing activity to London and other international financial centers.

On the day that President Kennedy proposed the IET, Henry Clay Alexander, chairman of Morgan Guaranty, told the bank's officers, "This is a day that you will remember forever. It will change the face of American banking and force all the business off to London."[3] The IET was then followed in

[3] Chernow, op. cit., p. 544.

1965 by a Voluntary Foreign Credit Restraint Program that the Johnson administration implemented and a Foreign Direct Investment Program designed to limit US corporations' exports of capital to finance their foreign expansion.

By the time Preston arrived in London in 1966, Dennis Weatherstone was a key figure in the trading room and a bit of a legend as a currency trader. One of Preston's first achievements was to persuade the bank's management in the mid-1960s that, having acquired the Guaranty Trust Company, it should trade in the new and rapidly growing, but still relatively unknown, Eurocurrency market. It became increasingly important in the second half of the 1960s, when US interest rates rose above banks' Reg Q ceilings on deposit rates, which created incentives for US banks to shift the locus of their activities to London.

The Preston-Weatherstone partnership took off when they extended the London dealing room activities. It would grow by leaps and bounds in the 1970s, when President Nixon took the United States off the gold-exchange standard and currencies and interest rates fluctuated considerably. Preston and Weatherstone also initiated work to create long-dated forward contracts, which were a variation of "parallel loans" made primarily to Scottish whiskey producers who set their stocks in cast oaks to mature for seven years before selling most of their production overseas. Thus, they entailed long-term currency risk.

While in London, one of Preston's roles included establishing a Eurobond trading function. Among US banks, Morgan became the acknowledged leader in bond underwriting and other aspects of corporate finance.

Preston was also involved in the creation of the Euroclear system in conjunction with John Meyer, who served as chairman and CEO of Morgan from 1969 to 1971. Meyer sought to develop modern systems that would allow for easier settlement of securities trades from the unreliable system that existed in the 1960s. He would subsequently help co-found the Depository Trust Company (DTC) of New York, which provided settlement services for the US securities industry.

Bruce Brackenridge, at Preston's direction, established the Euroclear securities depository as a cooperative in Brussels to facilitate the settlement of Eurobond trades. Unlike the experience with the founding of DTC, where virtually all important investment banks and securities custodians shared in the clearinghouse ownership, Brackenridge's initial efforts to syndicate shares in Euroclear failed. Consequently, Morgan experienced several years of significant losses before he was urged to try again. He ultimately succeeded when Morgan's role became the operator of the system instead of its sole shareholder.

Morgan continued to play a role as Euroclear's sub-depository of securities in major European markets where it had branches and expertise. It also acted as the agent for lending securities and cash to participants to facilitate timely settlement, utilizing its credit expertise. This worked well until Morgan Guaranty Ltd. in London began to rise through the underwriting league tables, which created false suspicions that Morgan was sharing data on competitors' positions.[4]

In 1968 Preston returned to New York as Head of the International Division, succeeding Walter Page, who moved up to the Corporate Office. Preston immediately set about expanding the footprint he inherited from Page, both in the Far East and Latin America. In Asia, Morgan had a representative office in Hong Kong, a 20% interest in the Bank of the Philippines Island (the country's oldest bank formed in 1851), a minor investment in a venture capital firm in Taiwan and a branch office in Tokyo. The latter is particularly noteworthy because Morgan was the first bank to be granted a banking license after World War II.

Morgan's dealings in Japan date back to the 1920s, when it was then a partnership and the only investment bank willing to raise funds for the country in the US bond market after the devastating Tokyo earthquake and tsunami in 1923. (See the Box on the Morgan-Japan connection.) Morgan was rewarded for this action three decades later, as the Japanese constitution incorporated its counterpart of the Glass Steagall Act as Article XXVI, which would technically have barred Morgan from engaging in investment banking activities.

In addition to the Tokyo branch, Morgan set up a number of entities in Singapore after it created offshore banking licenses in the early 1970s. A separate merchant bank and discount company were also formed as joint ventures with the Development Bank of Singapore.

Soon after, the government of Indonesia came calling for Morgan's assistance, as the country's foreign exchange reserves had been depleted by disastrous oil shipping contracts for the country's leading oil producer, Pertamina. Ken Raine, who headed the Singapore office, directed the Minister of Finance, Ali Wardhana, and the Governor of the Bank of Indonesia, Rachmat Salleh, to meet with Preston in New York to see if a solution could be found to their predicament.

---

[4] Somewhat surprisingly, Morgan Grenfell, which had been an important part of the Morgan banking family's history in London, was a bit player in the Eurobond market, even though JPMorgan retained a 30% stake in the firm.

Preston subsequently asked Rimmer de Vries to send some of his staff to Jakarta to help create a country prospectus. Although national account statistics had not been formally collected then, a group of ministers in the Suharto Government known as the "Berkeley Mafia" were working on creating them. Thereafter, Indonesia succeeded in raising a debt offering that alleviated the problem.

Throughout the 1970s, Morgan made an even bigger push to grow its business in Latin America under Preston's guidance. This occurred as the leading countries experienced sizable increases in their current account imbalances during the first oil shock in 1973–74. A staff of Morgan bankers, who either grew up in the region or who spoke Spanish and/or Portuguese fluently, descended on various capitals at a time when the competition was already well entrenched there. With the exception of an investment in Buenos Aires, Morgan set up representative offices in some countries in the region as its loan volumes expanded. By the latter part of the 1970s, Morgan had largely caught up with its American competitors in terms of its exposure to the region. Unfortunately, the big push into Latin America did not end well, as discussed in Chap. 5.

One of the most important decisions Preston made as head of international was to bring Dennis Weatherstone to New York in 1973. The circumstances were that Parker Gilbert, the co-head of Morgan Stanley, had informed Preston that Morgan Stanley wished to withdraw its stake from Morgan et Cie, which was a joint venture. Preston subsequently met with Alec Vagliano, his chief lieutenant in international banking, and Jack Bochow, the senior vice president (SVP) in charge of Credit for the International Division, to figure out how to respond.

Preston asked Vagliano to invite John Olds, who recently arrived from Merrill Lynch with experience in its investment banking departments in London and Paris. When Olds was asked if he had a view on the matter, he responded that Morgan would be hard pressed to find a joint venture merchant bank in London that was successful. Moreover, this was especially true when the US Treasury was about to reduce the interest equalization tax to zero in a matter of weeks. This would be the death knell for London-based institutions lending to US companies. This statement came as a complete surprise to the group, as the IET was not slated to sunset until 1974.

Vagliano asked if there was anything they could request from Morgan Stanley. Olds recommended they ask Morgan Stanley for their head of syndicate in London. The logic was that if Morgan was going to run the business alone, instead of as a joint venture, it would need someone steeped in syndicate practices, as Eurobond underwriters were notoriously unreliable. Soon after, Shep Poor, the head of syndicate in Paris, left Morgan Stanley to join

JPMorgan in London. Preston then determined it was time to bring Dennis Weatherstone to New York.

The environment in banking that Preston faced as he took over the reins in 1979 was as challenging as any leader of the House of Morgan confronted. A surge in inflation during the 1970s caused interest rates to spike, while Reg Q ceilings on deposit rates contributed to disintermediation as banks and thrifts competed with institutions that were not subject to them. Largely in response to this, the US banking industry was about to undergo an extensive transformation from a highly fragmented system that was tightly regulated to one that was increasingly deregulated. It would also experience the highest failure rate in US history in the 1980s, as many smaller banks and thrifts were unable to cope with the turbulent environment (Fig. 3.1). Accordingly, this period has been dubbed "the decline of banking."

As of the late 1970s, US banking was still predominantly a local business. There were close to 12,500 banks nationwide (15,000 financial institutions including thrifts), and only fourteen states allowed statewide branches. Until 1982, no state permitted out-of-state banks to open branches within their borders. Virtually the only avenue for New York City money center banks to grow in the regulatory environment of the time was to merge with banks in the same jurisdiction. Thus, the 1950s saw the formation of First National City Bank, Chase Manhattan Bank and the Morgan Guaranty Trust Company.

By comparison, by the mid-1990s the restrictions on interstate and intrastate banking had largely been eliminated with passage of the Riegle-Neal Interstate Banking Act of 1994. The number of US banks fell steadily beginning in the mid-1980s, a consolidation trend that has continued to present (Fig. 3.2).

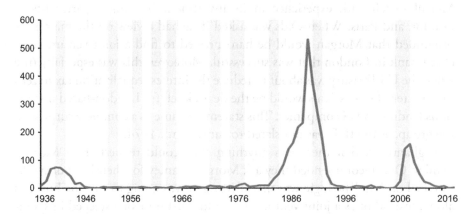

Fig. 3.1 Failures of US banks and thrifts. (Source: FDIC)

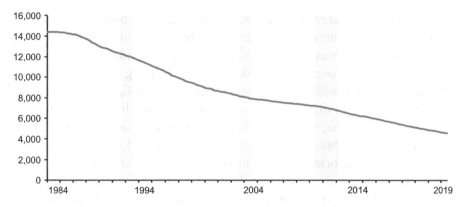

Fig. 3.2 Number of commercial banks in the United States, 1984 to 2019. (Source: The Federal Reserve)

Being a wholesale bank serving multinational clients, Morgan was relatively unaffected by the relaxation of prohibitions pertaining to interstate banking that ensued. Also, because Morgan funded its operations largely through the inter-bank market, it was well positioned for the changes in which deposit rates became market-based. However, these changes were more important for Morgan's principal rivals who were engaged in retail banking, as well as wholesale banking.

When Preston assumed the helm, there were ten money center banks in the United States that had sizable assets and which were involved in both domestic and international businesses. They included six in New York City (Bankers Trust, Chase Manhattan, Chemical Bank, National City Bank [Citibank], Manufacturers Hanover and Morgan), two in Illinois (Continental and First Chicago) and Bank of America and Security Pacific on the West Coast.

Morgan's primary competitors were the other New York City-based banks, which were involved in both wholesale and retail banking. They had experienced rapid growth in the 1970s mainly from expansions of their international operations and from lending to less developed countries (LDCs). By the mid-1970s the percentage of total earnings attributable to foreign operations ranged from 45% (Chemical) to 70% (Citibank) with Morgan's tally standing at 60%.[5] The key issue they faced was whether to continue to grow their businesses by expanding international lending or alter their business models for an environment in which capital market activity was proliferating worldwide. They would pursue varying strategies in the ensuing decade.

---

[5] James Freeman and Vern McKinley, *Borrowed Time*, Harper Business, 2018, p. 200.

Morgan's principal rival, Citibank, was the largest US bank, the most innovative and also the most diverse internationally. It was run by Walter Wriston, who served as chairman and CEO from 1967 and was widely considered to be the most influential commercial banker of his time. Along with George Moore, Wriston is credited with creating the certificate of deposit, or CD, that would become prevalent in the 1970s. He was also an ardent advocate for lending to LDCs contending that they afforded excellent opportunities for banks, because "countries don't go bust." Wriston also sought to expand Citi's presence globally by establishing branch offices abroad, especially in Latin America. As discussed later, his successor, John Reed, would alter Citi's strategy to emphasize serving consumers by utilizing technology including automatic teller machines (ATMs), widespread use of credit cards and online banking.

Chase Manhattan also experienced a major expansion of its international business under the leadership of David Rockefeller, who had extensive contacts with government and business leaders worldwide. In the 1970s, Chase added nearly forty new branches, representative offices, affiliates, subsidiaries and joint ventures outside the United States, including the first rep office by a foreign institution in the Soviet Union since the 1920s and the first US correspondent to the Bank of China since the Chinese Revolution in 1949.[6] Willard C. Butcher, who succeeded David Rockefeller as chairman and CEO in 1980, stayed loyal to Rockefeller's vision of developing a global bank that was involved in both wholesale and retail banking.

Chemical Bank differed from other money center banks by growing its domestic business through a series of acquisitions, first of regional banks and eventually megabanks. In 1980 its Chairman Donald Platten began restructuring non-consumer banking operations and setting up separate divisions for multinational corporations, large domestic corporations and middle-market businesses.[7] Chemical would go on to become the leading consolidator of the US banking industry, beginning with purchases of regional banks in Florida and Texas in the 1980s before undertaking acquisitions of Manufacturers Hanover and Chase Manhattan in the 1990s.

Bankers Trust, which had underperformed in the mid-late 1970s, made the biggest break of any money center bank. In 1980 it made the decision to exit retail banking under the direction of its CEO, Alfred Brittain III, and it eventually sold its network of bank branches. It chose to focus exclusively on wholesale banking and sophisticated financial transactions, viewing Morgan Guaranty as the role model for banking success.

For his part, Lew Preston knew that even though Morgan Guaranty was widely admired, it could not rest on its laurels. The reason: Banking and

---

[6] JPMorgan Chase & co., op. cit., p. 13.
[7] Funding Universe, Chemical Banking Corporate History.

financial markets were in tremendous flux and there was excess capacity in the industry. This meant Morgan would have to adapt to a continuously changing landscape or risk falling behind its rivals. During his stint in London he was quick to see how multinational corporations required sophisticated advice to solve their problems, and he believed Morgan had the requisite expertise to serve them. Preston would spend the remainder of his tenure trying to balance the need for Morgan to transform itself while staying true to its core values.

Box: Morgan's Special Relation with Japan

For the past 100 years, JPMorgan has enjoyed a special relationship with the government of Japan. The origins were a trip Thomas Lamont, a Morgan partner who became a spokesman for the bank, took to Japan in 1920 to establish ties with Japan's government. Three years later an earthquake erupted in the vicinity of Tokyo-Yokohama, Japan considered floating its first bond issue in America since the Russo-Japanese War. Lamont, however, advised Governor Inouye of the Bank of Japan against doing so, and he arranged a $150 million earthquake loan, which at the time was the largest long-term foreign loan placed in the US market.[8]

According to Chernow, the House of Morgan believed it had a stake in Japan's success and prosperity, and it felt obliged to perform political favors on behalf of Japan. Its government reciprocated in 1927, when the emperor of Japan awarded Jack Morgan with the Order of the Sacred Treasure and Thomas Lamont with the Order of the Rising Sun.[9]

More than fifty years later, Morgan Guaranty sought approval to become the first American bank since 1952 to win branch approval. John Meyer, who followed Thomas Gates, as Morgan's CEO and chairman, led the efforts along with Jack Loughran, a long-serving Morgan employee who headed its representative office in Tokyo.

One story that Bob Wynn, who headed business with Japan out of New York, told was that Loughran excitedly phoned Meyer to inform him that the Ministry of Finance had approved a branch opening in 1969, but not later. When Meyer did not seem excited, Loughran asked why. Meyer said that he was about to attend a JPM board meeting in which the board had approved the opening of a branch on Park Avenue, and he was worried he wouldn't be allowed to open two branches in the same year! (Both branches did open.)

Another story relates to Meyer visiting Japan afterwards to call on clients and government officials.[10] This was a time when the "Mo-rugahn ginko" (Morgan Bank) was held in the highest esteem everywhere, and especially in Japan, such that the head of Morgan was regarded almost as a demi-god. Meyer and several junior colleagues were invited to a cocktail reception, where there was a book for guests to sign. In a fashion typical of Meyer, he signed his name, wrote "Morgan Guaranty Trust Company," and in the space for position he wrote "bank employee."

[8] Chernow, op. cit. pp. 234–6.
[9] Ibid., p. 236.
[10] I am grateful to Bill Vogt for relating these stories.

4

Market Shocks

Before Preston could formulate a course of action for Morgan's future, he had to grapple with a series of shocks that impacted the global economy and financial markets from 1979 to 1983.[1] The first was a spike in oil prices that proved to be considerably greater than the oil shock in 1973–74.

At the start of 1979, newspapers and the media were full of stories about mounting demonstrations against the Shah of Iran and the possibility the Shah could be deposed. By mid-January it was clear the protestors had gained the upper hand, as the Shah left Iran for exile and the Ayatollah Khomeini returned to Tehran greeted by several million Iranians. Within a few weeks the monarchy was replaced by an Islamic Republic with Khomeini serving as the spiritual leader.

Amid this upheaval, a strike by workers at Iran's nationalized oil refineries that began in November of 1978 resulted in the country's oil production being reduced from nearly 6 million barrels per day to about 1.5 million bpd. One of our tasks in the International Economics Department was to assess the implications of this shortfall for the global economy and world financial markets. The department received considerable recognition during the first oil shock in 1973–74, when *World Financial Markets* published in-depth assessments of oil markets and the impact that a quadrupling in oil prices had on the external payments positions of leading oil exporters and oil importers. Now, for the second time in a decade, Morgan's international economics team was being called on to provide another assessment.

---

[1] The shocks in this chapter are discussed in greater detail in my book, *Global Shocks: An Investment Guide for Turbulent Markets*, Palgrave Macmillan, 2016.

© The Author(s) 2020
N. P. Sargen, *JPMorgan's Fall and Revival*, https://doi.org/10.1007/978-3-030-47058-6_4

While the entire department was engaged in the exercise, Rimmer relied heavily on Irene King to formulate the department's views on the price of oil and the size of the Organization of Petroleum Exporting Countries (OPEC) current account surplus. As the lead bank for the governments of Saudi Arabia, Kuwait and other Middle Eastern countries, Morgan Guaranty had long-standing relations with these countries, and its senior executives benefited from ongoing discussions with leaders in the region. As the senior economist for the Middle East, King was an acknowledged expert on the region and oil markets, and representatives from the region would regularly share their views with her, Rimmer and Rod Wagner, who headed the Middle East and Africa division.

It did not take long to observe the impact of the shortfall on oil prices. The price for West Texas Intermediate—the benchmark for crude oil produced in the United States—surged from $10 per barrel in December of 1978 to nearly $16 by early April of 1979. The Carter administration then began a phased deregulation of price controls for domestically produced oil that had been imposed by the Nixon administration during the first oil shock. The intent was to provide incentives for greater domestic production of oil and alternatives. Meanwhile, the price of crude oil continued to rise over the next twelve months, and it approached $40 per barrel in March of 1980.

The quadrupling in oil prices, in turn, contributed to massive payments imbalances between OPEC and the oil-importing countries: OPEC's combined current account surplus swung from a small deficit in 1978 to a surplus of $60 billion in 1979. At the peak in 1980, OPEC's surplus stood at $110 billion—twice as large as in the first oil shock.

While surging oil prices posed a threat to the global economy, it also provided opportunities for multinational banks such as Morgan Guaranty to boost revenues by lending to the governments of oil-importing countries to finance their deficits. Norman Klath was responsible for overseeing the team's estimates of the external borrowing requirements for oil-importing countries. For the leading economies in the Group of Ten (G-10) countries that had ready access to international capital, the financing could be obtained either through international capital markets or by borrowing from multinational banks. By comparison, the developing countries were almost exclusively reliant on bank financing.

The ability of developing countries to withstand higher oil prices and interest rates in the mid-1970s left most bankers optimistic that the recycling of petrodollars would proceed as smoothly as it did during the first oil shock. Indeed, as growth slowed in the industrial economies in 1979 and 1980, bankers were eager to lend to the governments of these countries because lending to domestic borrowers was slowing. They could also earn large spreads on the developing country loans, which would help offset revenue losses in other areas.

In an attempt to reduce risks, large banks such as Morgan would syndicate these loans to other banks and link the interest payments on them to the London Inter-Bank Offered Rate (LIBOR). It fluctuated on a six-month basis in line with short-term US interest rates. In this way, the banks believed they were effectively transferring the risk of higher US interest rates and of currency weakness in the developing countries back to the borrower.

One of my principal assignments was to develop a framework to rank the creditworthiness (or ability to repay debt) of twenty developing countries where Morgan Guaranty had its greatest exposure. The inputs came from the individual country economists, who prepared detailed analyses of the growth prospects and external financing requirements for the countries and regions they followed. I was responsible for assembling the data in a format that made it easier to compare the performance of countries within their regions and across regions.

When the time came to brief senior management, I was nervous because John Olds was an experienced Asian hand who asked insightful questions and was not hesitant about asserting his views. Our team's assessment was that the leading Asian countries, on the whole, were creditworthy and we were comfortable with Morgan's Asian exposure.

Many countries in the region were pursuing successful export-led development strategies, in which they were able to grow rapidly while keeping budget deficits and inflation under control. My colleague Jai Yang noted that countries in North Asia such as South Korea and Taiwan were heavily dependent on oil and other raw material imports, but they had also demonstrated a remarkable ability to adjust to external shocks. Similarly, another team member Ching-mai Wu contended that Southeast Asian economies such as Malaysia, Singapore and Thailand were dynamic, well managed and had a history of currency stability.

The two economies that we believed posed the greatest risks were Indonesia and the Philippines, as they tended to run larger external deficits and occasionally had to devalue their currencies to maintain their competitiveness. We were also unsure how their populace would react if it was necessary to curtail government spending.

I was relieved when Olds agreed with our assessment and told us to keep a close eye on them. To lessen credit risks in the region, bankers in the Pac Rim area emphasized project finance by private companies while diminishing the financing of balance of payments deficits that the public sector incurred.

The environment in Latin America was very different. Instead of export-oriented strategies, these countries sought to industrialize their economies behind a wall of high tariff barriers. Their governments also tended to run large budget deficits that in many instances were monetized by their central banks. This resulted in inflation being much higher than in other parts of the world, and their governments often had to devalue their currencies to restore competitiveness. Based on the objective indicators we collected, our assessment was that Latin America contained the greatest risks of defaults and debt reschedulings, which was also evident from the region's long history of currency and debt crises.

The co-heads of Morgan's Latin American division, Jackson Gilbert and Tony Gebauer, nonetheless were eager to increase their lending to the region for a variety of reasons. First and foremost, the Latin countries, especially the so-called MBAs—Mexico, Brazil and Argentina—had the largest borrowing requirements, and the added interest they paid—the spread over LIBOR—was very lucrative. Consequently, they were the most profitable areas for banks to extend credit, and Gilbert and Gebauer wanted to be sure Morgan maintained its market share in the region. They contended that our ranking system was flawed because it did not give countries credit for being able to attract capital from abroad. They could not conceive that this condition could change abruptly if lenders became less confident about the ability of these countries to service their debt.

Our economists who covered the region, Jim Nash and Arturo Porzecanski, were fairly sanguine about the growth prospects for Mexico, Brazil, Venezuela and Argentina. As commodity exporters, these countries benefited from surging prices of raw materials and agricultural commodities throughout the 1970s, and the expansion in their exports meant that they were earning the foreign exchange required to service their external debt obligations. Nash also pointed out that Venezuela was an oil exporter, and the Mexican government was boosting its production of oil to make it energy self-sufficient. Porzecanski, who covered the Southern Cone (Argentina and Chile), was encouraged by the market-oriented reforms in Chile and the attempts to diversify the country's reliance on copper, but he believed Argentina warranted closer scrutiny because of its history of political instability and currency crises.

In making our appraisals, our department also took into account conditions in the industrialized countries: They were the primary markets for developing country exports, and they could affect their debt-servicing costs through changes in interest rates and currencies. We were mindful that a global recession during the first oil shock eventually caused prices of oil and other commodities to decline and that this could happen again.

The industrialized economies, however, appeared to be weathering the second shock better than the first. The principal reason was rising inflation expectations had become more ingrained in the United States and other parts of the world. Businesses passed along higher input costs into product prices, and wages were increasingly indexed to inflation. As long as incomes rose with inflation and jobs were secure, consumers were not compelled to cut back on spending.

By the fall of 1979, the mood at Morgan was cautiously optimistic for several reasons. First, the bank's close ties with Saudi Arabia and Kuwait meant that Morgan was a major recipient of deposits from them and other OPEC members. Second, Morgan's revenues surged as a result of lucrative loans to LDCs. Third, the bank also had close ties with the largest oil and natural gas companies in part due to Lew Preston, who oversaw lending to the sector in the first part of the 1960s. Fourth, the bank had a very strong balance sheet with one of the highest capital-asset ratios in the industry and a AAA credit rating from both Moody's and S&P. Therefore, senior management believed the bank was well positioned to withstand the impact of higher oil prices.

While Morgan's management was optimistic that international banks could once again recycle petro-dollars from oil exporters to oil-importing countries, it was also cognizant of the risks that rising oil prices posed for the US and the global economies. The main uncertainty was how the phenomenon of rising inflation expectations and interest rates would play itself out. Some observers contended that rising inflation per se was not a problem for the United States as long as the economy was fully indexed to it. However, most economists recognized that the inflationary process created distortions, because some prices were fixed while others were adjustable. Also, as inflation in the United States reached double digits for the first time in post-war history, no one could be sure when it would peak or at what level. The true cost of inflation often was not fully evident until fiscal and monetary policies were tightened and the economy inevitably weakened.

For global investors, the resurgence of inflation hurt the US dollar's appeal as the world's reserve currency. Countries in Europe such as Germany, Holland and Switzerland pursued monetary policies that were geared to limit the increase in inflation, but they were frustrated when inflation in the United States spiraled. As long as they permitted their currencies to appreciate against the dollar without intervening in the currency markets, they could maintain control of their money supplies. However, as global investors exchanged dollars for deutsche marks, Dutch guilders or Swiss francs, the inflows of money into these countries surged, and the central banks in these countries found it increasingly difficult to keep their money supplies and inflation in check. The leading European governments responded by agreeing to establish narrow bands for their currencies to fluctuate against one another in order to limit the fallout of a weaker dollar on their economies.

Against this backdrop of accelerating inflation and a plummeting dollar, the Federal Reserve found itself increasingly on the defensive. It geared monetary policy to control inflation by raising the federal funds rate—the interest rate banks borrowed from one another to meet reserve requirements. However, confidence in the Fed's abilities to control inflation waned under the leadership of G. William Miller, whom President Carter appointed to be chairman in March of 1978. Miller previously served as the chief executive for Textron, and he had no background in economics or financial markets. Even more disturbing to market participants was his unwillingness to listen to economists in the Federal Reserve and the Carter administration about the need to raise interest rates to combat inflation. Most economists believed Miller was completely out of his realm of competence, and that the economic environment was likely to deteriorate further as long as he served as Fed chairman.

To bolster investor confidence, President Carter announced a Cabinet shakeup in early August of 1979, in which Miller would replace Michael Blumenthal as Treasury Secretary, and Paul Volcker would become chairman of the Federal Reserve. Markets rallied on the news, as Volcker brought considerable experience on both domestic monetary policy and international economic policy. He previously served as president of the New York Federal Reserve Bank and before that as Under Secretary for International Monetary Affairs at the US Treasury Department. In these roles he earned the reputation of being an inflation fighter and an advocate of a strong dollar, which made him a popular choice on Wall Street.

I was personally happy with Volcker's selection, as I served under him at the Treasury in the early 1970s and respected his expertise in international economics and his dedication as a public servant. At the same time, I wondered what changes he would make to restore confidence in US monetary policy and the dollar. During his stint at the US Treasury, Volcker was a strong advocate of the Bretton Woods system of fixed exchange rates. Yet, he presided over the breakdown of the system and the subsequent adoption of floating exchange rates.

As Volcker assumed the duties as Fed chairman, it was widely assumed he would continue to set a target level for the federal funds rate, but increase the rate more aggressively. Instead, Volcker announced that he planned to alter the Fed's operating procedures, whereby it would target the rate of growth of the money supply and allow the level of the federal funds rate to adjust as needed. This development surprised the markets, because Volcker appeared to be shifting policy in a direction that monetarists such as Milton Friedman had long advocated. If so, it marked the second time in his career in which he deviated from policy stances that he previously advocated.

The impact of this announcement on financial markets was profound. Once the Federal Reserve announced its targets for money supply growth, market participants immediately shifted attention to the weekly money supply numbers that were released every Thursday at 4:30 p.m. When the money supply exceeded the upper band of the target zone, short-term interest rates would surge; conversely, when the money supply came in below target, interest rates would decline. The volatility in the federal funds rate was unprecedented, as it would fluctuate by several percentage points on a weekly basis.

Like other market participants, those of us at Morgan were trying to figure out what all of this meant. Toward the end of 1979, I attended an event in Rochester, New York, where Lew Preston presented his assessment of the situation to clients of the bank. He concluded his remarks by saying that it appeared the Fed had "crossed the Rubicon" in establishing its new procedures to control the money supply and inflation. However, he also believed it was too early to determine the ultimate impact on the economy and financial markets. To this, I could only whisper "Amen."

As 1980 began, the central issues market participants weighed were how high US interest rates would go and whether rising rates would push the economy into recession. The responsibility for this call resided with Morgan's US Economics Department, our sister group that was located around the corner from our offices. The unit was headed by Milton Hudson, who replaced Jack Noyes as Chief US Economist upon his retirement. Hudson's key lieutenants were Will Brown and Walter Cadette, who spent their entire careers in the department. Brown was responsible for formulating Morgan's US economic forecast, while Cadette was a regular contributor to the department's publication, *The Morgan Guaranty Survey*.

Upon joining Morgan, I naturally assumed that the domestic and international economics departments worked closely together, especially with the global economy becoming more integrated. However, this was not the case due to a rivalry that started at the top. Rimmer and Milt maintained professional decorum with one another, but they rarely exchanged views and their staffs were discouraged from interacting, fearing that the other department would scoop them on information. This made no sense to me. I believed it was essential for both departments to understand the respective views on the domestic and international economy and share information. At the same time, I was loyal to Rimmer, and it seemed at times that I was engaging in covert operations whenever I met with the domestic economists.

Fortunately, this interchange became easier over time, as Hudson expanded his department by tapping the Board of Governors of the Federal Reserve and the New York Federal Reserve. He landed an impressive group of economists that included Dick Berner, Bill Dudley, Jim Fralick, Ed McKelvey and Steven Roach, who eventually would all move on to other Wall Street firms.

Dick Berner was a close friend, who I first met while he was in the International Department of the Board of Governors. He received his Ph.D. at Wharton under Lawrence Klein, a pioneering econometrician who later became a Nobel laureate. Berner helped build the Board's econometric model that linked the global economies, and he brought this expertise to Morgan. He introduced me to his colleagues who worked with him at the Board, and I benefited immensely from their knowledge and sound judgments. Rimmer also appreciated their expertise, and the informal barriers between the two departments began to come down.

While the new recruits had first-hand knowledge of how the Fed conducted policy, they too had to figure out the ramifications of the change in operating procedures that Paul Volcker introduced. The main uncertainty was how high the federal funds rate would rise to clear the market for bank reserves.

During the 1960s and 1970s, the US economy was very sensitive to small increases in the funds rate, because commercial banks and savings and loan associations faced regulatory ceilings (Reg Q) on deposit rates that could be paid. As the ceilings were reached and inflows into these institutions dried up, these institutions were constrained in making new loans to households and corporations, thereby weakening the economy.

When interest rates surged to double digits in the late 1970s, investors began to seek out and find alternatives to traditional bank deposits. Brokerage firms and other financial institutions created money market mutual funds, which pooled investors' funds to purchase commercial paper that corporations increasingly used to obtain short-term funding. Because money market funds operated without reserve requirements or interest-rate restrictions, they became a popular alternative to deposits at commercial banks and savings and loan institutions.

In order to enable banks and thrift institutions to compete effectively, President Carter signed into law the Depository Institutions Deregulation and Monetary Control Act of 1980. The legislation allowed depository institutions to offer competitive returns to depositors, and it established a committee to oversee the complete phase-out of interest rate ceilings within six years.[2]

The shift to monetary targeting provided the first opportunity to see how resilient the US economy was to rising interest rates when banks were no longer subject to financial disintermediation. To the amazement of market participants and policymakers alike, short-term interest rates surged in the first quarter above 20% while yields on US Treasury bonds reached levels never before imagined.

Both the magnitude of the rise in interest rates and the inverted shape of the Treasury yield curve were viewed as indicators that a recession was likely. In reflecting back on the experiment many years later, Volcker observed:

> I do not think that any of us embarking on this policy felt we were going to end up with bank lending rates at 21 percent in the United States. I think that happened because people dependent on bank lending did not follow a nice conceptual textbook approach and say, "the interest rate is a little higher, so we'll pull back a bit" … So they kept borrowing and implicitly thinking "well this interest rate is awfully high today, but maybe it will come down tomorrow, so we'll keep at it." And the credit expansion continued until, to exaggerate a little bit, this became a policy of restraint by bankruptcy.[3]

Amid these developments, investors confronted yet another surprise in the spring, when the Carter administration in conjunction with the Fed imposed controls to limit extension of new credits to consumers. When commercial banks interpreted the action as being designed to curtail exiting credit to borrowers, consumer spending plummeted and the economy plunged into recession. Policymakers, in turn, responded by canceling the experiment soon after. Reflecting on this failed experiment, Volcker later observed:

> We designed what we thought was a modest, market-mimicking restraint on some parts of consumer credit. This was something we anticipated would have a modest restraining effect on the economy, supplementing our control over reserves. It turned out to have a huge psychological effect. I never saw anything like it. There was a sharp reaction by consumers that single-handedly drove the economy into recession in a matter of weeks. I believe that this was the last time there was any experimentation in direct control of credit.[4]

---

[2] Matthew Sherman, "A Short History of Financial Deregulation in the United States," Center for Economic and Policy Research, July 2009.

[3] "Monetary Policy Transmission: Past and Future Challenges," address by Paul A. Volcker to Conference on Financial Innovation and Monetary Transmission, Federal Reserve Bank of New York, April 2002, p. 4.

[4] Ibid., p. 4.

During the brief period of credit controls, US interest rates fell by nearly one half from their peak level. Once the controls were eliminated, however, interest rates surged again, as households quickly resumed their spending and the economy emerged from recession in the second half of 1980. There were two main takeaways from this experience that helped shape my views on the US economy and on policymaking in the future. The first lesson was that the US economy was much more sensitive to the overall availability of credit than to the cost of credit. The second lesson was the law of unintended consequences—that is, policy changes could produce results that were vastly different from what was intended.

In addition to a sea-change in US monetary policy, market participants also had to contend with the most comprehensive overhaul of economic policy since the New Deal following Ronald Reagan's election as president in November of 1980. Reagan campaigned for office on the theme that reduction in the role of government was key to revitalizing the US economy. The 1981 Program for Economic Recovery had four major policy objectives: (1) reduce the growth of government spending; (2) lower the marginal tax rates for both labor and capital; (3) diminish government regulation; and (4) reduce inflation by controlling the growth of money supply.

The crux of Reaganomics was a belief in "supply-side" economics, a concept that Art Laffer, a fellow Stanford Ph.D., had popularized during the Nixon era. The central idea was fairly simple: Economic agents—households and businesses—would respond significantly to reductions in marginal tax rates and government regulations by boosting output and employment. Accordingly, the Reagan administration's top priority was to lower personal and corporate tax rates, and it succeeded on this front. However, the administration was unable to achieve a reduction in government spending, and the federal budget deficit ballooned to post-war record levels.

In the wake of these developments our economists had to assess how the mix of expansionary fiscal policy and restrictive monetary policy would impact the global economy. While US interest rates remained stubbornly high, one desirable effect was the dollar surged against the key currencies, as investors became convinced policymakers were determined to end the period of currency weakness. Foreign investors also began to invest in US Treasuries, attracted by a combination of high interest rates and an appreciating dollar.

For the most part, Morgan Guaranty was able to traverse this period of heightened market volatility reasonably well. The reason: Dennis Weatherstone and Bob Engel were savvy market professionals who understood currency and interest rate risk. As a global wholesale bank, Morgan was accustomed to funding its operations in financial markets, and it had an excellent coterie of traders. By comparison, the heightened market volatility would prove to be more trying for banks that were less involved in trading.

By early 1982, there were clearer indications that the US and global economies were weakening, and prices for gold, oil and other commodities began to subside. Nonetheless, Fed officials were concerned that inflation expectations were too high, and Paul Volcker contemplated additional monetary tightening.

5

Crisis Erupts

While those of us in the International Economics Department were encouraged by the United States' commitment to fight inflation and the effort to stabilize the dollar, we also realized that the global environment was becoming less favorable for developing countries. By the early 1980s, the key Latin American borrowers had debt service ratios (interest and amortization on external debt relative to exports) that far exceeded the 20% threshold that had previously been considered excessive.

However, our Latin American bankers maintained that the leading countries could borrow to cover any shortfalls in their foreign exchange reserves, and consequently traditional measures of debt serving capacity were not relevant for them. This argument carried the day, as senior management increased the credit limits for the region. Morgan's management was by no means alone, as virtually all the multinational banks plowed considerable new money into the region. Walter Wriston, chairman and CEO of Citibank and the dean of the international financial community, asserted that "Sovereign countries do not go bankrupt."

Rimmer and others in our department were uncomfortable with this line of reasoning, as it presumed that countries that took on too much debt could always obtain additional financing. However, I found myself torn about whether a developing country debt crisis was looming, partly because forecasts made during the first oil shock turned out to be too pessimistic. In 1981, I received a call from Charles Piggott, who succeeded me at the San Francisco Fed, telling me that early warning system I had developed was flashing red for a large number of countries. Rather than believe my own invention, I told him there were flaws in the model. It assumed that the

© The Author(s) 2020
N. P. Sargen, *JPMorgan's Fall and Revival*, https://doi.org/10.1007/978-3-030-47058-6_5

incidence of defaults and debt reschedulings increased significantly when a country's inflation rate reached double digits. But my model did not take into account that many developed countries including the United States were also running double-digit inflation rates. A year later it dawned on me that I had constructed a credible early warning system, but I lacked the courage of my convictions.

Amid this controversy, I told Rimmer that it was important for me to tour the Asia region, so I could get a first-hand impression of how it was faring. I trusted the judgments of my colleagues, Jay Yang and Ching-mai Wu, but thought it was essential for me to see officials in the region to get their take of the situation. In each country I visited, the Morgan name enabled me to see the top policymakers, and I came away reassured that we were making the correct appraisal: The region appeared to be in good shape, but we needed to continue monitoring the Philippines and Indonesia closely.

I also was able to spend a week in Japan, where my objective was to learn about the government's plans to abolish exchange controls and to liberalize the domestic financial system. The highlight of the visit was a meeting with Toyoo Ghyoten, the top official for International Economic Affairs at the Ministry of Finance. He lived up to his reputation as being very cosmopolitan and knowledgeable about international finance, and I came away convinced that these changes would make Japan a much more important player in international capital markets.

My role did not call for me to meet with policymakers in Latin America, which would have helped me formulate a more definitive view of the region. Instead, I came to rely on what our bankers in the region and economists were telling us. One development, however, that gave me some pause was a luncheon meeting that Rimmer and I had with Senator Bill Bradley from New Jersey. Bradley had a reputation for being one of the leading experts on international financial issues in the Senate, and he had just returned from a fact-finding visit to Mexico. He was remarkably frank with us and indicated that Mexico was in very poor shape from both an economic and a political perspective. In his assessment, Mexico was an accident waiting to happen.

When Rimmer informed our Latin American bankers about the conversation, they were very dismissive of Bradley's assessment. They reacted by asking Rimmer to feature Mexico in the August issue of *World Financial Markets* with an upbeat appraisal of the country. As I headed off for a three-week vacation in Cape Cod with my family, I couldn't help wonder which of these views was the correct one.

It didn't take long to find out which assessment was correct. One week into my vacation, I was shocked to read a *New York Times* article reporting that

Mexico had run out of foreign exchange reserves and was seeking financial assistance from the US government, the Bank for International Settlements (BIS) and the International Monetary Fund (IMF). My initial assumption was that Mexico was an isolated event, and I hoped that our forthcoming article had not been published. Otherwise, our department would be embarrassed by what happened. As news about the situation unfolded, however, it soon became apparent that Mexico's problems were having ripple effects on Argentina, Brazil, Venezuela and other Latin American borrowers.

Upon returning to the office after Labor Day, I headed immediately for Rimmer's office and asked him how bad the situation was. His first words to me were, "Nick, this is very serious. I've never seen Dennis so scared." When I asked why Dennis Weatherstone was so worried, Rimmer explained that the events in Mexico had spawned a cessation in bank lending to many developing countries, and that if it continued, it would force them into default. Considering that Morgan Guaranty and the other money center banks had exposures to the Big Four Latin American countries that exceeded their own capital, the banks themselves could be imperiled.

I next asked Rimmer what was being done to head off a crisis. He explained that officials were trying to arrange bridge financing from the US government, Bank for International Settlements and the International Monetary Fund before a longer term plan could be hammered out. The developing country debt crisis was slated to be the focal point of the annual World Bank/IMF annual meetings later in September. But the situation was becoming very complicated, partly due to political developments in the major borrowing countries.

The biggest borrowers from the banks were the so-called MBAs—Mexico, Brazil and Argentina—followed by Venezuela. Collectively, as of end-1982, these four countries had bank loans outstanding totaling nearly $190 billion, of which Brazil and Mexico totaled $68 billion each. Morgan had loans outstanding to the four borrowers totaling $4.1 billion, representing most of its capital.[1] Its share to each of them was between 1.5% and 2.5% of all bank loans they received, and 7%– 8% of the loans from US money center banks for Venezuela and Mexico and 12%–14% for Brazil and Argentina.

In Mexico, the outgoing president, Lopez Portillo, shocked the international banking community by nationalizing the Mexican banks, introducing controls on foreign exchange and blaming foreign creditors for the country's problems. These developments created a panic in the Mexican inter-bank market, as international banks refused to roll-over credits to Mexican

[1] Internal memorandum, March 1985.

institutions. While the incoming president, Miguel de la Madrid, was believed to be less nationalistic, he would not assume office until December.

Elsewhere, the political timetable also worked against the formulation of a speedy solution. Argentina was considered to be the weakest link in the chain, as the country was experiencing a bout of hyper-inflation and its foreign exchange reserves were being depleted. In the midst of the war with Britain over the Falkland Islands, the Argentine army assumed effective control of the government in July, and it was distracted by events inside the country.

There was more reason to be hopeful that Brazil might escape the crisis. The Brazilian authorities had made considerable progress in reining in the country's budget deficit, and the economy was considered the strongest in the region. The main complicating factor was that the military government, which assumed control in 1964, was preparing a transition of power to a democratically elected government. With the first congressional elections slated for November, the Brazilian officials who were involved in debt negotiations lacked authority to act.

Venezuela was considered to be the renegade of the group by Morgan's senior management, because its external debt burden relative to exports was considerably below that of the MBAs. Yet, it was demanding the same type of concessions from banks that the more heavily indebted countries sought. For Morgan's executives, Venezuela was an example of a country which had the capacity to repay its debt but which was unwilling to do so when other borrowing countries were seeking concessions.

In formulating plans for bridge financing and eventual term financing, the commercial banks formed advisory committees so that they could speak with one voice. As the largest bank lender to Latin America, Citibank assumed the leadership role for negotiating with both Mexico and Argentina, with William Rhodes serving as the chairman for the respective advisory committees.

In the case of Brazil, Morgan Guaranty was appointed to co-chair the Advisory Committee, with Tony Gebauer serving in that capacity. Both Fed Chairman Paul Volcker and New York Fed President Anthony Solomon supported the move, as they were concerned that Citibank favored reducing bank exposure to the country. Lew Preston was pleased that Morgan was assuming the key role in the negotiations, especially considering that it did not have as long-standing a relation with the country or as much exposure to it as Citi had.

Within Morgan, there was by no means a unified view on how the developing country crisis should be handled. The heads of the Latin American division, Jackson Gilbert and Tony Gebauer, maintained that the developing countries were facing a liquidity crisis or shortage of foreign exchange. They urged Preston and Weatherstone to increase exposure to the main Latin borrowers. From their perspective, the latest developments were not a full-blown crisis, and the bank should take advantage of the very large spreads over LIBOR these countries would have to pay. Their opinions carried significant weight, considering how much money the bank was making on loans to the region.

The other faction within the bank was led by Rimmer, John Olds and Rod Wagner. They believed the problem confronting the borrowing countries was one of insolvency, not illiquidity. In their opinion, the less developed countries (LDCs) had taken on more debt than they could service, and the solution required that these countries bring their finances under control. In order for the countries to do so, the banks needed to stretch out and roll over existing obligations, but they should not add to these countries' indebtedness.

One advantage Rimmer had in making his case to Preston and Weatherstone was the respect *World Financial Markets* commanded in shaping public opinion on international financial issues. In our staff meetings to discuss the upcoming issues of the publication, Rimmer indicated our focus would be to describe the causes of the crisis and its magnitude and then to present a strategy to resolve it. While the audience was the international financial community, encompassing both public and private sectors, his ultimate mission was to convince the senior management of Morgan that the bank should not view the situation as business as usual. Indeed, it should be prepared for a very long workout.

Our department's assessment was that in the wake of two oil shocks, the developing countries had taken on too much external debt, and their debt burden needed to be reduced over time. Our analysis showed that the incidence of defaults or debt reschedulings rose significantly when ratios of external debt outstanding to exports were in the range of 160% to 200%. Above that range, the prospects for countries to service their debt were very poor.

The main message for bankers was that while countries could postpone the day of reckoning by obtaining additional financing, such funding only worsened the situation over the long haul. Debt-servicing problems, moreover, had been compounded by the surge in US interest rates and the dollar in the early 1980s. While banks believed they had transferred the interest rate and currency risks to the borrower, these risks were ultimately transformed back to the banks as credit risk.

The final blow was the recession in the United States and other industrial countries, which sent commodity prices plummeting and made it more difficult for the LDCs to earn the foreign exchange to service the debt. This meant that the burden of adjustment would mainly fall on the LDCs by way of import reduction and economic austerity.

A more difficult issue to gauge was the external financing requirements for the borrowing countries. The amount of refinancing they would need depended, to a large extent, on the rate of economic growth that was being underwritten. This was a key issue in the negotiations between borrowers and lenders. Meanwhile, it was becoming increasingly apparent that our department's previous estimates of financing requirements were too low. We soon discovered that as countries began to encounter problems rolling over bank debt in the early 1980s, they increasingly relied on short-term financing (original maturity of less than one year), and this information was not readily available. At the same time, we uncovered that the magnitude of capital flight from these countries was much greater than we had realized.

Given the magnitude and complexity of the debt crisis, it was readily apparent that it would take considerable time for the developing countries to make the requisite adjustments and for the banks to rebuild their capital. It was also clear to us that coordinated action was required on the part of the developing countries, the banks and the creditor governments. In our opinion, there was only one body—the International Monetary Fund—that could assume the central role in the coordinating process. But we also realized the IMF's role would have to be expanded.

Traditionally, the IMF's role was to establish necessary conditions that troubled countries had to meet to be eligible for assistance from it. If countries met these criteria and thereby received the IMF's "good-housekeeping seal of approval," other creditors typically would roll over existing obligations on more favorable terms. In the context of the developing country debt crisis, however, many regional banks in the United States and smaller banks abroad were seeking to reduce their exposures to the problem countries. Therefore, for the first time, the IMF would also have to stipulate conditions that the commercial banks needed to meet for it to negotiate with the debtor countries.

As I reflected upon this strategy, I imagined the IMF to be the ringmaster for a three ring circus involving the debtor countries, the commercial banks and the creditor governments. The magnitude of the task was daunting: The circumstances varied considerably across countries, and the interests of the individual banks involved were not always aligned. While the underlying approach was soundly based, the big question was whether it was possible to pull off such a delicate balancing act.

Fortunately, some positive developments in global markets helped stave off the day of reckoning. One was the effect that global recession was having on prices of oil and other commodities, which had been plummeting since the second half of 1981. These price declines provided relief to countries that imported oil and other raw materials by reducing expenses. At the same time, they helped to break inflation expectations in the industrial countries, and bond yields began to recede from their lofty levels.

For its part, the Federal Reserve remained concerned that inflation expectations were still too high, and it continued its policy of targeting bank reserves until the spring of 1982. By then, it was abundantly clear that the US and world economies were in the throes of the worst recession in the post-war era. Fed Chairman Volcker finally relented and he lowered short-term interest rates.

The decline in interest rates, in turn, contributed to a rally in stocks. However, the secular period of weakness that began in 1966 did not end until August of 1982, when the developing country debt problems finally convinced investors that inflation was headed significantly lower. In early August, Henry Kaufman of Salomon Brothers, a long-time bear who had earned the nickname Dr. Doom, helped spark a massive rally on Wall Street, when he forecast a significant decline in government bond yields. Even though the US economy was mired in recession and the developing country debt crisis was unfolding, financial markets rallied throughout the balance of the year amid expectations that the prolonged period of soaring inflation and high interest rates was coming to an end.

As we gathered for the officer's holiday party in December, the mood was one of hope and fear. We had reason to celebrate as the US economy showed signs of emerging from recession, and both the stock market and the price of Morgan's shares had risen significantly. At the same time, my colleagues and I were well aware of the daunting task that the bank faced trying to extricate itself the problems in Latin America and other parts of the world. While Morgan had weathered the crisis as well as any money center bank, I wined and dined on the sumptuous feast wondering if Morgan would be forever transformed by all that happened. The year ahead, 1983, could be pivotal for the future of Morgan Guaranty.

6

Time to Say Goodbye

As 1983 unfolded, while multinational banks were extending bridge loans to debt-burdened developing countries, Morgan's management turned its attention to formulating a strategy that would guide bank lending to these countries in the future. Lew Preston and senior management concurred with our department's assessment that we were in for a long workout period and a quick restoration of voluntary bank lending to developing countries was not in the cards. Indeed, the best we could hope for was to prevent a cessation of bank lending to developing countries.

The strategy that Morgan's senior management adopted, called "managed lending," contained several guiding principles.[1] The first was the rejection of a global approach to the LDC debt problem in favor of a case-by-case approach. While it was increasingly apparent that the problem countries could not repay their outstanding debt obligations, Morgan was very resistant to calls for debt relief, because it would set a dangerous precedent. Once relief was granted to one country, management believed all developing countries would seek assistance, whether or not they needed it.

Therefore, Morgan rejected calls for a formulaic solution that could be applied to all countries. Instead, it favored an approach that tailored the solution to the needs and circumstances of individual countries. The international economics department played an important role in developing projections for the respective economies and their funding requirements for the balance of the decade.

---

[1] For further discussion, see Nicholas Sargen, "Managed Lending: An Assessment of the Current Strategy toward LDC Debt," *NYU Journal of Law and Politics*, Spring 1985.

© The Author(s) 2020
N. P. Sargen, *JPMorgan's Fall and Revival*, https://doi.org/10.1007/978-3-030-47058-6_6

At the same time, Morgan's management realized it would take considerable time for banks to replenish their capital and strengthen their balance sheets. If banks were forced to incur sizable losses on their loans, bank capital would be depleted and their profitability would be wiped out. In this regard, the roll-over process was beneficial to banks, because it enabled them to keep developing country loans on their books at par value. A favorite expression of bankers at the time was "a rolling loan gathers no loss."

Fortunately for the banks, the regulatory bodies acquiesced to this procedure at the urging of the US government. Regulatory bodies pursued forbearance, in which they allowed banks to mark the value of LDC loans at par as long as countries paid the interest on their borrowings. In fact, banks were merely lending countries the money to keep interest payments current. This situation was vastly different from the 2008 Global Financial Crisis (GFC) in which financial institutions were subjected to mark-to-market accounting on the value of their securities. Thus, the LDC debt crisis played itself out in slow motion whereas the GFC was at warp speed.

Ultimately the strategy of managed lending was designed to buy time for the LDCs to adjust by reducing their budgetary and current account deficits and for the banks to strengthen their balance sheets. The strategy effectively permitted the banks to act as a cartel in supplying new credits to developing countries. The objective and actions, however, were completely different from that of most other cartels. Rather than reducing the quantity of loans to LDCs to bid up the price, the objective was to maintain or increase the quantity of loans to LDCs.

One of the key challenges Morgan and other money center banks faced was how to keep smaller and regional banks in line. They had become involved in LDC lending much later than the money center banks, and lending to developing countries was not as critical to their operations. Furthermore, there were considerable differences between US and European banks with respect to their regulatory environments and geographic concentrations of lending. In light of these differences, banks and regulatory bodies soon realized the need for collective action to limit the number of dropouts or "free riders." To avoid such an outcome, Morgan's management favored a "burden sharing" concept in which banks would agree to roll over their existing obligations and to extend new credits on a pro-rata basis.

Morgan's management realized that if it played a leadership role in keeping bank syndications intact, the bank had to demonstrate its commitment to assist the major borrowers. One way was to increase its overall exposure to the MBAs moderately, so they would receive positive net transfers of resources, thereby lessening the incentive to default. The principal exception was

Venezuela, where the bank reduced its exposure in subsequent years because of management's concern that the country was a free-loader.

Morgan's management reached out to the leadership of Deutsche Bank about forming a behind-the-scenes steering committee to attain their goal of keeping the coalition of banks together. Morgan had close ties with Deutsche Bank, which it considered its European equivalent, and Kurt Viermetz, who was responsible for German and continental European business, had started his banking career there. Deutsche's management was quick to agree, and an initial meeting was held in London where the two sides could collaborate on a common strategy.

I was asked to become a member of Morgan's delegation that was headed by Jack Ruffle, the firm's controller. My role was to present the views of the International Economics Department on individual countries, as well as to take copious notes on what was discussed at the meetings. It was an opportunity to observe the customary role Morgan executives played brokering deals with a consortium of banks to ensure the stability of the world's financial system.

From this perch, I could see the challenges Morgan and Deutsche faced in trying to keep regional US banks and other European banks committed to maintain their exposures to troubled countries. It also caused me to wonder how long Morgan and other money center banks would be playing a "mop up" role until developing countries could regain access to international borrowing and capital markets.

This and other topics were discussed at a conference of international economists hosted by Wharton in February of 1983. The conference had to be adjourned early when a freak snowstorm hit the Eastern seaboard, and I wound up taking a long train ride back to New York City with Bruce Brittain, a fellow economist and friend. Bruce had joined Salomon Brothers after working in Citibank's international economics department, and our conversation revolved around what it was like working for a securities firm versus a money center bank. Bruce's position was in the Bond Market Research Department headed by Dr. Henry Kaufman, the most famous economist on Wall Street, whose publication *Comments on Credit* was followed closely by market participants and whose statements could move markets on a regular basis.

What resonated was how excited Bruce was working for "Solly." He said the people he interacted with were very bright and hard charging—in his words "the biggest group of over-achievers I've ever encountered." He also described Salomon as a laboratory for financial innovation, in which the firm pioneered the creation of mortgage-backed securities and the application of derivatives such as financial futures, options and interest rate and currency swaps. I was mystified by what he was describing, as I had only heard the terms before but had no understanding of what they were. Bruce mentioned that the firm's Monday morning sales and trading meeting were the equivalent of a university lecture hall in which the attendees were barraged with sales priorities from a collection of knowledgeable product specialists. When our train finally arrived in New York City, we agreed to stay in touch and compare notes.

On the trek back to my home in Ridgewood, I tried to absorb what Bruce had told me. In the end I was left wondering how Morgan and other commercial banks would be able to compete with firms such as Salomon Brothers that seemed to have everything going their way. I was well aware of the slowdown in international bank lending that ensued after the LDC debt crisis, and for the first time corporations were raising more of their funding through the issuance of bonds. This was the area where Salomon was the acknowledged leader.

During the summer, Bruce approached me about getting together for lunch. When we met I was surprised to learn he had decided to leave Bond Market Research to become the product specialist for the foreign exchange area. He then asked if I would be interested in the position he was vacating. My response was I was very happy at Morgan, but would think about it and get back to him.

Several weeks later, I was contacted by Salomon's H.R. department to set up a round of interviews. When I arrived at the firm's headquarters at One Water Street (which was commonly referred to as the Belgium Waffle building because of its design), I was immediately struck by how different Salomon was from Morgan Guaranty. The firm's trading floor was double storied and the largest in the world with a commanding view of New York harbor and the Statue of Liberty. There was a swirl of activity going on like I had never seen before in contrast to the decorum at Morgan. Even more intriguing was the sight of Salomon's chairman and CEO, John Gutfreund, who sat in a semicircular desk at one end of the trading floor smoking a cigar while surveying the scene. I had never seen a chief executive before with a desk that wasn't in a corner office.

I was next escorted to the Bond Market Research Department, which was located on the opposite side of the trading floor from the main reception area. When I entered the department I was struck by how quiet it was and similar to Morgan's Economics Department, except it had a magnificent view of Manhattan and the harbor.

Henry Kaufman looked exactly as in pictures and media and was extraordinarily gracious. He mentioned how much he respected Morgan and that he was a client. When I asked what he was looking for in considering me for a position, he began by saying the department was called Bond Market Research and not Economic Research for a reason: Its purpose was to identify relative value in the bond market, for which I would use my knowledge of economics to render advice. I nodded as if I understood, but hoped he wouldn't press me, as I knew little about domestic or international bond markets.

Kaufman also discussed the tradition of bond research at the firm, which began with Sydney Homer, who co-authored a book titled *A History of Interest Rates*.[2] It spanned four millennia of interest rates beginning with the Babylonians. Kaufman was hired by Homer, and he subsequently hired Marty Leibowitz, who headed Bond Portfolio Analysis that pioneered the use of mathematics and quantitative techniques to analyze bonds.

Following my meeting with Kaufman, I was introduced to Jeff Hanna, who headed International Bond Market Research and oversaw its publications. Hanna was Bruce Brittain's boss, and the person to whom I would report if I was hired. He discussed how Salomon had been influential in the development of floating rate notes (FRNs) and other instruments that gave investors protection in a rising interest rate environment. He also mentioned how the unit developed strategies to separate currency and interest rate risk for international bonds that included the use of options. I, once again, nodded as if I understood what he was talking about. At the end of the session, he introduced me to Deryck Maughan, a British citizen who had recently joined Salomon from Goldman Sachs, to become the product specialist for international bonds.

I came away from the meeting extremely impressed by the quality of people I met and by how innovative Salomon was. I was also well aware that the firm was on a roll, as bond financing was displacing bank loans as the primary funding vehicle for corporations. When I didn't hear back from the firm, I assumed they had moved on and hired someone else, and I settled back into my routine at Morgan. Then, during the last week of the year, I received a call from Salomon indicating they would be making me an offer for a substantial pay increase.

Now that the ball was back in my court, I had to confront the most difficult decision since my offer from Morgan in 1977. In the meantime I had come to admire the firm and had developed a coterie of friends not only in New York and the other US offices but in Asia, as well, and I felt part of the Morgan

---

[2] Sydney Homer and Richard Sylla, *A History of Interest Rates*, Wiley, 1963.

family. While money was an important factor, considering I had to save to send four sons to college one day, it was not decisive. Rather the key consideration for me was whether commercial banking or investment banking and securities was the future of international finance. My main worry was that if I stayed in my current role I would become outmoded at some point, as financial innovations proliferated and I did not understand them. Nor was I aware about how involved Morgan had become in "financial engineering," as I was not exposed to this area.

One of the most difficult things I had to do was tell Rimmer of my decision to leave the International Economics Department. I knew it would be difficult for him, as we had developed a close relationship, and I assured him that I appreciated all he and the firm had done for me. I also told him that I was taking a risk working for a firm that was dominated by traders and I might not like it. If so, he told me I would be welcomed back.

When I left Morgan in January 1984, several things were evident about the firm. One was Lew Preston was fully in charge. He proved to be a decisive leader in navigating the firm through extreme market volatility and the developing country debt crisis. He did not blame the bankers in Latin America or the senior credit officers for not warning him, but immediately focused on what needed to be done to repair the bank's balance sheet and restore the bank's profitability. Under Preston, Morgan also played its traditional role backstopping the financial system. The bank formulated the strategy of managed lending that bought time for banks and their borrowers to adjust, and it worked continuously to assure that regional banks and those in Europe continued to roll over loans to LDCs.

Second, Morgan Guaranty survived the LDC debt crisis better than any of its competitors. A *New York Times* article in April 1983 titled "The Wealth and Aura of Morgan" provided the following assessment: "Morgan is so well run and so profitable that it is the paragon of the banking industry."[3] But the article went on to note that "all is not as placid as it seems at Morgan…Most challenging, however, is Morgan's struggle to plot its future in a rapidly changing financial world, where the rule of the game are shifting." Despite these concerns, the article cited Preston declaring that the bank would stick to its basic business and not lower its sites. It further quoted him referring to Citibank's CEO Walter Wriston, "He's running a financial conglomerate and we're running a bank."

Third, while Preston had reservations speaking publicly about the need for the bank to transform itself, he understood early on that Morgan could not

[3] Robert A. Bennett, April 10, 1983.

stand still. He addressed his senior management team on several occasions about his desire to see the firm become a universal bank, in which it could provide customers both commercial and investment banking capabilities. However, it was blocked from doing so domestically by Glass Steagall, and he began to explore ways to circumvent it as early as 1982. In the meantime, Morgan expanded its securities and trading capabilities abroad beginning in London in 1979 with the creation of Morgan Guaranty Limited (MGL), which became a leading underwriter of Eurobonds and developed extensive trading capabilities in foreign exchange, gold and financial futures and options.

Fourth, amid all this Preston continually struggled with the need to transform the firm without compromising Morgan's unique culture. He was constantly mulling: Who are we? What do we stand for? What is our mission? How do we stay unique?

What was especially important to me was how it proved to be a class act when I left the firm. I received a warm sendoff in the chart room from colleagues and friends from other departments. Everyone wished me the best in my new endeavor, although some thought I was "too nice" for a trading firm like Salomon Brothers.

As I was getting settled at Salomon, I was gratified to receive a handwritten note from Dennis Weatherstone. He thanked me for my service and wished me the best at Salomon Brothers. He concluded the note whimsically by writing, "Perhaps we will have to increase the pay economists receive." What more could a Morgan employee expect?

Part II

Formulating the Plan

7

Origins of Morgan's Transformation

By early 1984, several things were readily apparent about Morgan. First, it had weathered the Less Developed Country (LDC) debt crisis better than its competitors, and it was in position to solidify its standing within the banking industry. Second, Lew Preston at the same time knew Morgan had to be transformed so it could compete not only with money center banks and foreign banks but also with securities firms that were in the ascendancy. The big unknown was how Morgan as a commercial bank could break into the investment banking and securities world when Glass-Steagall barriers stood in the way.

These themes were articulated in a *New York Times* article "The Wealth and Aura of Morgan" written in the spring of 1983.[1] The article began by noting how Morgan was so well run and so profitable that it was considered the paragon of the banking industry:

> Bankers Trust openly tries to emulate it, and even Walter V. Wriston, Citicorp's supremely self-confident chairman, often uses Morgan as a model of profitability and a yardstick by which to measure how well a bank is run. Last year, for example, Morgan—the nation's fifth largest bank holding company with assets of $58.6 billion—earned 78 cents on each $100 of average assets, more than any other of the 15 largest bank holding companies.[2]

---

[1] Robert A. Bennett, *New York Times*, April 10, 1983.
[2] Ibid., p. 1.

© The Author(s) 2020
N. P. Sargen, *JPMorgan's Fall and Revival*, https://doi.org/10.1007/978-3-030-47058-6_7

The article then went on to describe the principal challenge Morgan faced in plotting its future in a rapidly changing financial world:

> As other banking companies thrust boldly into new fields and push for inter-state banking, Morgan's top officers are questioning whether their bank can continue along its tried but narrow course—shunning customers that aren't very, very rich and doing business only with governments and the largest and most prestigious of corporations.[3]

As Preston contemplated transforming Morgan in the 1980s, he first had to assess how the competitive landscape in financial services was changing and then weigh Morgan's strengths and weaknesses in order to formulate a coherent strategy for the firm. The backdrop for making these decisions was one of considerable excess capacity within the banking industry. Merger activity among US banks picked up in the mid-1970s when inflation and interest rates surged, and Reg Q interest rate ceilings limited banks' ability to compete with institutions that were not subject to them. To alleviate this challenge, amendments to federal and state legislation pertaining to bank holding companies were enacted that allowed banks to accept deposits in states where they were not domiciled.

What was not foreseen at the time was the profound changes in the US banking industry that would ensue over the next two decades. The pace of merger activity subsequently ballooned from 1980 to the mid-1990s when a total of 6347 mergers took place.[4] This tally equaled 43% of all banks in 1980.

A Brookings study in 1995 noted that this period is "undoubtedly the most turbulent period in U.S. banking history since the Great Depression."[5] The number of US commercial banks declined by 36% to just under 8000 in 1994 from nearly 12,500 in 1979. (Note: This tally excludes thrifts.) Most of this reflected reductions in the number of small banks, and the share of assets they held was cut in half while that of so-called megabanks (those with assets of more than $100 billion) doubled (Table 7.1).[6]

There were two major drivers of change in the banking industry. First, on the asset side, US banks were being disintermediated, as corporate customers increasingly tapped capital markets and foreign banks to fund their activities.

---

[3] Ibid, p. 2.

[4] Stephen A. Rhoades, Board of Governors of the Federal Reserve System, "Bank Mergers and Industrywide Structure, 1980–94," January 1996.

[5] Allen N. Berger, Anil K. Kashyap, Joseph M. Scalise, "The Transformation of the U.S. Banking Industry: What a Long, Strange Trip It's Been," Brookings Papers on Economic Activity, 1995.

[6] Ibid., Table 1, p. 67.

Table 7.1 Transformation of the US commercial banking industry

	1979	1994
Total number of banks	12,493	7926
Small banks	10,014	5636
Total industry assets	3.26	4.02
(trillions of 1994 dollars)		
Share of industry assets (%)		
Megabanks	9.4	18.8
Small banks	13.9	7.0

Source: Berger, Kashyap, Scalise, Brookings, Federal Reserve call reports

Table 7.2 US commercial banks and external competition

	1979	1994
Total credit market debt	$8.27	$17.14
(trillions of 1994 dollars)		
US bank share	25.8%	17.0%
Total nonfinancial corporate debt (trillions of 1994 dollars)	$1.58	$2.75
US bank share	19.6%	14.5%
Foreign bank share	5.6%	13.4%

Source: Berger et al., Brookings, Federal Reserve

The share of credit market debt of individuals, businesses and governments financed by US banks fell to 17% in 1994 from nearly 26% in 1979[7] (Table 7.2). Over this period the share of US corporate debt financed by foreign banks rose to 13.4% from 5.6%. This development was especially relevant for Morgan, because its customer base was predominantly Fortune 100 companies and foreign governments that had ready access to financing from capital markets and foreign banks.

By comparison, the second major drivers of change—a shift away from regulated deposit rates to market-based funding for banks along with liberalization that allowed banks to accept deposits outside the jurisdiction of their headquarters—were less of a challenge for Morgan's business model. The reason: Morgan Guaranty was a wholesale bank, not a retail bank. Therefore, it routinely funded its activities by borrowing in the inter-bank market rather than via customer deposits. Throughout its history Morgan never encountered problems on the funding side.

The change in banking regulations nonetheless had an indirect impact on Morgan, because its principal competitors engaged in retail banking and they

---

[7] Ibid., Table 4. p. 74.

benefited from the consolidation in the banking industry. As the *New York Times* article noted:

> What concerns Mr. Preston is that, once Federal Law allows interstate banking, if it ever does, other banks might merge into gargantuan institutions, making Morgan small by comparison. This would put Morgan at a disadvantage in serving its own clients because it could not make big loans to individual clients as its competitors did.[8]

To counter this threat Morgan's management was able to increase its capital in a 14-month stretch by $900 million to $3 billion as of the first quarter of 1983.

Morgan's principal rival at the time was Citibank—the largest US bank, the most innovative and also the most diverse internationally. Under the leadership of Walter Wriston, who served as chairman and CEO from 1967 to 1984, Citi's network of branches expanded globally as a way of increasing its opportunities outside the highly regulated domestic market. Wriston saw the highest rewards as being available in less developed countries, and when he assumed the helm as CEO, Citi had more than 200 branches abroad, far surpassing that of Chase Manhattan and Bank of America. By the mid-1970s, 70% of Citi's total earnings came from its overseas obligations.

At the same time, Citi was venturing into the application of consumer technology via deployment of automated teller machines (ATMs) and credit card facilities under the direction of John Reed who succeeded Wriston in 1984. He would take the bank in that direction, which would have a major influence on US banking (Table 7.3).

Table 7.3 Technical and financial innovations affecting US banking

	1979	1994
Number of ATMs	13,000	109,080
Real cost of electronic deposit	0.091	0.014
Real cost of paper check	0.012	0.025
megabanks		
Notional value of derivatives/assets	0.82	11.45
Other noninterest income/op. income	7.0	20.9
small banks		
Notional value of derivatives/assets	0.00	0.00
Other noninterest income/op. income	3.5	8.3

Source: Berger et al., Brookings, Federal Reserve

---

[8] Ibid.

Preston had no inclination to follow Citi's lead, especially as Morgan had no experience in retail banking. What Preston did not say publicly, but he believed to be true, was that Citi's schizophrenic strategy—that served both corporate and retail clients—was eating itself out of house and home.

Preston believed Morgan's core competencies encompassed advising elite corporations and governments on highly sophisticated transactions and creating innovative financing techniques (the power of ideas) for its customers. One of its most innovative transactions linked debt warrants to zero-coupon bonds, which gave investors a chance to buy more debt from the issuer in the future at a fixed price while lowering the overall cost to the issuer. Citibank became one of Morgan's first underwriting clients using this financing arrangement.

To expand its capabilities Morgan became the first bank to open a subsidiary in 1981, Morgan Futures Corporation, which dealt in the potentially lucrative business of financial futures. Morgan had seats on the major commodity exchanges in New York, Chicago and London, and it also ramped up its trading activities in gold and precious metals. These units dealt with central banks, government and large corporations, rather than with individual speculators or small industrial users.

Another competitor, Chemical Bank, pursued a strategy of growing its domestic business through a series of acquisitions, first of regional banks and eventually megabanks. In 1980 its Chairman Donald Platten began restructuring non-consumer banking operations and setting up separate divisions for multinational corporations, large domestic corporations and middle-market businesses.[9] Thereafter, Chemical engaged in a series of acquisitions to expand its operations into Florida (via a 1982 merger with Florida National Banks), New Jersey (via a merger with Horizons Bank holding company initiated in 1987) and Texas (via a 1987 merger with Texas Commerce Bank).

Chemical under Jimmy Lee's stewardship also created a new business called loan syndications, which became a lucrative business that it dominated. This transformed large-client commercial banking, because a lead bank could arrange large financing quickly for clients, especially for M&A deals. Financing leveraged buyouts (LBOs) for private equity firms also became a big business that was both profitable and risky. Morgan, by comparison, had no prior experience in servicing small- and medium-sized firms. Consequently, it was slow to enter this business.

---

[9] Funding Universe, Chemical Banking Corporate History.

Table 7.4 Return on equity: investment banks versus largest banks

(Average annual after-tax rates of return)					
	1979	1980	1981	1982	1983
Largest investment banks	19%	30%	30%	30%	24%
Ten largest bank holding companies	16%	16%	14%	13%	13%

Source: JPMorgan

Table 7.5 Market valuations: bank stocks versus industrial stocks

(Ratio of market value to book value)					
	1979	1980	1981	1982	1983
S&P 400 Index	1.23	1.43	1.18	1.33	1.53
35 largest banks	0.76	0.80	0.78	0.79	0.90

Source: JPMorgan

While Morgan's management ruled out retail banking and the middle market, Preston long considered the prospect of turning Morgan into a universal bank, in which it could provide an array of commercial and investment banking services to its corporate customers. In the wake of the developing country debt crisis the timing was propitious: The profitability of major investment banks measured by return on equity far surpassed the largest commercial banks (Table 7.4) and market valuations of large banks were well below industrial company stocks (Table 7.5).

As Preston searched to find the model for the JPMorgan of the future, one firm that Morgan's management found appealing was Morgan Stanley. The reason was not so much that it did business "in the Morgan Way." Rather, its management was able to take a firm that was heavily concentrated in corporate finance via underwriting and M&A and transform it into a global investment bank with strong sales and trading capabilities. Moreover, Morgan Stanley's executive team—Dick Fisher, Parker Gilbert, Bob Greenhill and Lewis Bernard—were able to do so without sacrificing the firm's culture.

The main challenge Morgan Guaranty and other money center banks faced in pursuing this course was how they could build a securities business when Glass-Steagall restrictions blocked them from doing so in the United States. Morgan's path to break into the securities business, therefore, entailed expanding its international capabilities in London, Frankfurt, Zurich, Paris, Amsterdam, Melbourne, Toronto and Tokyo.

The transformation began in 1979 with the creation of Morgan Guaranty Limited (MGL), which became the launch pad for underwriting Eurobonds.

Preston assigned Tony Mayer, who had run project finance, Eurobond syndication and private placement to establish the entity. At the same time, a specialized unit called Territory Five was renamed International Financial Management (IFM) and taken over by Roberto Mendoza.[10] Its purpose was to attract multinational clients who needed sophisticated cross-border advice. MGL's objectives were to: (1) provide IFM with the means to raise money in the markets; and (2) build securities expertise, which could then be transferred to the United States when Glass-Steagall barriers fell.

Initial results were encouraging. As Chernow points out, by 1984 MGL was the second largest underwriter of Eurobonds (and the leader among US banks), up from #46 in 1980.[11] With this success Morgan's management was able to sell its 33% stake in Morgan Grenfell in 1984.

However, there were also growing pains along the way. In 1985–86 banks were adding to their secondary reserves by selling subordinated debt obligations with fixed terms. MGL created an alternative floating-rate note structure, in which the coupon was adjusted every six months based on LIBOR. The twist was that to ensure the debt would be treated as primary capital, the term of the loan was unlimited, or "perpetual." The team in London quickly lined up three bank issuers—all based in the Asia-Pacific region. However, due to the size of the issues, they had to revert to New York for capital before they could bring the deals to market.

Weatherstone and Bob Engel had given the green light to David Band and Tony Mayer to ramp up MGL's activities. However, they kept MGL on a short leash rather than permanently increasing its capital, which would have required approval from the New York Fed. By this time, the firm had allowed Shep Poor to retire, and when the deals brought to market sales were minimal. This meant the deals had to be re-priced. When syndicates refused to sell the deals, MGL was forced to buy back the bonds or let the price slip away. In the process, MGL's capital was wiped out.

Morgan's management ultimately had to seek approval from Gerald Corrigan, president of the New York Federal Reserve, to recapitalize MGL, this time for $250 million with an identical amount of sub-debt on call. This was embarrassing to Morgan's management, because regulators and securities firms were watching to see if banks could be trusted to get back into the

---

[10] Robert Teitelman, "Morgan Enters the Morgan Era," *Institutional Investor*, January 24, 1996, p. 54.
[11] Chernow, op. cit. p.

securities underwriting business. Ray Wareham subsequently came up with the idea of splitting the "perpetuals" into interest-only and principal-only tranches, which were promptly sold to UK insurance companies. With the gains from these sales, MGL was finally properly capitalized for its underwriting and trading activities.

The broader issue that Morgan's management confronted was that new issuance in overseas markets was primarily in debt markets, which was necessary but not sufficient for success in the US market. Notably, there was no bulge bracket for debt issuance in the Eurobond market, syndicate discipline was lax and underwriting was client-centric with limited market depth. Morgan also suffered from a lack of knowledge and experience in syndicate practices—who to include in the management group, how much to allocate to syndicate members, how much to over-allot, how to stabilize a new issue and when to free it up to trade without influencing the price. All of these were learned the hard way with inevitable setbacks.

When the US markets began to open up in the latter part of the 1980s, these challenges reappeared, but the weaknesses were even more pronounced. Distribution had to be built from scratch, and structures were considerably more complex. Even more daunting was that equity issuance, not debt, was the sine qua non to success, and the so-called bulge bracket was dominant. Given these challenges many observers (myself included) wondered why Morgan didn't acquire businesses instead of building them.

Nonetheless, as discussed in the next chapter, Lew Preston was undeterred that it could transform itself into a universal bank, although many of Morgan's "old guard" executives were less sure.

One event that helped to convince Morgan's management to continue its quest was the collapse of Continental Bank in 1984. The Chicago-based bank was the seventh largest in the United States and the largest in the Midwest, with approximately $40 billion in assets. While the bank had conservative roots, its management pursued a rapid growth strategy in the late 1970s, such that it became the largest commercial and industrial (C&I) lender in the country. Problems surfaced in July 1982, when Penn Square Bank failed, which risked losses on Continental's $1 billion in speculative energy-related loans right before the developing country debt crisis surfaced. These events caused investors to re-examine the bank's risk-pricing and lending practices.

Continental took actions to stabilize its balance sheet thereafter. However, when its tally of nonperforming loans increased by $400 million to $2.3 billion in the first quarter of 1984, rumors of its insolvency sparked a massive run by depositors on May 10. The following day the bank borrowed $3.6 billion from the Federal Reserve Bank of Chicago.

Paul Volcker subsequently contacted Preston about arranging a consortium of banks that would extend a credit line of $4.5 billion to further shore up Continental. Whereas Morgan once again assumed its traditional role of trying to stabilize the situation, Citibank was far less accommodating. Its chief negotiator, Tom Theobald, balked and reportedly said, "When my house is on fire I call the fire department and my insurance company, not my neighbor."[12] When Wriston ultimately acquiesced, he claimed that by holding out Citibank got better terms than if it had immediately accepted the Fed's demands.

While Wriston did not believe the government should have rescued Continental or its bondholders, Preston was worried that scores of Midwestern banks that had sold Fed funds to Continental amounting to three times their capital. Beyond this, Continental's near failure served as a wake-up call for Morgan's management about the risks of relying heavily on loans to grow its business. Continental, after all, had long been admired as a conservative institution that seemed well managed, and which many referred to as the "Morgan of the Midwest."

The rescue of Continental ultimately entailed keeping it alive with the injection of Federal Deposit Insurance Corporation (FDIC) funds that protected all the banks creditors including uninsured depositors and bondholders. During Congressional hearings, Comptroller of the Currency C.T. Conover explicitly stated that regulators were unlikely to allow the nation's eleven largest multinational banks to fail. Congressman Stewart McKinney reportedly responded, "Let's not bandy words. We have (created) a new kid of bank. It's called too big to fail. TBTF, and it is a wonderful bank."[13]

Soon after, Morgan stepped up its efforts to lobby the Federal Reserve about breaking down Glass-Steagall barriers. In 1982, Preston formed a study group under "Johnnie" Wissell, who ran Public Finance and Municipal Bond departments, and Rachael Robbins, who ran the Legal department, to find a way out. After weeks of study, the group concluded any loosening would likely be progressive and based on demonstrated performance as banks branched out from underwriting and distributing government and municipal bonds.

The key finding was Morgan should exploit the language of the Glass-Steagall Act itself in which the bill drafters had left an exclusion—that the banks must be "engaged principally" (but not exclusively) in commercial

---

[12] Philip L. Zweig, *Wriston*, Crown Publishers Inc., 1995, p. 817. Ironically, Theobald later became the CEO of Continental after he lost out to John Reed as Wriston's successor.

[13] Federal Reserve History, Failure of Continental Illinois, May 1984.

banking businesses. Preston, at first, was skeptical that Morgan could re-enter the US corporate bond business by taking advantage of a loophole in the act. He ultimately came around to the idea and was fortunate to have Alan Greenspan on Morgan's Board to test the waters.

Two years later, in December of 1984, Morgan issued a report titled "Rethinking Glass-Steagall" in which it presented the case for allowing bank holding company subsidiaries to underwrite and deal in corporate securities.[14] The report examined the arguments most commonly made to justify the preservation of the artificial barriers to competition imposed by Glass-Steagall and found these arguments to have little merit:[15]

> Historical research reveals that the Act did not play a major role in restoring the stability of the banking system; review of the risks and rewards entailed in corporate securities activities shows that permitting bank holding companies to diversify in this way would enhance, not diminish, the system's stability; an analysis suggests that no unmanageable conflicts of interest would arise from the affiliation of banks and securities firms.

In his book on Walter Wriston, Philip Zweig mentions that Preston tried to persuade Citi to join Morgan in lobbying to dismantle Glass-Steagall, but was unsuccessful.[16] One reason was Preston had a much better rapport with Volcker than Wriston, and Volcker was also more comfortable with Morgan being in the securities business than Citibank, which was much more aggressive.

Over the next three years, Preston would continue to lobby Volcker for relief on Glass-Steagall to little or no avail. Morgan's management at one point even considered giving up its bank charter and dropping deposit insurance in order to enjoy full banking services.[17]

An article in *Fortune* magazine in April of 1986 titled "Morgan Guaranty's Identity Crisis" commented that while the bank posted record quarterly earnings, it came from a large bet on its investment portfolio that interest rates would decline.[18] This was an interest rate swap in which Morgan would receive a fixed rate and pay a floating rate in anticipation that interest rates would decline. Otherwise, Morgan's loan portfolio was stagnant: "So dismal is the

---

[14] J.P. Morgan & Co., Rethinking Glass-Steagall, December 1984.
[15] Ibid.
[16] Zweig, op. cit., p. 808.
[17] Ibid., p. 808.
[18] Gary Hector, "Morgan Guaranty's Identity Crisis," Fortune, April 28, 1986.

profit outlook in commercial lending that Morgan is considering a revolutionary move: giving up its commercial bank charter so it can plunge into investment banking. The decision would rattle the banking industry like an earthquake."[19]

Preston subsequently concluded that access to the Fed's discount window outweighed the advantages of becoming an investment bank. Somewhat later, however, Morgan sent an inquiry to Edward George of the Bank of England about the possibility of switching the bank's domicile to England and was given a positive indication.

On a cold mid-November afternoon in 1986, all of the senior officers were gathered in the board room beneath the silver chandeliers. Preston had called the meeting to make a go/no go decision on the bank's securities strategy. There was no question it had been a hard slog to get Glass-Steagall repealed. Members of the Investment Bankers Association had done all in their power to keep the banks from intruding on their turf. They had lobbied Congress, their corporate and government clients, and hired MBAs away from the banks on the premise that Glass-Steagall would never fall—anything to keep the banks at bay.

A formal presentation to kick off the proceedings indicated how far Morgan lagged in critical skills and revenue streams from businesses like mergers and acquisition advisory services to trading debt, equity and commodities. As the meeting wore for almost three hours there was a notable divide between the old guard who favored the status quo and those who now staffed the revenue-generating divisions of the bank. Toward that end, Preston, who had remained silent throughout, went round the table asking each participant (the Corporate Office excluded) where he stood.

Only three were enthusiastic for proceeding: Mendoza, Olds and Nicholas Potter, who headed JPMorgan Investment Management (JPMIM). However, Potter had ulterior motives. He had a memo prepared by a partner of Davis Polk and Wardwell, which looked after JPMIM's affairs, that they would not be able to purchase any securities underwritten by Morgan due to Chinese Wall restrictions. When asked how Goldman Sachs and other investment banks were able to do so, Potter demurred, saying the choice for Morgan was between going "retail" and following the client base into the capital markets. In fact, it later was revealed that Potter was in unauthorized discussions with one of the largest insurance companies about a sale of JPMIM as an independent investment advisory arm.

---

[19] Ibid.

Everyone in the room waited for Preston's decision. Looking around the table, he said, in effect: We are going to finish what we have started. While Preston and Weatherstone had made the decision, it was far from the end of second-guessing. Morgan's senior management was still split into two factions—the old guard, who was moved to supernumerary functions, and the younger generation who ran the profit-making divisions. In the end, it did not matter, as there had been a changing of the guard.

In the meantime, Morgan's management opted to play a waiting game, expanding its tentacles in the securities business while conforming to Glass-Steagall. By late 1987, it received the opening it was waiting for when Alan Greenspan succeeded Volcker as Fed chairman, and he proved more sympathetic about phasing out Glass-Steagall.

Box: JPMorgan in the Securities Business—A Historical Note

The beginnings of the "House of Morgan" can be traced to Junius S. Morgan's admission to become a partner of George Peabody & Co. in 1854. Peabody was a London-based merchant bank specializing in business with the United States. Its business in the 1850s included promoting and investing in Cyrus Field's project to lay a telegraph cable across the Atlantic, and leading its first issue for American railroad in London in 1853. Upon George Peabody's retirement in 1864, the name of the firm was changed to J.S. Morgan & Co., which it retained until it became Morgan Grenfell & Co. in 1910.

J. Pierpont Morgan, Junius' son, joined with Charles H. Dabney in 1864 to form a partnership that evolved into Drexel Morgan & Co. in 1871. It represented an alliance between the interests of J.S. Morgan & Co., represented by Pierpont Morgan, and Drexel & Co. of New York and Philadelphia. This alliance solidified the positions of the Morgan firms in the United States, while also establishing a close correspondence between the Drexel house and prominent banking houses in London.

The new arrangement established an international network of partnerships located in London, Paris, New York and Philadelphia. While legally organized as separate firms, the four houses acted in concert. Pierpont Morgan was the leader of the New York house, and in 1895 he became the senior partner in all four firms.

During the last quarter of the nineteenth century, the Morgan firms were active in financing prominent sovereign and corporate issuers in securities markets, often competing or cooperating with the prestigious Baring and Rothschild houses. They included leading or participating in syndicates for sovereign borrowers such as France (during the Franco Prussian War), Norway, Sweden, Italy, Chile and Argentina, as well as cooperating with the Rothchild firms in arranging a private purchase of US Treasury bonds to replenish US gold reserves. By the

(continued)

(continued)

end of the century, the Morgan firms had attained a stature equal to these firms, and in the American context superior to them.

Among issues for corporate clients, railroad securities figured prominently in the late nineteenth century. The Morgan firms earned prominence for recapitalizing the Erie, the B&O and the Northern Pacific, among others. JPMorgan & Co. was also instrumental in forming via mergers several corporations that would dominate US industry including the General Electric Company in 1892, the establishment of United States Steel in 1901 and the foundation of International Harvester in 1902.

As they reached the stature of acknowledged financial leaders, the Morgan firms were also called upon to assist other firms in difficulty. In 1895, the Bank of England looked to J.S. Morgan & Co. and to Barings' holdings of Argentine securities while the firm was resuscitated. The most famous rescue occurred during the Panic of 1907, when the financial community looked to Pierpont Morgan to organize the relief of banks and trust companies experiencing heavy withdrawals.[20] This earned JPMorgan & Co. the reputation of being a de facto central bank before the Federal Reserve was created.

When J.P. Morgan died in 1913, his son J.P. Morgan Jr. succeeded him as senior partner in each of the Morgan firms. They reached the height of their dominance in issuance of securities in the 1920s. Private banks led the vast majority of all issues during the decade, with Morgan taking the largest single share.

As some of the country's most influential bankers, the Morgan partners became prominent targets for those dissatisfied with the structure of US financial markets. Thus, during the Congressional "money trust" investigation of 1912, as well as a Senate investigation of 1933, Morgan firms and partners were the focus of inquiries that sought to establish that a small number of banks exercised control over securities markets. The Senate inquiry culminated with passage of the Glass-Steagall Act that led to the separation of commercial and investment banking.

---

[20] See Bruner and Carr, op. cit.

8

Buy or Build?

Once Morgan's senior management was committed to transition the firm into securities and investment banking it had to develop a strategy to pull it off. There were two directions in which the bank could go. One was to gain expertise via acquisitions that the regulatory authorities would sanction; the other was to build a capability in securities and investment banking organically.

For Lew Preston the choice was clear. Morgan would primarily build the business internally. However, he was open to consider targeted acquisitions that were good strategic fits provided the price was right.

Preston's aversion for making a major acquisition reflected two primary considerations. First, he believed Morgan's unique corporate culture was the key to its storied success. It emphasized putting customers' interests first, and it stressed the importance of teamwork over individual accomplishment. He and most other senior managers of the bank had spent their entire careers at Morgan, and they could not conceive doing business any other way. They worried that if Morgan acquired a firm with a different set of values, it would create disharmony among employees that would harm the bank.

The second consideration related to Morgan's history. Throughout the post-war era, it was involved in only one merger, that with the Guaranty Trust Co. of New York to form the Morgan Guaranty Trust Company in 1959. According to Chernow, Morgan was languishing in the 1940s and 1950s while losing ground to its principal rivals.[1] The merger with the Guaranty Trust Co. virtually fell into its lap, as the Board of Guaranty Trust was looking to replace its CEO, and Morgan's management was highly regarded. The fit

---

[1] Chernow, op. cit.

© The Author(s) 2020
N. P. Sargen, *JPMorgan's Fall and Revival*, https://doi.org/10.1007/978-3-030-47058-6_8

proved to be excellent as the two banks had numerous relationships between them and complementary characteristics: JPMorgan brought a prestigious name and high-end clients while Guaranty Trust brought significant assets that were nearly four times the size of JPMorgan. Despite this, Morgan was considered the buyer and nominal survivor, and JPMorgan employees became the primary managers of the new company.

This transaction breathed new life into Morgan, which re-emerged as one of the most powerful and prestigious financial institutions in the world.[2] Through the merger Morgan regained its status as the world's largest whole-sale bank, and it stood fourth in total assets behind National City (that became Citibank), Chase Manhattan and Bank of America.[3]

During the second half of the 1960s and continuing into the 1970s Morgan Guaranty became a pioneer institution for trading federal funds (holdings of reserves at the Fed), and the bank expanded its trading operations in money markets and capital markets, becoming the most active dealer in Treasury and municipal securities.[4] It then went on to expand its global presence and was a major player in the Eurocurrency markets. Among the key players in this transition were Ralph Leach and Dennis Weatherstone, who both came from Guaranty Trust.

While the merger with Guaranty Trust proved to be a "win-win" arrangement for both entities, Morgan's management did not want to expand its business in wholesale lending in the mid-1980s by merging with a major bank. Also, it had no interest in building a branch network for retail banking. Instead, management focused on laying the groundwork for Morgan's eventual entry into the securities and investment banking business.

One of the first steps management took was to continue to build a "fortress balance sheet" that could withstand unforeseen shocks to the financial system and at the same time enable Morgan to expand its business. An article in *Fortune* magazine in 1986 noted that Morgan was the only US commercial bank whose bonds were rated AAA by Standard & Poor's.[5] Its primary capital, which is the cushion regulators consider as a bank's last line of defense in the event of a run, was equal to 8% of assets, 45% more than the minimum regulators require. Morgan's reserve against possible loan losses equaled 2.14% of loans, more than twice what Citibank set aside, even though both institutions had equal percentages of problem loans. In fact, Morgan was the only major

---

[2] Ibid.

[3] Ibid.

[4] Ibid., p. 540.

[5] Gary Hector, "Morgan Guaranty's Identity Crisis," *Fortune*, April 28, 1986.

bank with a reserve cushion bigger than its problem loans. Despite this, Preston is quoted saying, "It is absolutely unrealistic to think we are going to go back to the low-loss experience of the past."[6]

Among the actions Preston took to signal Morgan's transition into investment banking were a series of organizational changes among senior management. The first was a press release on February 13, 1985, that assigned new duties to three of its executive vice presidents: Bruce Brackenridge became head of the Administrative Division; James Flynn, who had run the Operations Division, became head of a newly formed Financial and Information Systems Division, and John Ruffle, who had been treasurer of JPMorgan and chief financial officer, was given added responsibilities. An internal memo stated that the purpose of these changes was to ensure the company's success "to adapt to changes in our business environment without sacrificing the core strengths that have made Morgan distinctive."[7]

One year later, a second reorganization was announced that combined into one division Morgan's commercial lending group and the few investment banking operations it was allowed. Robert Engel, who had served as head of the bank's treasurer's division, was placed in charge of the combined group. A Morgan spokesman estimated Engel would oversee roughly 10,000 of the company's 13,500 employees worldwide, and the division would generate between 75% and 80% of the bank's profits.[8] A Merrill Lynch banking analyst, Lawrence M. Cohn, offered the following observation about the change:

> They are taking the existing commercial bankers and trying to make them more aware of the investment banking products that are there. And their chances of marrying several different kinds of cultures together are better than most, because Morgan has a long, long tradition of being organizationally run on a highly integrated sort of basis.[9]

Nonetheless, the enormity of what Morgan's management was attempting should not be underestimated: Namely, it was seeking to retrain commercial bankers who were skilled at assessing credit risk to become investment bankers who understood securities transactions and who could assess market risks.

One of the reasons Engel was selected for this assignment was he brought a background in trading and was considered a favorite among younger officers.

---

[6] Ibid.

[7] JPMorgan memo to employees, February 13, 1985.

[8] Kenneth Gilpin and Eric Schmidt, *New York Times*, February 14, 1986.

[9] Ibid.

In his new role, however, he would have a much tougher assignment—namely, weeding out people who could not make the transition:

> One former trader fondly remembers watching Engel wander along the trading floor, wearing a blue shirt—so frayed that his elbow showed through, stopping to place a hand on young traders and chat briefly. Former Morgan executives expect Engel in his new job to wander through the bank wielding an ax.[10]

The principal reason is Morgan needed to retrain its employees so it could be competitive with investment banks, while pruning those who could not make the cut. An example: When I joined the bank in the late 1970s it had approximately 8000 employees, but by the mid-1980s the head count had increased to 13,500 people. By comparison, Salomon Brothers generated profits in 1985 that were 83% of Morgan's with a headcount that was one third as large. Thus, while Morgan compared favorably with rival commercial banks in terms of productivity as measured by assets or revenues per employee, its productivity per employee lagged most investment banks considerably.

Engel acknowledged this by stating, "First you have the reorganization. Then the weeding out begins."[11] The vision of Lew Preston and Morgan's senior managers was that bankers had to become more sophisticated about financial market transactions, as well as understand their clients' needs and the array of products to serve their needs. Using this framework, the ideal Morgan banker was a hybrid of "the courteous, gentlemanly commercial banker of Morgan's past and the brash, deal-oriented investment bankers of Wall Street."[12]

The key challenge for Morgan's management was whether they could marry the two prototypes—commercial banker and investment banker—without producing a culture clash. The route management chose involved retraining bankers and analysts to become knowledgeable about how capital markets functioned. McKinsey & Company was hired to advise Morgan's management about "best practice" techniques in the financial services industry, and they told Morgan's management that the firm was lagging Citibank.

The training program was then devised internally by Marnie Gislasson and Til Guldimann, and they hired two top professors from Harvard to teach classes on financial markets. Part of the appeal for new recruits was they could attend the training sessions and receive the same background as MBAs. But

---

[10] Hector, op. cit.
[11] Ibid.
[12] Ibid.

the training process also continued to stress the importance of Morgan's culture and doing business the right way.

The potential for a culture clash, nonetheless, would become apparent in the mid-to-late 1980s, when Morgan's management sought to beef up its corporate finance area, first in London and subsequently in New York. In London, financial deregulation associated with the launch of the Big Bang in 1986 created an opportunity for Morgan to add to its list of clients in the United Kingdom. Preston and Weatherstone had selected Sandy Warner to lead the effort several years earlier, and Warner responded by sending signals to old-line bankers to lift their game or accept lower compensation. Many who weren't up to the task departed for other banks, and Warner, in turn, responded by stepping up recruiting from outside.

For a while, the London office seemed like a carousel. A flock of senior managers departed for New York while others arrived in London. Amid this, there was potential for groups to split into factions. However, Warner was credited for having a stabilizing influence and for ensuring that groups cooperated with each other.

Based on this, Preston and Weatherstone gave Warner an even more challenging assignment in mid-1987. They selected him to take over corporate finance for the Americas and to help mold traditional relationship bankers into becoming investment bankers. Their new roles would require them to do much more than arrange loans and offer cash management services. Henceforth, they would have to become the principal contact for underwriting securities, as well as for offering advice on derivatives and M&A.

In September of 1988, Warner sent a memo to the corporate finance unit that laid out its mission to understand each client's business, management objectives and financial needs. He emphasized that "the competition was Goldman Sachs and Morgan Stanley," and he stated that "we must leverage our resources to achieve greater productivity."[13] Warner then announced a reorganization to create fourteen client teams, each headed by a senior banker that would provide a full array of services to corporate clients. Given the importance of credit, a special group was set up that was independent of the client teams.

During the reorganization, many bankers who had been successful under the former arrangement struggled to adapt. Some could not handle the demands created by having to market new products. Others—especially those in their fifties—did not want the pressure and travel loads involved in

---

[13] Robert Teitelman, "Morgan Enters the Warner Era," *Institutional Investor*, January 24, 1996, p. 60.

competing with thirty-year olds from Goldman, Morgan Stanley and other investment banks.

For Morgan's competitors on Wall Street this goal of molding traditional bankers into investment bankers was a far stretch. From their perspective, the name of the game in the securities and investment banking world is compensation, not prestige. Moreover, the gulf in the mindset between bankers and traders is huge.

I witnessed this first hand when I joined Salomon Brothers, which was the epitome of a firm run by traders. Salomon was on a roll then and was ramping up hiring in most areas, and it held an offsite at the Arrowwood conference center in Westchester to build camaraderie between the old guard and new hires. The session began with speeches by John Gutfreund, the CEO, and Tom Strauss, the president, about the firm's goal of becoming a financial super-power where customers could satisfy all of their needs at one place, which Strauss dubbed "one-stop shopping." Their speeches were followed by talks by various area heads including fixed income, equities, derivatives and international, each of which made me realize how much I had to learn about the securities business.

Following the speeches, we convened for a sumptuous dinner that rivaled any I had at Morgan. Thereafter, I witnessed something I'd never seen before: The tables were cleared and senior executives became engaged in high stakes poker games, where the bets that were placed exceeded several thousands of dollars, much as described in Michael Lewis' book, *Liar's Poker*.[14] It was then I fully realized how different Solly's culture was from Morgan's, and I worried I might not fit in. Fortunately, there was still a place for me, as none of my colleagues on the research side participated, and we all wondered what we were witnessing.

A while later I contacted a former colleague from Morgan who had switched from the International Economics Department to become a banker covering Turkey. When I told him how different Salomon Brothers was from Morgan, he told me that working at Morgan was not the same as before. Bankers were now being graded on a scale of one to five, and those in the bottom group were told their performance needed to improve or they would be let go. This created considerable pressure to adapt to the changing environment, where the mentality had become "sink or swim." He was fearful he might not make the cut even though he was highly educated with a Ph.D. in Economics from Columbia University.

---

[14] Michael Lewis, *Liar's Poker*, W.W. Norton & Company, 1989.

One of the biggest challenges for Morgan's senior management was how to reward individuals who achieved high performance ratings. Previously, the range in pay increases between the top performers and those rated less highly was fairly narrow. During my best year, for example, I received a pay increase in the low double digits, but inflation was also close to double digits, so my real pay raise (after inflation) was much smaller. While I was content and realized I had a great job with a wonderful firm, people who were on the front line facing considerable pressure to produce top-line results would question whether they were being properly compensated for their results and hard work.

This issue came to the forefront once Morgan decided to go down the path of investment banking and securities trading. The reason: Morgan's bankers were well compensated within the commercial banking world, but their pay was well below levels investment banks and securities firms paid. Preston understood there would have to be a significantly wider differentiation in compensation between star performers and the rank and file, but he at the same time was leery of paying top performers what rival institutions would offer them. He feared getting into a bidding war for the top talent on Wall Street could shatter Morgan's team spirit.

One of the most visible test cases for the bank was Rafe de la Gueronniere, a former backgammon teacher who built Morgan's highly successful gold-trading operation before heading its government bond trading department. He eventually left Morgan for Paine Webber, where he became a member of the firm's executive committee and was believed to have made three to four times his compensation at Morgan. De la Gueronniere's departure may have been the catalyst to convince Preston that top money producers had to be rewarded properly. Thereafter, for the first time in its history, a Morgan trader earned more than the chairman's compensation, which at the time was $1.2 million.[15]

While this episode may have been a test case for Morgan, it paled in comparison with what was happening at other Wall Street firms. At Salomon Brothers, I worked with a currency options trader who took huge positions in Australian dollars and New Zealand dollars using the firm's capital to back his trades. In 1985, he bet the ranch and won, reportedly earning the firm about $100 million on his trades, for which he received compensation of $10 million. The next year he made additional outsized bets, but wound up losing most of what he had gained the prior year. While he was let go for this, he did not have to relinquish his prior year's bonus.

---

[15] Chernow, op. cit.

When I realized what was happening, I could not understand how Salomon could be so short-sighted and I asked executives at the firm how they could allow this practice. The response was that this was the way the game was played on Wall Street, and firms had to either go along or risk losing top talent. Preston, however, did not want Morgan to play this game.

The problem for Morgan was it had to compete with firms that were prepared to dole out bundles of money to star producers. This was especially apparent in the area of M&A, where the bank had only been successful on a few deals during the 1970s and early 1980s. In the middle 1980s, Morgan responded by putting one of its acknowledged stars, Roberto Mendoza, in charge of the group. Mendoza had been very successful in helping to build Morgan's Eurobond business and had a razor sharp mind to compete in M&A. However, the team he inherited lacked his talent, and Preston was not willing to bid for established stars to build a competitive business.

The bottom line: It was not easy to build a securities and investment banking business from scratch, and it was also costly. First, it was expensive to retrain commercial bankers and not all would make the cut. Second, Morgan had to be prepared to pay outside hires more than its existing employees. This not only added to salary expense, but it also risked a clash between the old guard and new hires.

At the same time, as the size of the firm nearly doubled, Morgan had to seek new quarters in the United States and abroad, which added considerably to costs in the second half of the 1980s and early 1990s.[16] Jim Boisi was brought on-board as a vice chairman of Morgan with his extensive experience as a real estate lawyer to find new premises in New York City. Initially, the intention was to buy 25 Wall Street which Citi had taken over because the owner was delinquent on taxes. The property was supposed to be auctioned, but Citi found out that Morgan intended to enter a low ball bid, so they increased the minimum which made the project uneconomic from Lew Preston's point of view.

Attention then turned to the old City Service property at 60 Wall Street which had also been the headquarters of Merrill Lynch until they moved to a building originally built for US Steel that was adjacent to the World Trade Center. After the 60 Wall Street building was razed, the firm of Dinkeloo & Roach designed a modern building which was looking for a sponsor. Boisi negotiated through a dummy corporation, and Bruce Brackenridge hired

---

[16] The main requirements outside the United States were to rebuild the historic office in Paris on Place Vendome and to replace the Angel Court facility in London by taking over an old school building on the Embankment and converting it into a modern office.

Phillip Johnson as a consultant. Changes were made to the podium to allow for more trading floors among other things.

A controversy arose over the projected costs especially as it was proposed that the building has its own emergency power supply and part of an elevator bank was to be rededicated as a channel for fiber optic cables to permit maximum flexibility on the trading floors. This controversy was a reprise of an earlier disagreement over putting computers on every desktop a few years earlier.

Preston was not a technologist, and he agonized over the cost of proliferating personal computers. He considered confining them to a few departments such as International Financial Management and various research departments. However, Rod Lindsay carried the day, when he argued that management did not consciously want to allow some employees to be considered first class citizens and others second class.

When Preston balked at the expense of the new headquarters, a row developed between various members of senior management. Jack Tai, who headed the Real Estate Group, pointed out that Japan Inc. was buying trophy properties all over the United States from golf courses to office buildings. He noted that, based on negotiations he had with Dai-ichi Mutual Life, the cost of the base building could be recouped by selling a 50% stake for approximately $1 billion. Preston thought the idea was preposterous, and he worried it would be seen as a sign of weakness. Yet, Citibank had already done something quite similar with its headquarters as 399 Park Avenue.

Preston left the decision up to the board. When he turned to Rod Lindsay for his views, Lindsay's message was that in the day and age when technology was changing so rapidly, headquarters buildings should be viewed like "razor blades." Then, Frank Carey, chairman of IMB, turned to Jack Tai and asked: "Jack, can you find me some of that money to buy our headquarters in Armonk?"

Thereafter, Morgan's Board endorsed the transaction enthusiastically, and the deal with Dai-ichi was completed. More amazingly, when Dai-ichi ran into liquidity issues a few years later, Morgan bought the 49% interest back at 50 cents on the dollar. And, after the Chase/Chemical/Manny Hanny merger, 60 Wall Street was sold again—this time to Deutsche Bank. Razor blades indeed!

While the process of building a securities business from scratch was proving both challenging and costly, Morgan's management never strayed from its objective. In the spring of 1987, the firm named David W. Fisher president of JPMorgan Securities Inc., a newly formed subsidiary of JPMorgan & Co. The unit became the sixteenth largest securities firm in the United States, and it was initially capitalized at $250 million, which was the same as Morgan Guaranty Limited.

JPMorgan Securities Inc. was initially authorized to underwrite and deal in government securities and money market instruments. Morgan's management had also approached the Board of Governors of the Federal Reserve for permission to engage in investment banking activities including underwriting and trading commercial paper, municipal revenue bonds and mortgage-backed securities. At the same time, Morgan's management expected to encounter lawsuits from firms in the securities industry who would challenge Morgan's request on grounds that it violated Glass-Steagall. However, with the funding for the securities unit, Morgan's management was making a clear statement of its intent to enter the securities and investment banking businesses.

9

Industry Shakeup

When Morgan contemplated entering the securities business in the mid-1980s, the environment was favorable for both stocks and bonds. Interest rates had fallen from record levels as inflation and inflation expectations receded, while economic growth and corporate profits were strong following the 1982–83 recession. As investors flocked into financial assets, securities firms expanded their operations to meet growing customer demand.

Bond yields stopped declining in early 1987, however, and they began to rise for the first time in several years. The principal reason was Japanese investors, who had become the largest buyers of US Treasuries, began to scale back their purchases as the US dollar plummeted against the yen: The dollar fell from a peak of Y265/US$ in 1985 to about Y150/US$ by the first quarter of 1987. In order to stabilize the dollar and financial markets an agreement called the Louvre Accord was reached in February between the Group of Three (G-3), in which the Federal Reserve agreed to raise short-term interest rates while the Bank of Japan and the Bundesbank agreed to lower interest rates.[1]

This agreement appeared to be effective for a while, as US bond yields stabilized while the US stock market surged to record highs. However, the markets turned volatile in August, when Paul Volcker stepped down as chairman of the Federal Reserve and was replaced by Alan Greenspan. While Greenspan was highly regarded, investors were unsure about his credentials as an inflation fighter and immediately tested his resolve. Greenspan responded by

---

[1] Previously, in September 1985, an agreement called the Plaza Accord had been reached to produce an orderly decline in the US dollar via coordinated easing of monetary policies in the United States, Japan and Germany.

© The Author(s) 2020
N. P. Sargen, *JPMorgan's Fall and Revival*, https://doi.org/10.1007/978-3-030-47058-6_9

raising short-term rates by 50 basis points to reassure investors, which normally would have calmed financial markets. Instead, market volatility increased when the Bank of Japan and Bundesbank both nudged interest rates higher, as Treasury Secretary Baker considered such action to be a violation of the Louvre Accord.

By mid-October, US financial markets were in turmoil, as G-3 policymakers bickered openly. On Monday, October 19, press reports indicated that Secretary James Baker no longer favored currency intervention to support the dollar, which was near free-fall. Treasury bond yields surged by 50 basis points to 10.5%, and the stock market plummeted, closing down more than 500 points for a 23% decline.[2] This, in turn, contributed to a worldwide stock market rout.

While policymakers were ultimately able to calm markets by collectively easing monetary policies, the stock market crash was a wake-up call for securities firms that the period of steady increases in stock prices was over. Soon after, job hiring by securities firms came to an abrupt halt, as Wall Street firms realized the good times were over and there was considerable overcapacity in the industry. One year later, for example, employment at US securities firms was 7% below its peak in 1986, while overall trading volume had contracted by 33% over the same period.

The impact was especially apparent at Salomon Brothers, which on the day of the stock market crash announced it would lay off 1000 employees in London and a firm-wide hiring freeze was in effect. These developments came on top of surprising news in the spring, when Lewis Ranieri, who pioneered the firm's lucrative mortgage-backed securities (MBS) business and rose to become vice chairman, was suddenly fired by John Gutfreund. The only explanation was a cryptic statement by Gutfreund that Ranieri's skills in building a business didn't extend into managing it. Many of my colleagues at the time wondered if anyone's job was safe if a person of Ranieri's stature could be dismissed so easily.

These developments were the precursor of yet more surprises. The most important for those of us in Bond Market Research was the announcement at the end of 1987 that Henry Kaufman would be departing the firm to run his own company. Previously, we were able to take comfort that research was a bastion of stability in an otherwise volatile firm. But we now realized that perception of the firm's invincibility had been breached, and the future was

---

[2] For more detail on events leading to the October 1987 stock market crash, see Nicholas Sargen, *Global Shocks*, op. cit., Chapter 5.

highly uncertain. Thereafter, for the first time since I joined the firm, there was a steady drain of top talent away from Salomon by its principal competitors.

Salomon Brothers was by no means alone in succumbing to competitive pressures in financial services. Many "White Shoe" firms that were not heavily involved in brokerage and trading were nonetheless grossly undercapitalized for the new world of global finance. At the same time, with the exception of Merrill Lynch, many of the brokerage houses did not generate enough "product" for their salesforce to distribute. What was becoming clear was that the registry of collapse was expanding markedly to eventually impact firms such as Dillon Read, DLJ, Eastman Dillon, First Boston, Harriman Ripley and Kuhn Loeb, among others.

Amid all of this, the investment banking competition was disappearing faster than new entrants were being created, even as commercial banks were navigating Glass-Steagall to re-enter investment banking. Against this backdrop of growing turmoil in the securities industry, Lew Preston wanted to be sure that Morgan would follow the examples of famous London merchant banks that traced their histories back well over a hundred years. They included names such as Barings (1762), Kleinworts (1786), Morgan Grenfell (1838) and Hambros (1839). But even for these venerable firms, only one—the House of Rothschild—still retains its original ownership structure.

Preston's goal was to restore Morgan to its former prominence as a firm to whom the securities markets looked for leadership in the origination, structuring and placement of securities issues. It had played that role from the beginnings of a "Morgan house" in the 1850s until 1933, when JPMorgan & Co. elected to serve its clients as a commercial bank following passage of the Glass-Steagall Act, while five of its partners withdrew to form Morgan Stanley & Co. in 1934. Preston's vision was to recreate a modern-day version of Morgan as a "universal bank" that could engage in both wholesale banking and investment banking activities.

In early 1988, Preston shared his thoughts about what was happening in the financial services arena and the challenges it posed with Morgan's senior management team. He began by noting how difficult it was to map out a strategy for the firm given the complications from: (1) rapid growth in the number of employees contrary to the industry trend; (2) the transition in the firm's business model that was underway; (3) the risks and complexities of the businesses it was involved in; and (4) the costs of supporting activities that had gone "sky-high."[3]

---

[3] Senior management meeting, January 18, 1988.

Preston candidly admitted he did not know exactly what Morgan would look like in 3–5 years, but he had a general idea: Namely, Morgan would become a "hybrid" institution that would add securities powers to its business but would not surrender its core banking business. The open question was when Morgan would be granted securities powers. He acknowledged that Morgan had explored the possibility of withdrawing from the Fed and taking advantage of the powers the FDIC would allow if they were the regulator. It also considered the possibility of turning Morgan into an investment bank and eventually selling Morgan Guaranty. However, he considered this an extreme solution, and he did not want to publicize it.

Preston acknowledged one of the biggest challenges Morgan faced was there was no role model for it to emulate, and it had to be flexible in a rapidly changing environment. The firm, at the same time, had numerous competitive advantages including its capital, client base, reputation for fair dealing, long presence in global markets, experience and skill set and hopefully the ability to offer the array of financial services and products that clients desired.

Preston concluded by sharing one of his greatest concerns: Namely, he did not want to saddle his successors with huge fixed costs and highly volatile or insufficient revenue streams to cover them. Accordingly, he recognized the need to develop business plans for new activities to monitor progress and to step up or slow down activities, as well as the need for cost containment.

Soon after, Preston followed up by creating a Management Committee whose goal was to integrate policy and planning (for which Morgan's corporate office was ultimately responsible) with daily management. Its purpose was to foster more efficient analysis of issues, faster decision making and better communication. The Managing Committee comprised Preston (chairman), Weatherstone (president), Jack Ruffle (vice chairman) and five senior executives who were in the running to one day succeed Preston and Weatherstone—James Flynn, Roberto Mendoza, John Olds, Kurt Viermetz and Sandy Warner.

From this group John Olds was given the responsibility for overseeing the build-out of JP Morgan Securities and the Corporate Planning Group (CPG). Olds was ideally suited for these responsibilities, as he was a strategic thinker who had prior experience in investment banking. Before joining Morgan in 1972, he worked for Chemical Bank in London and subsequently for Merrill Lynch in Paris. Olds earned the respect of Lew Preston early on both for his native intelligence and also for his knowledge of investment banking. In 1982

Preston asked him to head a task force for circumventing Glass-Steagall, and he would go on to head Morgan's Far East banking area.

As Olds set out to build the securities business in 1988, the year-end goals called for JPMorgan to have $1 billion in capital invested in securities subsidiaries that supported consolidated assets of $29 billion with a total headcount of nearly 2000. Of those, the entities within the Securities Group represented about two-thirds of the capital investment and headcount and 80% of the assets.

When Olds took charge of growing the securities business, it was a fledging operation that did not remotely resemble full-fledged broker-dealers such as Goldman Sachs or Morgan Stanley. One of the main obstacles was activities were conducted in various subsidiaries of the holding company and there was no central administrative function in place. The main unit involved in domestic underwriting activities was JPM Securities Inc. (for money market instruments, government securities and mortgaged-backed securities), with separate subsidiaries for equities and futures. MGL in Europe and JP Morgan Securities Asia Ltd. handled underwriting and distribution in those regions. Morgan was also under contract to run the Euro-clear operations center in Brussels, which was a highly profitable operation, and there were additional support groups to service various client activities.

Apart from integrating these entities and bringing them under a central administrative unit, Olds was conscious of the expense that would be incurred in quartering the traders and salespeople in modern trading floors in New York, London and Tokyo by the end of 1990. His belief was that Morgan had the opportunity to become a full-fledged broker-dealer globally, but it needed to have the staying power to do so. The goals over the next two to three years were to (1) expand client coverage; (2) tighten costs and controls; (3) continue training and resource development; (4) undertake selective investments in systems; and (5) achieve greater organizational clarity and integration while maintaining regulatory flexibility.

When Olds briefed senior management on what would be entailed, many members who had spent their entire careers at Morgan thought this vision was a tall order and some believed it was an impossible task. While they did not stand in the way of proceeding in this direction, they were unsure the firm could pull it off. When Preston asked Nicholas Potter, head of Investment Management, his thoughts, Potter's response was Morgan had to select among two choices—either to combine commercial and investment banking or to become involved in retail banking. When Preston heard this, he responded by saying, "I've heard enough. Onward." This was his way of saying retail banking was not a viable option; therefore there was no alternative to the direction the bank was pursuing.

By the end of 1988, Morgan had made considerable progress toward attaining its goals and it had stemmed losses in London. However, it was still a long way from being a full-fledged securities firm. For example, debt and equity trading represented nearly half of the total revenues of three major firms—Salomon Brothers, Morgan Stanley and First Boston—compared with about one quarter for Morgan.

Accordingly, the CPG plan for 1989 emphasized the need to expand the array of new products and investor coverage, with the goal being to develop a client base of 300 to 400 institutional investors worldwide. One theme that both Preston and Olds stressed was Morgan would have to compete for business on the basis of superior execution, market insight and research-based ideas, but above all with a view to serving clients' needs. By doing this, Morgan hoped to differentiate itself from firms that were more interested in clearing their own inventories than in adding value for their clients.

The Planning unit set stretch goals for the securities business for the next few years, and it perceived there was a possibility of an industry shakeout in the United States, London and Tokyo beginning in 1989. This call proved to be prescient, as the period of rapid expansion in the securities industry during the 1980s led to considerable excess capacity, growing pressures on operating margins of securities firms and ongoing staff reduction.

The shakeout in financial services first became apparent in Morgan's London office during the launch of the "Big Bang" in 1986. With many UK merchant banks not involved in securities underwriting, Morgan had capacity to both lend and underwrite securities. It was very effective in carving out a niche set of clients in the oil and gas sector that required sophisticated cross-border advice.[4]

But Morgan was not immune from being caught up in the deregulation frenzy. Like many other institutions at the time, its London office had gone on a hiring spree in anticipation of growing its UK business. However, when revenues fell shy of expectations, the office had to pare back spending, and it began to push old line bankers out the door.

Tougher markets also spawned rapid changes in managements and frequent departures and promotions at firms such as Salomon Brothers, Kidder

---

[4] Teitelman, op. cit., p. 56.

Peabody, Smith Barney and Nomura Securities. The firm that came under greatest scrutiny, by far, was Drexel Burnham Lambert. It had grown rapidly throughout the 1980s primarily due to Michael Milken's efforts to create a market for high yield bonds ("junk bonds") that enabled firms with below investment grade credit ratings to finance their growth. Junk bonds also became a vehicle for leveraged buyouts (LBOs) in which private equity entities acquired old line businesses with considerable cash holdings by issuing them to finance acquisitions. The period culminated in the massive buyout of RJR Nabisco by Kohlberg Kravis Roberts (KKR) in 1989, just before the collapse of Drexel Burnham.

Milken's activities had been under scrutiny by federal investigators throughout the 1980s due to alleged unethical and illegal behavior. In 1986, arbitrageur Ivan Bosky, a client of Drexel, pleaded guilty while implicating Milken for several illegal transactions, including insider trading and stock manipulation. For two years, Drexel insisted nothing illegal had occurred, even when the Securities and Exchange Commission (SEC) formally sued the firm in 1988. However, when Rudy Giuliani, then US Attorney for the Southern District of New York, considered indicting Drexel under the powerful Racketeer Influenced and Corrupt Organizations Act (RICO), Drexel's management entered plea bargain talks. In March 1989, a federal grand jury indicted Milken on ninety-eight counts of racketeering and fraud, and one later Milken pleaded guilty to six counts of securities and tax violations. Drexel, which was the fifth largest investment bank in the United States, was not able to overcome the blow to its reputation, and it was forced into bankruptcy in February 1990.

The downfall of Drexel did not directly impact Morgan, because it was not involved in underwriting junk bonds. However, Morgan was seeking it to expand its M&A activity and leveraged finance was an important feature of the business. One of the ethical questions that Preston and Morgan's senior management struggled with was whether the bank should be involved in hostile takeovers, which had become prevalent in the 1980s. Roberto Mendoza believed it was necessary to do so. He convinced Morgan's management that it should become the advisor for Hoffman-La Roche's bid for Sterling Drug Inc. at the beginning of 1988.

Both firms were clients of Morgan, and Preston had to weigh whether representing the acquirer would breach Morgan's standard of providing the best and most professional advice to its client. In the process, Preston laid down several markers it would consider in basing a decision. Specifically, it would not advise a hostile takeover under the following circumstances: (1) if doing so would involve a breach of confidentiality; (2) if it would impair the quality or objectivity of advice Morgan provided; and (3) if one client would gain an advantage because of Morgan's relation with the other.

One of Preston's over-riding concerns was that Morgan should not be perceived as "joining the pack." He was well aware that as Morgan became more involved in the investment banking business, there would be numerous situations in which its standards would be tested, and he wanted to make sure that the firm stayed true to its values and standards.

Nonetheless, Morgan received adverse notoriety for its stance. A *New York Times* article titled "How Morgan Bank Struck Out" questioned whether Morgan had stayed true to its principles[5]:

> In a highly visible advertising campaign, the Morgan Guaranty Trust Company has been holding itself out as the bank that stresses its "relationship" with its clients. "We don't promote M&A deals just to generate fees," heralds one ad that proudly shows an empty tombstone—symbolic of a takeover deal that wasn't done, presumably because it wasn't in the client's interest.

The article went on to state that in the eyes of many, Morgan violated that credo by agreeing to advise La Roche's unsuccessful hostile takeover of Sterling. The article concluded by noting the controversy over the deal and the gloating by many securities firms says much about the state of the takeover business and the future role commercial banks might play.

Throughout the 1980s, the vision of many of the largest commercial banks and investment banks was to become a "universal bank" that could provide "one stop shopping" for its customers. This became especially important as US banks increasingly competed with European institutions, where universal banking was the norm. As Dennis Weatherstone observed at the end of the decade[6]:

> In most financial centers, the principal competitors of U.S.-based international banks are now universal banks. Looking ahead, the European Community has chosen the universal banking model for the banking firms that it will license to

[5] Leslie Wayne, February 7, 1988.

[6] Remarks to the International Symposium on Banking and Payment Services sponsored by the Board of Governors of the Federal Reserve System, Washington, D.C., June 7, 1989.

do business throughout the unified Europe of 1992. Such banks can offer their clients integrated banking and securities services in every major market in the world—including the United States…

All this means that pressure for reform is likely to intensify in the United States and Japan—the only major industrialized countries that still try to segment their banking and securities industries with artificial barriers. Make no mistake: We understand and support the gradual financial industry reform that U.S. bank regulators have been pursuing—history and politics make it necessary. But I firmly believe that converging activities and international competition are sweeping us toward a new order, where universal banking will be the norm worldwide.

Weatherstone went on to observe that securities firms also were chipping away at Glass-Steagall provisions and have a growing volume of bank-like assets and liabilities[7]:

They make bridge loans to assist mergers, they arrange loan syndications, and they trade foreign exchange. They sell commercial paper, which is not a lot different from certificates of deposit, to obtain unsecured funding; and they gather savings from the public through money market funds. American and Japanese securities firms, moreover, have established or purchased banks in a number of countries.

Amid these developments, the megabanks, especially Morgan, Bankers Trust and eventually Citicorp, began to make forays into investment banking and securities trading and distribution. Anti-trust policy became more lenient during the Reagan and George H. W. Bush administrations, which were less concerned than prior administrations about loss of competitiveness resulting from mergers of large financial institutions. Fed Chairman Alan Greenspan was also more open to allow commercial banks and investment banks to compete directly with one another than his predecessor, Paul Volcker.

In 1989 the Federal Reserve permitted JPMorgan to be the first commercial bank to underwrite a corporate debt offering. By the late 1990s, when Glass Steagall was repealed, the firm had built its investment banking operations to emerge as a top-five player in securities underwriting.

---

[7] Ibid.

Box: Competition from Investment Banks

During the 1980s, Morgan and other money center banks faced increased competition from investment banks, as corporate customers increasingly tapped capital markets for funds. The initial impetus came from record high interest rates in the early 1980s and Japan's emergence as the world's largest capital exporter. Unlike OPEC, which deposited surplus funds with global banks, Japanese institutions, especially life insurance companies and trusts banks, directed their investments primarily to the US bond market. US corporate borrowers, in turn, increasingly raised money from capital markets and by 1983 international bond issuance had surpassed syndicated banking lending.

Within the securities industry a power shift was occurring in the late 1970s and early 1980s. Morgan Stanley stood atop other securities firms in the mid-1970s, as it benefited from strong ties with oil companies during the first oil shock, arranging 40% of the money they raised.[8] Morgan Stanley also had strong control over syndications with its key corporate clients, and it routinely insisted on being the sole lead manager on securities it underwrote.

A few years later, however, corporate customers placed greater importance on the ability of securities firms to underwrite and distribute securities than on traditional relationship banking. By the end of the decade Morgan Stanley had to relinquish its policy of being the sole manager on syndications, as other firms—notably Salomon Brothers, Goldman Sachs, First Boston and Merrill Lynch—demonstrated their prowess in underwriting and distributing securities.

One of the key developments that transformed the securities industry was the SEC's decision to allow "shelf registration." The ruling allowed issuers to offer and sell securities to the public without having to issue a separate prospectus for each offering. This decision was beneficial to trading-oriented firms such as Salomon Brothers, which was especially adept at pricing and distributing securities. In 1981, to obtain the requisite capital that would finance its expansion, Salomon Brothers was sold to Phillips Brothers (PHIBRO), a commodities trading organization. By 1984, however, Salomon's management team was fully in control of the combined entity, and a year later its CEO, John Gutfreund, appeared on the cover of Business Week with a story titled "King of Wall Street."[9]

Another mega-merger occurred in 1988 when Credit Suisse (CS), a Swiss-run bank, acquired a 44% stake in First Boston (FB), a premier US investment bank, to form a global investment bank, Credit Suisse/Frist Boston (CSFB). The sale occurred when First Boston was unable to redeem money it had lent for a leveraged buyout of Ohio Mattress Company as the junk bond market collapsed. Credit Suisse subsequently bailed out FB by acquiring a controlling stake in CSFB. Although such an arrangement between an investment bank and a commercial bank was technically in violation of the Glass-Steagall Act, the Federal Reserve permitted the transaction, because it concluded the public and financial markets were better served than allowing FB to fail.

---

[8] Chernow, op. cit., p. 623.
[9] Business Week, 1985.

10

Should Morgan Rescue Citi?

One institution Morgan's management monitored closely in 1989 was Citibank for a very special reason. Two years after it tried to put its Less Developed Country (LDC) loan problems to rest, Citi was embroiled in yet another crisis, this time due to mounting problem loans for commercial real estate and highly leveraged buyout (LBO) transactions. This was merely the latest in a series of booms and busts for Citi throughout the twentieth century (see the Box: "What Makes Citi Crisis Prone?" at the end of this chapter).[1] By-mid 1990, Citibank's non-accrual loans as percentage of equity capital were nearing 100%, which some observers viewed to mean Citi was "technically insolvent."[2] As this information leaked into the markets, Citicorp's share price plummeted by about 70% from its 1989 peak of $34.

One story that circulated within Morgan for years was that Lew Preston and Dennis Weatherstone could have acquired Citi for a price of $10/share, but they opted to pass. Upon hearing this, the reaction of most Morgan employees was bewilderment as they wondered, "How could management have rejected an opportunity that would have transformed Morgan into a financial powerhouse?"

This popular rendition, however, is not accurate. The correct story is that Preston and Weatherstone were approached by Gerald Corrigan in late 1990 about acquiring a 10% stake in Citi along with a mandate from the Federal

---

[1] The box discusses the main thesis of Freeman and McKinley's book, *Borrowed Time: Two Centuries of Booms, Busts, and Bailouts at Citi*, op. cit.

[2] Ibid., pp. 246–247. House Committee Chairman, John Dingell, Democrat of Michigan, asserted this in Congressional hearings on Citicorp in July 1991, although FDIC Chairman William Seidman disputed this assertion.

© The Author(s) 2020
N. P. Sargen, *JPMorgan's Fall and Revival*, https://doi.org/10.1007/978-3-030-47058-6_10

Reserve to "fix" Citi's problem. However, they passed on making the investment once they considered all the negative ramifications for Morgan.

The backdrop is that Morgan and Citi were rivals with common business interests, and they collaborated when problems arose in the financial system. These episodes included the LDC debt crisis and the problems involving Continental Bank in the 1980s, as well as the financial difficulties facing New York City in the mid-1970s. Because of their power and influence, they were the two banks the Federal Reserve and other regulatory bodies would consult to solicit views on the banking industry and possible regulatory changes.

Walter Wriston and Lew Preston were widely acknowledged as the deans of the industry, and they respected each other even though their styles were completely different. Wriston was a champion of free market economics and a vocal critic of government involvement in the economy and banking, and his relationship with Paul Volcker was testy at times. By comparison, Morgan's chairmen and CEOs including Preston were accustomed to working closely with the Federal Reserve and other regulatory bodies, and Volcker was a personal friend of Preston.

During the LDC debt crisis executives from the two institutions shared a common goal of ensuring the consortium of banks would maintain exposures to the respective borrowers. Thus, as noted in Chap. 5, Citibank chaired the steering committees for Mexico and Argentina while Morgan, at Volcker's request, chaired the committee for Brazil. However, the relationship between Morgan and Citi changed when John Reed succeeded Wriston in 1984.

Reed's prior experience was in technology and consumer credit cards, and he was unfamiliar with international banking and problem loans to LDCs. Nor did he have long-standing relationships with counterparts in other financial institutions. As Reed was learning the ropes, he was willing to go along with the negotiations to rollover loans to troubled LDCs in the hope they could grow their way out of their debt problems. In doing so, he backed the Baker Plan that was implemented in 1985. It extended new loans to the indebted countries in return for market-oriented reforms that included privatization of state-owned entities, corporate tax reduction and trade and investment liberalization.

Reed's stance changed, however, when these efforts failed to produce the desired results and several countries threatened to withhold debt service payments, including the two largest borrowers, Mexico and Brazil. As Reed inserted himself into the debt negotiations his relations with Paul Volcker became strained, because Reed felt Volcker was calling the shots for the banks.

Tensions heightened during the negotiations over Mexico's debt rollover in 1986, as Philip Zweig observes[3]:

> Now the banks were forced to choose sides. Morgan's Lewis Preston allied with his friend, Paul Volcker. "There was a suspicion," Preston recalled, "on the part of other banks that packages might have advantages for Citibank that they might not have for others." So Morgan Bank for one, in sometimes acrimonious discussions with Citibank, pushed to get the deal done and chastised Citibank for demanding options skewed in its favor.

By 1987, Reed decided that Citi would stop pretending the troubled loans would be fully repaid. He wanted to put the issue behind him by writing off LDC loans so he could focus on his ultimate goal of creating a global and national consumer bank through the expansion of Citi's network of ATMs and credit cards. Reed's tactic was to first garner the support of Paul Volcker in a series of meetings with the Fed chairman in which Reed indicated he would like to set aside a sizeable reserve for LDC debt. Volcker responded that he was amenable to the idea, but he favored gradual reserving, rather than taking one big hit.[4]

The gradualist approach posed a problem for Reed, because it would imply no growth in Citi's earnings for a prolonged period. For a bank that had been built on the premise of 15% annual compound earnings growth, this was a tough pill to take. Reed's opening to take a more aggressive posture occurred in late April, when the Brazilian government declared a moratorium on its international debt. This was the final straw for him. After briefing Volcker, Treasury Secretary James Baker and Walter Wriston, Reed went ahead and asked Citi's Board of Directors to add $3 billion to its existing loan-loss reserves.

Once the approval was granted, Reed tried to contact Preston to forewarn him of the decision. Preston was in a meeting and would not take the call even though his executive assistant, Pat O'Hara, said it was urgent. After three attempts to get hold of Preston, Reed finally reached Jack Ruffle. Reed subsequently contacted Lew Preston, John McGillicuddy of Manufacturers Hanover and Tom Clausen of Bank of America (BoA) shortly before the press release announced the action. Following the announcement prices for Brazilian and Mexican debt that traded in the secondary market plummeted,

---

[3] Zweig, op. cit., p. 850.
[4] Ibid., p. 847.

as did the share prices for Manny Hanny and BoA. However, Citicorp's stock price surged.

Reed was roundly criticized by Preston and other bankers for making a unilateral decision that impacted the entire banking industry. As other money center banks were forced to follow suit in adding to provisions for LDC loans, a precedent had been created whereby banks signaled they would accept less than 100 cents on the dollar for their loans. It also resulted in the banking industry reporting a combined loss of $10 billion in the quarter, which was the worst quarter, and 1987 the worst year, in US bank history.[5]

Although Morgan's share price rallied on the news because of its strong balance sheet, Preston and Weatherstone were angered by what they considered reckless behavior by Reed. (They had little regard for Reed in general, whom they disrespectfully referred to in-house as "the brat.") They were particularly worried that Citi's unilateral action would lead to changed attitudes and expectations by both debtors and creditors that could ultimately result in a decline in the values of the banks' LDC portfolios. At the same time, it could break down the fragile coalition among banks, large and small, that Morgan was trying to spearhead.

Two years later in September of 1989, Preston and Weatherstone concluded their concerns had proven to be well founded. They observed that as a result of a deterioration in conditions in three of the four major borrowers—Argentina, Brazil and Venezuela—the prospects for resumed debt servicing and further restructuring of their debt had virtually collapsed.

The arrearages in these three countries were estimated to have resulted in more than 37% of Morgan's LDC debt portfolio being placed on non-accrual status.[6] Preston noted that such large arrearages did not bode well for debt negotiations with these countries, because most non-money center banks had insisted that such arrearages be cleaned up for them to provide new money. Furthermore, he acknowledged that the debtor countries were increasingly unwilling to service their debts, because they regarded debt reduction as inevitable. Consequently, none of the three was engaged in serious negotiations.[7]

In the end, it was Morgan's former chairman John Meyer who came up with the solution. Over lunch with Preston and Rod Wagner, Meyer asserted there was no way such a disparate group of lending institutions could ever agree on either the size of a write-off or the underlying value of the loans. His

---

[5] Ibid., p. 855.
[6] Presentation to Morgan's board by Lewis T. Preston in September 1989.
[7] Of the major borrowers, Mexico was in the best shape economically and politically, and it was the only one still at the negotiating table.

suggestion was that Morgan needed to figure out a way to turn the illiquid loans into publicly traded bonds and let the market determine the clearing price. This meeting marked the start of the Brady Bond initiative, in which 30-year US Treasury bonds were used as collateral to back the developing country loans and turn them into marketable debt instruments.

Negotiations over pricing the Treasury bonds that were used to secure the first tranche of Mexico's bonds were drawn out by US Treasury Under Secretary David Mulford, who was a former investment banker. The impasse was finally resolved when Mulford visited Morgan's trading floor, sitting alongside a team of bond analysts, who determined the pricing to the fourth decimal point.

Recognizing this new reality, Preston recommended to Morgan's board that the time had come to "put the LDC problem behind us" by writing off 100% of its troubled loans to LDCs. Because Morgan had the means to do so, management believed the action would strengthen the bank's position within the financial community. Furthermore, by reducing its LDC loan book, Morgan would be in better position to expand into trading activities and investment banking. At the same time, Preston recognized that Morgan's attempt to reduce its LDC debt exposure would result in a further reduction in the market value of LDC debt. He noted that Morgan's actions would impact other money center banks that still had sizable LDC exposure. However, one consolation was their capital positions had improved relative to where they were in the mid-1980s.

One of the most adversely affected banks was Citibank, which felt compelled to take additional provisions of $1 billion for LDC loan losses. This development was only one of many issues John Reed was wrestling with then. As he was seeking to put the LDC debt issue to bed, Citibank had been ramping up lending to commercial real estate developers, while targeting about fifteen or so in the New York area including Donald Trump. Some competitors believed Citi's objective was to corner the New York commercial real estate market.[8] Because these developers had projects throughout the country, Citi's management team contended their risk was well diversified. At the same time Citi was increasing loans for leveraged buyouts. The reason: Walter Wriston had viewed junk bond financed takeovers as a way for mid-sized companies to no longer be captive to regional banks.

Meanwhile, both areas were plagued with problems that could derail the deal. In mid-1989, Citi's profitability began to tank. One of the most visible signs of trouble occurred in October, when Citibank and Chase failed to

---

[8] Ibid., p. 843.

make good on the commitment to assemble $3 billion for the management and the pilots' union of United Airlines (UAL) to acquire the company with the participation of British Airways. When the $300 per share bid fell through, partly due to disagreements between UAL's management and the major labor unions, UAL shares plummeted, and Citicorp's share price dropped by about 15%.[9] Takeover stocks and junk bonds were dealt a blow they did not recover from for several years, and Citibank wound up with egg on its face as the broken deal wound up being Wall Street's nominee for the year's worst deal.[10]

Later in 1989, Reed would confront an even bigger problem, when regulators took control of the Bank of New England, which was significantly overexposed to real estate and was forced to unload assets. This caused bank regulators to come down hard on other institutions that had large real estate exposure. Philip Zweig quotes Reed's reaction as follows: "That just killed the market. From then on you couldn't sell buildings for love or money."[11] Thereafter, the US commercial real estate market plummeted in the first quarter of 1990, and the sell-off continued for the rest of the year as the economy slipped into recession. Reed placed the blame on regulators, calling the downturn a "regulatory recession."[12]

By then, Morgan's Corporate Planning unit had become concerned that Citi's problems could spread throughout the banking system and potentially impact Morgan. Accordingly, it prepared a thorough analysis of both Citicorp, the holding company, and Citibank for Morgan's senior management. One of the recommendations was that Morgan should limit any further exposure to Citi. In reaching this conclusion the internal report acknowledged there was scant public data with respect to Citi's asset holdings and risk concentrations, the stability of its funding sources and expenditures on technology and capital expenditures. Nonetheless, the Corporate Planning Group was confident that Citi's financial predicament was serious and warranted caution.

Morgan's assessment was that the core of Citi's problem was it was significantly under-capitalized and also poor at assessing credit risk, with Reed and other senior executives having little prior experience in lending.[13] Citi's capital deficiency relative to earnings posed a dilemma for its management, because the bank had a history of rapid (double-digit) earnings growth, and it could no longer grow its way out of its problems. Instead, Citi's management would

---

[9] Ibid., p. 866.

[10] Sarah Bartlett, "United Airline Deal: A Costly Fiasco," *New York Times*, October 25, 1989.

[11] Zweig, p. 868.

[12] Ibid., p. 868.

[13] Freeman and McKinney contend the problem grew worse when Tom Theobald left for Continental Bank in 1987, because he was one of few senior managers who was experienced at assessing credit risk.

have to take dramatic steps to shrink its balance sheet, but this could destabilize its access to funding sources.

Moreover, Reed showed no inclination to do what was required, and he completely ignored criticisms of the way he was managing the bank. In April of 1990 he announced a dividend increase of 9.9% when Citi's write-offs of bad loans soared by 79% while first quarter earnings plunged by 56%.[14]

While Citi might be able to hide the full extent of its problems for a while, Morgan's management worried the market could force Citi's hand once they became known. Indeed, a *Wall Street Journal* article that came out after the release of first quarter earnings noted that shareholders and taxpayers should be concerned that Citi's reserves only covered one half of its nonperforming loans and its common stock equity was well below that of almost all its rivals.[15] The article went on to state that by some estimates, Citicorp needed $2 billion in additional capital and reserves. By 1991, nearly 43% of Citi's $13 billion in commercial real estate loans were nonperforming, and it had lent up to 80% or more of the value of the properties. This put Citibank's investment underwater, with values plunging by 40% or more.[16]

The Planning unit's report acknowledged that Citi had scaled back some unprofitable businesses, including real estate lending, leveraged finance, venture capital and other areas. However, lackluster earnings also highlighted its anemic capital formation, which increased the probability the bank's "AA" credit rating would come under scrutiny before year-end. Meanwhile, Citi's access to external primary and secondary capital had largely dried up.

Morgan's senior management was briefed on the precariousness of the situation in mid-1990, with Citi facing potential liquidity problems with each re-pricing of its public debt. It was becoming apparent that any delay in taking bold action could result in permanent impairment of Citi's real estate and leveraged loans. Accordingly, Morgan's management concluded Citi's Board of Directors needed to be apprised of the seriousness of the situation. In their view, bold action from the Federal Reserve would be required to restore investor confidence if Citi's financial conditions continued to deteriorate.

After reflecting on this development, Dennis Weatherstone contacted Gerald Corrigan to alert him about Morgan's concerns. Corrigan requested an emergency meeting with Citicorp's Board of Directors that excluded John Reed to get the directors' perspective on the situation.

---

[14] Ibid., p. 242.
[15] Freeman and McKinney, op. cit., p. 241.
[16] Ibid., p. 369.

Corrigan and William Taylor, who headed bank supervision at the Board of Governors, subsequently met with Reed to discuss the consequences of the Citi's real estate exposure. They also pushed him to take actions that Morgan had recommended—namely, shrink its balance sheet, cut its dividend and raise capital even if it meant diluting existing shareholders.[17] Corrigan indicated that for the next two and a half years, all major decisions would have to be cleared by the Federal Reserve and the Office of the Comptroller. The message was that Reed would have to transition Citi to a safer business model while also raising $4 billion to $5 billion of new capital.

At the beginning of November, Corrigan escorted Reed to Dennis Weatherstone's office for him to hear specific actions that Morgan thought Citi needed to take to lessen the risk of a crisis. They included the following measures: (1) Citi should shrink its balance sheet from $230 billion to around $190 billion and then focus on restoring profit margins so it would be able to attract investors and increase its primary (Tier 1) capital in line with risk-weighted assets. (2) Citi should also reduce its head count considerably while developing a multi-year, companywide program of cost reductions. (3) Citi needed to scale back its network of domestic and foreign branches, which had expanded by more than 300 locations since 1987.

During the meeting, Corrigan proposed that Morgan should consider taking a 10% stake in Citi and "clean up" its problems by pursuing the course of action it recommended. Preston and Weatherstone responded they would get back to him after they had a chance to hash out what it would entail for Morgan.

In briefing Preston and Weatherstone on this matter, the Corporate Planning Group's assessment was that Morgan's top priority was to help regulators avoid a broader, systemic problem, and to protect Morgan from impairments from its substantial and diverse exposure to its largest global counterparty. Another issue discussed was whether Morgan should play a general advisory role as Citi deleveraged its balance sheet. Morgan had a lot to offer based on its extensive experience unwinding portfolios of taxable and tax-exempt securities, LDC debt and real estate. There were also opportunities for Morgan to assume or replace some of Citi's credit facilities, as well as to manage asset-backed securities. Morgan, however, had no interest in acquiring any of Citi's branch locations or its retail operations.

Morgan's senior management next discussed what conditions it would require if it were to take a significant stake in Citi. One was that Morgan should seek unlimited access to Fed funding, because the full extent of Citi's

---

[17] Ibid., p. 245.

problems were unknown and Morgan did not want to jeopardize its "AAA" credit rating. Another was it would need to assemble a team of senior staff that could be deployed to carry out the strategy without hobbling Morgan's own business. Roberto Mendoza's name was floated as Morgan's designated representative given his sophistication, extensive background in financial markets and reputation as a "problem solver." If Morgan's plan was successfully implemented, the Planning Group believed that Citicorp's share price might ultimately climb four to five times to $40–$50/share.

In the end, Preston and Weatherstone were not convinced that Citi could be turned around easily. They were also unsure how much control they would have over Citi once Morgan's people resided there, and whether it was worth the effort. They realized Reed was not happy with the forced arrangement, and he most likely would have posed obstacles to implementing Morgan's recommendations. For these and other reasons, Preston and Weatherstone declined Corrigan's offer.

Faced with Corrigan's ultimatum, Reed then focused on raising capital from other sources. In February 1991, it was announced that a member of the Saudi royal family, Prince Alwaleed bin Talal, had agreed to invest $590 million of Citicorp's common stock.[18] Previously, the Prince had quietly purchased 4.9% of Citi's common stock in the final months of 1990, and he would eventually own just under 15% of the company with the latest stake. The terms of the convertible preferred stock included an 11% dividend and an option to buy Citicorp common stock at a $16 strike price, when it was trading just below that level.

Years later, it was evident the deal had been very lucrative. When Prince Alwaleed made an additional investment in Citigroup in January 2008, *The Economist* summarized his initial investment as follows[19]:

> One of the greatest investments in the history of capitalism took place in 1991, when Saudi Arabia's Prince Alwaleed bin Talal acquired a 15% stake in Citibank at the absolute bottom of the market. Citibank was flirting with bankruptcy due to some spectacularly bad real-estate investments. The prince was rich to start with, but this investment, which proved lucrative beyond all expectations, made him the sort of fellow who buys an Airbus 380 as his personal jet.

With the benefit of hindsight, some may contend Morgan's management missed a golden opportunity to invest in Citi. However, the deal Corrigan

---

[18] Michael Quint, "Saudi Prince to Become Citicorp's Top Stockholder," *New York Times*, February 22, 1991.

[19] "Doing an Alwaleed," January 15, 2008.

presented to Morgan was more than a pure financial transaction. It would require Morgan to dedicate senior executives to help run Citi, and it did not guarantee the control Morgan would have over its rival. In the end, Morgan's management did not consider Citi as "franchise opportunity." One reason is Citi's business model was vastly different from Morgan's. Another reason is that Citi's culture would have clashed with Morgan's, possibility diluting the century-old reputation of the House of Morgan.

The idea that Morgan might acquire Citi outright, which many Morgan alums believed to have been on the table, was never a serious consideration. The extensive ramifications of the deal were much more complex than many realized and ultimately proved insurmountable.

Box: What Makes Citi Crisis Prone?

In their book, *Borrowed Time: Two Centuries of Booms, Busts, and Bailouts at Citi*, James Freeman and Vern McKinley observe that the 2008 financial crisis was just one of many debacles Citi has experienced since its founding more than 200 years ago. Their thesis is Citi was a well-managed bank for the first 100 years following its founding in 1812, because it could not rely on government entities to bail it out. However, its management style turned more aggressive once the Federal Reserve was established, and Citi could count on government backing when it got into trouble. According to the authors, Citibank's relation with the Fed and other regulators is a clear example of George Stigler's theory of "regulatory capture," in which government regulation ultimately operates for the benefit of firms in the regulated industry.

The most important episode in the bank's first 100 years was the panic of 1837, when it was on the verge of bankruptcy. John Jacob Astor came to its rescue by providing capital, and he installed his protégé, Moses Taylor, on Citibank's board. Taylor and his successors went on to lead the bank through decades of stability and growth, and Freeman and McKinley point to the legacy of financial conservativism they bestowed on Citi.

By comparison, the second hundred years of Citi's history have been marked by a series of booms and busts. Freeman and McKinley trace the shift to a more aggressive management style during Frank A. Vanderlip's tenure as president from 1909 to 1919, when he undertook a major expansion of the bank's overseas operations. Thereafter, "Sunshine Charley" Mitchell continued Citi's overseas expansion in the 1920s, and he encouraged his salesmen to sell shares in the bank to retail customers. When Citi's stockholders' equity plummeted by more than 80% from 1929 to 1932, Mitchell was blamed by Senator Carter Glass for causing the stock market crash, which led to the passage of Glass-Steagall legislation.

Five decades later, when Citi was in the midst of crises involving LDC debt and real estate, government involvement and regulatory forbearance were required to stabilize the bank. The situation became even more precarious in 2007–08,

(continued)

(continued)

when Citi incurred more than $50 billion in losses on its securities and bank loans and needed $45 billion of assistance from the FDIC to keep it afloat.

During each of these episodes, Citi was highly leveraged in order to boost earnings and equity return. This strategy worked in good times, but it also left the bank vulnerable in bad times. Citi's management argued their bank was global and well diversified, so it could afford to be more highly leveraged than less diversified institutions. Yet, its experience over the past 100 years suggests otherwise. Citi's management routinely under-estimated credit risks in developing countries, commercial real estate, LBOs and asset-backed securities. The irony is that Citi's management was consistently one of the most vocal critics of bank regulation, even though Citi became increasingly dependent on regulators to bail it out of crises.

11

Preston's Legacy

Inevitably, there are moments in the lives of great leaders which subtly, and often unexpectedly, reshape their decisions and the course of future events. For Lew Preston, who went to war at the age of 18 while many of his classmates went to college and who ultimately had a meteoric career that took him to the pinnacle of the most prestigious financial institution in the world, that moment came in the early 1980s.

The event was the Latin American debt crisis. It caught both Preston and Dennis Weatherstone completely off guard and left Morgan and other financial institutions in peril. It also helped convince Preston he had no choice but to transform Morgan.

According to one high-ranking Morgan executive, the crisis also changed Preston's leadership style and demeanor.[1] Previously, he was tough and self-assured. During his rise to the top he swept competitors aside while pursuing a dual strategy of international expansion and an end to restrictions imposed by the Glass-Steagall Act. After the LDC debt crisis, he turned cautious and less decisive about the path Morgan should pursue.

Stated simply, the thesis is Preston never recovered his panache after Latin America. Worried that somehow he might dishonor the mantle he had inherited from the twentieth century's most storied franchise, he deliberated long and delayed taking strategic decisions until the passage of time overcame most of the obstacles and threats he encountered.

---

[1] The name is withheld for purposes of confidentiality.

© The Author(s) 2020
N. P. Sargen, *JPMorgan's Fall and Revival*, https://doi.org/10.1007/978-3-030-47058-6_11

But there are competing interpretations, as well. One is that Preston instinctively knew Morgan's business model had to change, but he was stymied about how to proceed without compromising the company's core values and culture. Morgan, after all, had been involved in only one merger in the post-war era, and its culture was completely in-bred. Another view is that Preston was ill in the later years of his tenure, and this weighed heavily on his decision making.

One of the challenges in assessing the validity of these hypotheses is Preston and most of his colleagues are no longer alive to confirm or reject them. Another is that little has been written about him, even though he was the pre-eminent banker of his generation along with Walter Wriston, about whom much has been written.

Listings on the internet and obituaries devote most of their coverage to Preston's role as head of the World Bank from 1991 to 1995 rather than his career at Morgan, which spanned four decades. (See Box: Preston and the World Bank.) One reason is that in the words of *New York Times* columnist, David Binder, Preston was "almost painfully reticent"[2]:

> In the thick periodic anniversary volumes for his class at Harvard, 1950, others poured out page-long descriptions of their activities, offspring, divorces and other highly personal data. But Mr. Preston listed only his home address.

Preston did not even mention his wife, Gladys Pulitzer Preston, known as "Patsy." She was a granddaughter of Joseph Pulitzer, publisher of the *New York World* and *St. Louis Post Dispatch* newspapers, who founded the Pulitzer Prize. She also had many notable accomplishments of her own. Patsy was actively involved in promoting education for women in journalism, the arts and charities, and was recognized as an outstanding sportswoman. (She once caught a black marlin weighing 1320 pounds off the coast of Peru.) She was also an iconic model at the Eileen Ford agency and the innovator of the Bell Cane Company.

As a member of the Finest Generation, Preston did not like to talk about himself or his accomplishments. Moreover, Preston disliked giving speeches, even though he was able to overcome dyslexia with a prodigious memory and incisive thinking. Once a year, in preparation for the annual meeting of stockholders, he would plow through two ring binders with six-inch spines that

---

[2] "Lewis T. Preston, 68, Dies; Led World Bank into 1990s," May 6, 1995.

had been assembled to prepare him for what he called "our annual exercise in corporate democracy."[3]

In his book, *The World's Banker*, Sebastian Mallaby depicts Preston as a consummate Wall Streeter of the "old school" whose upright bearing was "calibrated to convince the wariest of clients that their money would be cared for prudently."[4] Among the attributes that propelled him to head Morgan were his intelligence, courtesy and inner steel. He was accustomed to exercise power privately "in a boardroom kind of way." Mallaby writes[5]:

> Sometimes he wouldn't speak at all, leaving visitors to glean his answers in his eyes. He wouldn't object, a novice would say after a meeting with the great banker—only to be told by an experienced reader of the man that the objection had been firm and final.

From this perspective, Preston comes across as a modern-day Teddy Roosevelt, who spoke softly, but carried a big stick. What this account does not convey, however, is his softer side and keen sense of humor (see Box with vignettes at the end). Preston was fond of giving his coterie of senior executives nicknames such as "Linz" for Rod Lindsay, "Vag" for Alec Vagliano, "Speedy" or "Spidoodle" for John Spurdle, "Vonk" for Fred von Klemperer and "Tiki" for Bob Wynn, a fellow Marine and head of Morgan's Japanese business out of New York. Also, one of his favorite quips when he asked a colleague a question was "And, what do you have on your alleged mind?"

So, one may ask, who was Lew Preston? The answer is complicated. The reason: Preston was both a stoic patrician and a tough Marine, an unlikely hybrid who was hard to fathom.

Upon graduation from St. Paul's School in Concord, New Hampshire, in 1944, Preston and his classmate, Alec Vagliano, both enlisted in the military, with Preston joining the Marines and Vagliano serving in the army. By the time Preston finished basic training, the war with Japan was over, so the Marines sent him to China, where he served in a detachment that tried to protect Chiang Kai-Shek's railways from Mao's guerillas.

From his time in China, Preston developed a healthy respect for General Joe Stillwell, whose caustic personality earned him the nickname "Vinegar

---

[3] At each of these meetings he could count on questions from a trio of gadflies—Evelyn Davis and the Gilbert brothers—to ask pointed questions. Toward the end of the 1980s a favorite hobbyhorse of theirs was Morgan's persistence in doing business in South Africa against the so-called Sullivan Principles.

[4] Sebastian Mallaby, *The World's Banker*, Penguin Books, 2004, p. 56.

[5] Ibid.

Joe." Stillwell was no admirer of Chiang, and his distrust of his Allies and a lack of resources meant he was continually forced to improvise.

Years later, some of Stillwell's leadership traits would manifest themselves in Preston's management style and personnel decisions. Notably, he was quick at sizing up a situation, understanding what needed to be done, and removing all obstacles, even when they involved close friends.

Returning to the United States as a sergeant, Preston was demobilized and entered Harvard, as did Vagliano. They both graduated in 1951, the year Preston captained the hockey team. Preston subsequently joined Morgan, while Vagliano continued on at Harvard Law School.

After a brief interlude, Vagliano followed in the footsteps of another colleague, Danny Davison, in joining Morgan.[6] Davison's forbears had already chalked up five generations with the House of Morgan when he joined the bank. He attended the Groton School, which had been founded in 1884 by his grandfather, and he enlisted in the US Army Air Forces during World War II. After the war, he attended Yale University, where he was a member of the Yale Political Union and the Skull and Bones Society. He earned a legal degree from Harvard Law School in 1952 and joined Morgan in 1955.

During the 1950s–60s, Preston, Vagliano and Davison were widely perceived as the up and coming generation of bankers at Morgan. The team that was assembled around them also attended the best boarding schools and colleges. They all took pride in the bank's AAA credit rating, reputation for innovation and adherence to strict rules of conduct. To be a Morgan man meant something more, something special. It was not so much a throwback to a bygone era as it was a commitment to a culture of excellence. It eschewed fads, revered its history and awarded promotions to people who had already proven their qualifications well before they were conferred their titles.

As the 1960s gave way to the 1970s, it was de rigueur to have international experience. Consequently, there was a steady stream of mid-level Morgan bankers who were assigned to overseas offices or affiliates. This was not surprising considering US institutions dominated global finance after World War II, and US corporations expanded worldwide while the US dollar emerged as the world's leading currency. The Bretton Woods era of fixed exchange rates, however, dissolved in the early 1970s, as inflation soared and President Nixon devalued the dollar on two occasions.

---

[6] Davison's scholastic career differed from Vagliano's only in attending Groton instead of St. Paul's, which was founded by his great grandfather, Endicott Peabody.

Morgan thrived in this new era of volatile currencies thanks to a group of unrivaled foreign exchange dealers in London led by Ernie Angel, Reg Barham and Dennis Weatherstone. In fact, they dominated the financial landscape better than the investment bankers of the day whose names were much better known.[7]

Not many people outside Morgan knew Preston then. What stood out early on in his career was his ability to grasp how the global economy and financial markets were becoming increasingly integrated. He understood that the US government's attempt to impose a withholding tax on foreign borrowers in the mid-1960s—the interest equalization tax (IET)—created incentives for US financial institutions to set up operations abroad to serve the needs of multinational corporations. His tenure as the head of Morgan's London office in the mid-1960s gave him a front row seat into the evolution of the Eurodollar market.

Thereafter, his stint as head of the International Division left him directly involved in the recycling of petro-dollars in the early 1970s. As the network of capital markets expanded globally and became increasingly linked, he understood that Morgan would have to become more involved in them.

The period from his appointment as EVP and head of international was characterized by expansion of Morgan's cross-border lending, as distinct from its footprint. Nothing so epitomizes this development as the rapid increase in Morgan's exposure to Latin America, even though the bank had virtually no local operations in the region. While Walter Page and Alec Vagliano were also a party to this strategy, they were by no means alone. Virtually all money center banks saw Latin America as a gold mine, which, in fact, turned out to be a money pit. The most ardent supporters included George Moore and Walter Wriston of Citibank, as well as George Champion and David Rockefeller of Chase Manhattan. Their strategies going back to the 1960s were to plant their banks' flag in branches around the world, especially in Latin America.

By comparison, one of Preston's strategic decisions was to exit virtually all of the joint ventures Morgan had been involved in or to buy their partners out. This became apparent with the breakup of the two Morgan firms' operating partnership at Morgan et Cie in Paris in 1967. Several years later, Preston exited the bank's 33% stake in Morgan Grenfell, and he bought out other partners in Australia United Corporation (AUC) in Australia and Morgan Guaranty & Partners in Singapore. Minority investments in Nigeria, Venezuela, Buenos Aires and Lebanon took somewhat longer to disengage.

---

[7] They included the Stans—Ross and Yassukovich—Hans Joerg Rudloff, Peter Spira and Rupert Hambro, who were darlings of the financial press.

One of the ways that Preston tried to shift resources to meet the perceived international opportunity was to merge the national and international divisions. Prior to 1979, employees with or without foreign language skills were assigned overseas for seasoning, but Preston realized this would not give the bank the boost it needed. When he asked Vagliano to assume the new post, he declined because his interests were predominantly in international markets.

As the senior ranks were being depleted, Preston needed to replace them, and people such as Rod Lindsay, Bob Engel and Sandy Warner were rushed through the London office to gain international experience. Peter Smith became head of the merged banking division after serving prior stints in Buenos Aires and Amsterdam. Bruce Brackenridge, who also returned from overseas, helped supervise the opening of new offices just as he had done so under Preston in London, when he opened the Frankfurt office and hired Kurt Viermetz.

Amid these changes at the senior management level, the strong partnership ethos that was a hallmark of Morgan began to crumble. It was replaced by a more rigid hierarchical structure, with Preston at its head and Weatherstone the second in command. All key decisions were made by them out of the New York headquarters.

It is not hard to imagine, therefore, the profound embarrassment that ensued when Mexico, Brazil and Argentina ran out of foreign exchange reserves in 1982 and were unable to service their debt. This proved to be just the first wave of a long list of developing countries that required their principal payments be rolled over and new lending be extended to keep their interest payments current.

To his credit, Preston did not blame others for what happened. Instead, he persevered, and in the best tradition of "Vinegar Joe" he took decisive actions to ensure not only that Morgan would survive the crisis, but that it would come out ahead of its peers. He partnered with Alfred Herrhausen of Deutsche Bank to keep syndicates with very different levels of exposure together, while also working with regulators to convince them of the need to forestall write-offs that would deplete the capital of banks. This was sold as another example of Morgan stepping to the fore in a financial crisis. In reality, though, Morgan's exposure in relation to its capital was more manageable than most of its competitors, and it came through the crisis way ahead of them.

At the same time, the LDC debt crisis appears to have had a lasting impression on Preston. Even though Morgan was adequately capitalized to write off the problem loans, he resisted doing so, because he still hoped for a way to make the bank whole. When banks with much smaller exposures such as the Bank of Boston and Lloyds Bank bit the bullet, lending solidarity began to deteriorate. Finally, when Citibank decidedly took its massive $3.3 billion write-off in 1987, the game of pretending the respective countries could service their debt was essentially over. Yet, it was only when Preston turned to Morgan's former chairman and CEO, John Meyer, for advice that he accepted the idea of turning illiquid LDC debt into marketable instruments backed by US Treasury bonds.

Even then, Preston could not countenance throwing away all his hard work of keeping the lending syndicates together. So while Morgan took the write-down after Citibank, the bank waited several years until the market had recovered to sell the bonds. Nick Rohatyn was moved from the swaps unit to start Latin American debt trading, and Morgan received a big boost from the profits that were embedded in the legacy bond portfolio. In this respect, at least, Preston got the last laugh.

The crowning blow to Preston, however, may have been the "Gebauer affair." In 1987, it was revealed that Tony Gebauer, who had co-headed Morgan's Latin America lending and who was also put in charge of the negotiations for Brazil, had misappropriated millions of dollars from Brazilian depositors' accounts from 1976 until August 30, 1985. Gebauer had moved on to Drexel in 1985 and therefore was beyond Morgan's immediate reach when charges were brought against him and he was remanded to the authorities and subsequently convicted. Nonetheless, the damage to Morgan's pristine reputation was evident, and some believed Preston was never the same: He seemed to turn inward, made strategic decisions haltingly and kept his cards close to his vest. Yet, this was the only scandal during his tenure as Morgan's chairman and CEO.

Preston was at his best in times of crisis, where he was cool and decisive. He saw plenty of them, both large and small. This was critical as he lead Morgan during difficult times and as he filled Morgan's traditional role as defender of the financial system. During the Yom Kippur War in the early 1970s, he helped calm the waters after the Saudis led an oil boycott of Western nations by helping to ensure that Japanese banks had access to interbank funding. This was vital to keep Japan's economy afloat, as it was 100% dependent on imported oil. Preston also played a role in maintaining bank funding during the Bank Herstatt failure in 1974 and during the Hunt Brothers' attempt to corner the silver market in 1980.

While Preston's feats in stemming banking crises were well known, he preferred to act quietly behind the scenes. One of the clearest examples is his decisiveness during the stock market crash on October 19, 1987, known as "Black Monday." The week before, signs of a correction were apparent, as policymakers in the United States clashed with their counterparts in Germany and Japan over their monetary policies that were intended to stabilize the dollar. That same week, the Iranians had launched a Silk Worm missile at a vessel in the Persian Gulf, which prompted a response from the US Navy. There was also a freak snowstorm in the United Kingdom that closed the London Stock Exchange the Friday before. When trading opened on Monday in the Far East, the dollar was near free fall and problems began to gather. When the futures exchanges in Chicago were about to open, margin calls on some participants were unmet. As sell-side volumes grew, particularly from users of portfolio insurance, both Chicago exchanges were forced to close and market participants shifted their sales (and shorts) to the Big Board.

Around noon, with rumors rife of the impending closure of the New York Stock Exchange (NYSE), Preston sprang into action. He organized a conference call with Gerald Corrigan of the Federal Reserve, James Baker at the Treasury and Howard Baker, President Reagan's Chief of Staff. Preston warned the participants that closure of the stock exchange would send the stock market into a downward spiral, and he dispatched them to call John Phelan, head of the NYSE, to tell him that under no circumstances should he close the exchange. Shortly thereafter Preston made a follow-up call to Corrigan to warn him that Bankers Trust was squeezing the two-year Treasury note, which was a common source of collateral at the Fed's discount window.

Once the dust had settled, the Treasury formed a task force to study the events leading up to the crash and to make recommendations for forestalling future crises. The speed with which the report was delivered, the specificity of its conclusions and the breadth of its recommendations surprised everyone involved. They were testimony to the respect Preston earned from his peers in the financial community and the influence he wielded.

Preston's effectiveness in forging alliances within the banking community to tackle common problems partly stemmed from the expansive networks he built with counterparts in the banking industry and with leaders of "white shoe" firms such as Morgan Stanley, First Boston, Smith Barney and White Weld. He developed this trait early on as a graduate of St. Paul's and Harvard and also as a de facto member of the Harriman family. During his career Preston expanded his international network as a member of the Group of Thirty, The Council of Foreign Relations, The Bilderberg Group that fosters ties between Europe and North America and the Pilgrim's Society that promotes close ties between the United States and Great Britain.

The open question is how effective Preston was in positioning Morgan for the future. When he became the leader in 1979, he essentially inherited a bank with four pillars—(1) corporate lending and finance; (2) trading of government securities, foreign exchange and gold; (3) investment management;

and (4) private banking. These areas, in turn, were supported by outstanding economic and corporate research and by an unrivaled domestic and international back office called Securities, Trust and Information Services (STIS).

As capital market transactions overtook bank lending in the early 1980s, Preston realized the bank would have to change its business model to become involved in investment banking and securities transactions. By 1984, he set in motion changes to restructure the firm and he actively lobbied Paul Volcker to circumvent the Glass-Steagall wall, mostly to no avail. Thereafter, he expanded trading activities abroad and more selectively in the United States until the Fed under Alan Greenspan began to relax Glass-Steagall restrictions. Morgan subsequently became the first commercial bank to be allowed to underwrite publicly traded securities in 1989.

By comparison, Preston seemed completely uninterested in beefing up Morgan's Private Bank, which he at times viewed as a dog walking exercise, and with the exception of Euro clear, he was content to milk STIS. Yet, these areas along with Investment Management commanded much higher price-earnings multiples from Wall Street analysts than revenues earned from trading securities, because their revenue streams were more predictable. For whatever reason, Preston failed to grasp the importance of the potential these areas offered Morgan to fund new business undertakings.

Equally surprising to some of his lieutenants was how tentative Preston became when he contemplated making acquisitions. After studying various possibilities in depth, he was Hamlet-like at times and invariably opted to pass. This was in direct contrast with his decisiveness in handling domestic and international financial crises. As one observer puts it, "It was as if all of the bank's history in the face of financial crisis had tempered and annealed him to act decisively; while decisions that affected the future of the bank were subjected to agonizing indecision."[8]

This meant the only recourse for Morgan was to build out businesses organically on multiple fronts. By default, the bank's strategy effectively became "build it and customers will come!" As would become evident in the 1990s, the problem with this approach is it took considerable time and money, and Morgan's profits and share price lagged its principal rivals.

To some extent, the reluctance to acquire banks may have reflected Morgan's history, in which its sole merger in the post-war era was with Guaranty Trust, a bank that was four times larger than Morgan. Ron Chernow contends it breathed new life into the House of Morgan. The merger, after all, was a

---

[8] Name withheld due to confidentiality.

virtual layup for Morgan, because the Board of Guaranty Trust wanted Morgan executives to run the combined entity.

That said, Preston never wavered in believing Morgan should avoid retail banking. In his view, Citi's strategy of pursuing both retail and wholesale banking was eating it out of house and home and had rendered it on the doorstep of becoming insolvent. He also knew that the path the retail giants were pursuing was unsustainable and completely alien to Morgan's culture. At the same time, he and Weatherstone failed to grasp the enormous buildup of personal wealth that began in the 1980s, and which would expand substantially thereafter.

Preston's reluctance to acquire businesses undoubtedly was also influenced by what he observed when his friends from white shoe firms began to retire and their businesses either folded or were taken over by traders. He admired how Morgan Stanley, under Dick Fisher and Parker Gilbert, maintained a culture of excellence during its transition from private to public. During the process it went from being a narrowly based investment bank to a market maker in a broad range of securities. However, as trading revenues grew and traders replaced bankers in leadership roles, management's orientation shifted from serving clients to the firm's proprietary positions. Preston was determined this should never happen to the House of Morgan.

The ongoing challenge Preston faced was he understood Morgan needed to change its business model, but he did not want to disrupt its cherished culture. His conviction was reinforced as he surrounded himself with members of the "old guard" who spent their entire careers at the bank and only knew how to do business "the Morgan way." He would push talented people to their limits and sometimes beyond, but even some who failed were kept on.

In the process, younger Morgan bankers saw a growing disconnect between the need for change and the impediments to change. Some even viewed Morgan's adherence to its culture as an impediment to change that was necessary.[9] They sought to make the firm less hierarchical and more responsive, but they would encounter resistance from their superiors, who were wedded to doing business as usual. This would become an even greater impediment in the 1990s, when Morgan's competitors were forced to embark on bolder strategies as they worked their way out of problem loans to developing countries, commercial real estate and highly leveraged companies.

During a board meeting in 1988, Preston collapsed and was taken to Beekman Downtown Hospital. A subsequent scheduled angioplasty was

---

[9] One colleague who rose to a prominent position in the firm declared to me that, "Morgan's culture was the problem!"

performed at New York Hospital, and some suspect that was when the first signs of cancer were diagnosed. The discovery wasn't all that surprising, as Preston was a chain cigarette and cigar smoker. In those days, it was not a requirement of either the NYSE or the SEC to make these issues public, and there is no way to know how, if at all, Preston's illnesses affected his decision making. However, Lee Raymond of Exxon, who served as chairman of Morgan's board, exercised his authority to ensure Dennis Weatherstone would succeed Preston as chairman and CEO, while Sandy Warner would become Morgan's president.

Looking back as his tenure as Morgan's leader, Preston is widely recognized for successfully navigating the bank during the tumultuous 1980s and for laying the foundation for its transformation into investment banking and the world of securities. During his reign, Morgan far surpassed all of its rivals, and it was the only US bank to retain a coveted AAA rating. In Sebastian Mallory's words, "Morgan was the country's pre-eminent bank, and Lew Preston was the country's pre-eminent commercial banker."[10] Still, while this was the legacy he passed on to his successors, only time would tell whether his strategy of expanding into the world of securities de novo would leave Morgan well positioned for the future.

Box: Preston and the World Bank

In 1990, Preston was approached by senior members of the Reagan administration to see if he would be willing to succeed Barber Constable as head of the World Bank. While he worried that the confirmation process would expose him to unwanted scrutiny, his sponsors had already figured out how to make the proceedings as painless as possible. Unfortunately, as Preston threw himself into his new job, tragedy struck when his only son died of cancer at the age of thirty-five.

During his tenure at the World Bank from 1991 to 1995, Preston oversaw the entry of the former Soviet republics into the institution after the demise of the Communist bloc. He strived to give it a larger role in restructuring the public sectors of member countries. He also met with Soviet President Mikhail Gorbachev and Russian President Boris Yeltsin to help former Soviet republics transition toward market economies. Preston also acted to make the World Bank more responsive to prevailing social issues, including tackling environmental issues and increasing lending for health, education and family planning.

Amid this, Preston took steps to trim the Bank's sprawling bureaucracy: The administrative budget had increased by nearly 50% as it took on added countries. Before assuming the post he consulted with Rimmer de Vries and others who were knowledgeable about the Bank, and one of his first steps was to slash 240 senior management positions.

(continued)

---

[10] Ibid., p. 56.

(continued)

Preston clashed on occasion with some of the executive directors for the various regions who attempted to tell him how to manage the World Bank. His overriding goal was to ensure the Bank's mission remained "the alleviation of poverty," and he judged performance not by the volume of loans but by the success of projects it financed.The *Financial Times* concluded that the World Bank had fallen into safe hands[11]:

Preston does not pretend to be a development expert, an intellectual or an economist. But he appears to have other, rarer virtues: steady nerves, sound judgment and enough confidence cheerfully to admit that he does not know all the answers.

Sebastian Mallaby, however, observes that Preston was a fish out of water[12]:

Preston was not running the World Bank because he had a compelling vision of its role; his anxiety about the Vision Thing mirrored that of the man who had appointed him. He lurked in his office on the twelfth floor of the Bank's headquarters building, his door guarded by Pat O'Hara, a devoted executive assistant who spent years with him at JP Morgan. O'Hara wielded a pencil and a big leather-bound Economist Diary; she would note down two or three appointments every day, and that was considered adequate. Even two or three years into the job, Preston could ride the World Bank elevator twelve stories down to the ground floor without being recognized by anyone. It is hard to believe so private a man could ever have inspired and fixed so public an institution.

Box: Preston Vignettes

Lew Preston's demeanor made him appear stern at times, and he could intimidate people merely by staring at them with his half-rimmed glasses ensconced on his nose. Those who knew him best, however, shared stories that revealed a softer, more humorous side.

One that Bruce Brackenridge loved to tell was the story of a round of golf that he and Preston played at Sunningdale, the legendary course just outside London. Born in a suburb of Glasgow, Brackenridge was an excellent golfer, having played on the team at Williams College. Preston, by comparison, was an avid tennis player. As the story unfolds, he was having a hard time finding the fairway that day, and his Scottish caddy trudged through sand and fescue searching for Preston's balls. When they came to the turn, Preston remarked to the caddy, "It's

(continued)

---

[11] Ibid.
[12] Ibid., p. 57.

(continued)

a funny game!" "Aye" said the caddy, but "it's not meant to be." Preston then asked the caddy if he'd like a drink. "No" said the caddy. "I think I'll walk over to the next fairway. It's the only one I've seen all day!"

Another favorite story of Morgan execs was about a trip Preston and his wife, Patsy, took to Asia. They first stopped in Manila, where it was a requirement in those days for Morgan executives to call on Jaime Cardinal Sin. The reason: The Catholic Church Pension Fund had nearly an identical shareholding interest as Morgan in the Bank of the Philippine Islands. As the gates of the compound opened, a diminutive figure appeared at the entrance, and the Cardinal, with an impish grin, said, "Mr. Preston, welcome to the house of Sin!"

12

Preston Passes the Baton

Soon after Preston addressed Morgan's board in September 1989 about provisioning for $2 billion of its LDC loans, he announced that he would be stepping down as chairman and CEO of JPMorgan and that Dennis Weatherstone would succeed him in those roles as of January 1, 1990. The press release stated that Preston would stay on to serve as chairman of the Executive Committee. Three other officers were elected directors and were named to new positions: Sandy Warner would succeed Weatherstone as president, and Roberto Mendoza and Kurt Viermetz were appointed vice chairmen.

While the timing of the announcement was a surprise, Preston's choice for Dennis Weatherstone as his successor had been a foregone conclusion among the ranks of Morgan's employees. From the time they worked together in London, beginning in the mid-1960s, through their collaboration in New York, it was increasingly evident that Weatherstone was Lew Preston's man and designated successor. Nor did it matter to Preston that Weatherstone's background was very different from previous Morgan leaders (Table 12.1).

At first blush they might seem an odd couple. Whereas Preston had a patrician upbringing, Weatherstone came from humble beginnings. His father was a postal worker, and he did not attend college. He joined the Guaranty Trust Company when he was a teenager, and shortly thereafter he served in the British Army Signal Corps and in North Africa.

When Weatherstone returned to rejoin the bank after the war, he went to school at night to learn trading skills. He was surrounded by clever people in the dealing room, and being clever himself, he thrived as a currency trader. Even though the United Kingdom had virtually no foreign exchange reserves and traded primarily with Commonwealth members, London was still the

© The Author(s) 2020
N. P. Sargen, *JPMorgan's Fall and Revival*, https://doi.org/10.1007/978-3-030-47058-6_12

Table 12.1 The pedigree of Morgan Guaranty chairmen and CEOs

Henry Alexander	1955–65	Vanderbilt/Yale Law
Thomas Gates	1965–69	University of Pennsylvania
John Meyer, Jr.	1969–71	University of Chicago
Ellmore Patterson	1971–77	University of Chicago
Walter Page	1978–79	Harvard University
Lewis Preston	1980–89	Harvard University
Sir Dennis Weatherstone	1990–94	No college
Douglas Warner	1995–2000	Yale University

pre-eminent center for foreign exchange dealing and international commerce. It would take years before New York and other foreign centers presented any real competition.

It wasn't until after the Guaranty merger with Morgan that it became clear Morgan had the clients and Guaranty had the expertise in markets. True to its roots, Morgan had durable relationships with corporate chiefs; but as barriers to trade and capital flows came down and US corporations began to expand overseas, their need for capital grew. And so did their need to find way ways to hedge their overseas exposure.

By the time Preston arrived in London in 1966, Weatherstone was a prominent fixture in the dealing room. He had managed to overtake his mentors, but was well liked and regarded as "one of the boys." Preston, a savvy lender, was also immersed in commodity markets, having covered the petroleum industry in the United States as it expanded steadily after World War II.

What made the partnership so effective was that Preston's expertise, unlike most bankers, went well beyond lending to corporations and raising money for them in capital markets. Rather, Preston was a hybrid banker-trader, and Weatherstone was a man of the markets. They both grew in stature and responsibilities in the latter part of the twentieth century, when the world of banking was being transformed by globalization, and large bank failures became common owing to speculative excesses and failure on the part of many to understand the risks they were taking.

Soon after Weatherstone arrived at Morgan's headquarters in 1973, Preston began to move people aside to make room for him. This enabled Weatherstone not only to head the foreign exchange dealing room but also to become treasurer of the bank in the late 1970s.

One of the first to leave was Ralph Leach, who like Weatherstone came from the Guaranty Trust side of the house. Leach's departure was noteworthy, as he had served on the Board of Morgan Guaranty Trust from 1969 until his departure in 1977. During the 1960s, Leach was a pioneer in trading federal funds—reserves banks held at the Federal Reserve.[1] According to Chernow, some banks at the time did not believe the federal funds market should be used to make trading profits. However, Leach proved to be highly successful in placing large bets on the direction of interest rates.[2] Under his direction, Morgan hired scores of young traders to take positions in Treasury bills, negotiable CDs, foreign exchange and Fed funds. A *Fortune* magazine article in 1966 noted that Leach "very likely handles more money in the course of a year than any other man in private industry."[3]

Not long after, another trader, Frank Smeal (also a former Guaranty hire), left Morgan to join Goldman Sachs. Smeal headed Morgan's municipal bond desk, and he earned accolades for his efforts to hold bond syndicates together during the New York City and State financial crises in the mid-1970s. Thereafter, Weatherstone assumed responsibility for the muni market, the Treasury market as well as currencies and gold. These markets were key to Morgan's eventual migration back to its roots as an investment bank, and it did not take long for Weatherstone to master them. The municipal market was particularly important for banks because of their tax free status, and bank holdings of municipals became a significant source of profits.

One of the most prominent departures at the senior executive level was Dan Davison. He served as a vice chairman of Morgan Guaranty and was the fifth generation of his family to be a Morgan banker. Davison left Morgan in 1979 after Preston won out as Morgan's president, and he went on to assume the top spot at US Trust, where he was credited for revitalizing the bank. This cleared the way for Preston to appoint Rod Lindsay, brother of the former New York City mayor, as president of Morgan, when Preston assumed the role of chairman and CEO in 1980. Weatherstone, in turn, was elevated to become chair of the executive committee, which was the stepping stone to become president of Morgan.

Another key departure was Alec Vagliano. As discussed in the preceding chapter, he succeeded Preston as the head of the international banking division. Early on, Preston pushed for the merger of the national and international divisions in order to extend the expertise and contacts developed in the US market to suit his vision of the bank's growing presence in the international arena. When Preston asked Vagliano to integrate the two divisions,

---

[1] Previously, Leach had been a high-level economist at the Board of Governors in Washington, D.C., where he was a tennis partner of Fed Chairman William McChesney Martin. See Chernow, op. cit. p. 530.
[2] Ibid., p. 540.
[3] Ibid., p. 540.

Vagliano declined.[4] As a polyglot, with years of experience in international dealings, Vagliano's interests were nearly exclusively in international markets.[5] Also, he thought it was unnatural and inefficient to separate commercial banking from capital markets, but this didn't translate into nursing domestic bankers to become proficient in the intricacies of dealing overseas.

The list of senior-level departures expanded fairly steadily in the 1980s. Some took early retirement, as they felt pressure to meet Preston's high expectations. As a member of the GE Board of Directors, Preston had observed the way Reg Jones dealt with his succession as CEO, which led to the appointment of Jack Welch and the exit of all his rivals for the top spot shortly after. Preston, in particular, admired the very public contest Jones had set up, as he thought it was a good way to keep senior leaders on their toes.

One of Preston's characteristic traits was the way he treated his senior managers as he was during his ascent through Morgan's ranks. If he gave someone a stretch assignment and they passed the test, they would then be handed an even more challenging assignment. While this characteristic is a tried and true way many CEOs use to separate performers from non-performers, some of Preston's lieutenants believed he often pushed people past their breaking points.

Curiously, those who failed were often kept in senior positions out of Preston's loyalty to them. However, this often instilled a deep sense of caution on their part—a quality that was not geared to advance corporate risk taking or to break down barriers as Morgan transitioned into investment banking. One consequence was that many of the MBA recruits that the bank hired in the 1970s and 1980s became convinced the bank was not committed to make the transformation, and they opted to leave.

In the end, the decision for Morgan to become a hybrid commercial-investment bank was Preston's decision. True to form, he kept his own counsel until the decision was confirmed at a long meeting of senior officers in late November 1986. The principal exception was Dennis Weatherstone, whose counsel Preston respected and on whom he could count to pursue the course he envisioned for the bank.

When Weatherstone succeeded Preston as chairman and CEO, it was as if it had been pre-ordained. Virtually every important decision that Preston made after he returned to New York was made in Weatherstone's presence, if not with his consultation.

---

[4] Peter Smith was then given the nod to replace Vagliano, and his experience in Latin America may have contributed to an ill-advised attempt for Morgan to catch up with Citi.

[5] According to one source, Vagliano reportedly played a key role in freeing the hostages from the US Embassy in Iran, among whom was his cousin, Morehead Kennedy.

But Weatherstone's style as a leader was quite different from his mentor's: He was widely regarded as being charming and a "people person," who was particularly adept at financial markets. However, Weatherstone, who had no banking experience, would discover that knowledge of markets was no substitute for running a bank. He was also more consultative than Preston, although some colleagues observed he generally favored those who agreed with him, not those who challenged him—a characteristic of many executives.

Like Preston, Weatherstone believed in keeping his managers on a short leash. On most days when Morgan Guaranty Limited (MGL) led a syndicate of underwriters for a new issue, the people in charge in London had to revert to Weatherstone or Bob Engel for authorization. This reliance ultimately led to not-too-subtle shifting of responsibility to New York.

Being a markets man, Weatherstone also contrived to beef up Treasury and trading earnings and insulate them as much as possible from losses. At the beginning of each year, the Private Bank was awarded a finder's fee of 0.5–1% of their clients' interest income (less the FDIC fee), which accrued to the Treasury Division. This had the effect not only of insulating Morgan's Treasury from poor decisions but also significantly understating the Private Bank's earnings. (Note: The precedent for this was a long-standing Bank of England policy that allowed the banks latitude to divert some of their profits into so-called inner reserves.)

Among the most important decisions Preston and Weatherstone made was the selection of Sandy Warner to become president of Morgan and eventual chairman and CEO. The decision was made in the fall of 1988 soon after Preston learned that he was suffering from cancer. In addition to Warner, the contenders included James Flynn, Roberto Mendoza, John Olds and Kurt Viermetz, who all served in the Management Committee. However, Flynn, who headed Operations, and Mendoza, who was the bank's top deal maker, were both considered long shots. And Viermetz had a similar markets' background as Weatherstone, which were thought to lessen his chances. Of the five, Olds had the most experience in the securities industry and was a strategic thinker.

In many respects, Warner's background fit the profile of other Morgan chairmen and CEOs. He grew up in a prominent family in Indian Hill, a wealthy suburb of Cincinnati, and he attended the Hill School in Pottstown, Pennsylvania. He then went on to attend Yale and was interested in pursuing a career in medicine. However, he discovered banking while working as a summer intern at Morgan in 1968, and enjoyed the experience immensely. One year later, he accepted a full-time position at the bank and entered the training program.

Warner's first assignment entailed calling on clients in northeast Ohio, and he soon was relocated to Morgan's New York headquarters. While there he made a favorable impression on his superiors, and in 1979 he was asked to serve as administrative assistant to the chairman, first John Meyer and then Elmore Patterson. He was only the fourth person to land such a coveted position, which had been started by Thomas Gates, Morgan's chairman in the mid-1960s. James Robinson III, who later became chairman of American Express, was the first assistant to be chosen.[6]

In 1973 Warner was rotated to cover District 9 that included Chicago, and he subsequently was assigned to cover the West Coast. The challenge that he faced there was to penetrate the lucrative California market that was home to prominent banks such as Bank of America, Security Pacific and Wells Fargo. He was recognized by his superiors for landing a remarkable amount of new business compared with his predecessors.

By 1979 Warner was running the bank's Midwest region, and he found himself dealing with venerable Morgan clients such as Ford and Chrysler. Two years later, he was assigned responsibility for running operational services, a marketing unit that sold noncredit services such as cash management to corporate clients.[7] Warner reorganized the unit and helped to develop a form of electronic checking for Morgan's network of correspondent banks.

Along the way, Warner's organizational skills were noticed by Preston and Weatherstone. As noted previously, he was picked to head corporate banking in London in 1983. Preston and Weatherstone wanted a person who was adept with clients and who had experience in operations to develop a corporate banking organization that could garner UK clients. Oil and gas lending proved to be the main entry point, as Morgan had established a strong relationship with British Petroleum in the 1970s.[8]

It didn't take Warner long to recognize the talent base that covered the UK oil and gas industry. The unit, which was run by James Berliner and driven by Tom Ketchum out of New York, had a coterie of highly talented people who would eventually rise to senior management positions at Morgan and other institutions. They included Ramon de Oliveira (who would go on to head equities and high yield), Peter Hancock (who would run fixed income and derivatives), Rod Peacock (who became co-head of M&A for Europe), Charles Stonehill (who would run European equities for Morgan Stanley) and

[6] Teitelman, op. cit., p. 52.

[7] Ibid., p. 53.

[8] Ibid., p. 56. Morgan's petroleum team in conjunction with Lazard's had pioneered the financing of BP's Forties Field in the North Sea.

Alexander Cato.[9] Warner reportedly paid homage to the group, on one occasion telling them, "What we've got here is the equivalent of the corporate finance group of Goldman Sachs & Co. And I'm going to let people know about it."[10]

In 1985 with oil prices falling, Warner downsized the London unit, but he also lobbied for key people to be placed in prominent positions. Tom Ketchum was moved to Hong Kong to run Asia-Pacific, while de Oliveira and Hancock were assigned to MGL. De Oliveira began to develop Morgan's equity business out of London before moving to New York to run high yield.

In 1986, Warner was appointed the general manager of the London office and was Morgan's senior executive in the United Kingdom. One year later Warner was promoted to executive vice president, and he returned to New York City to take charge of corporate finance for the Americas.

While Warner commanded loyalty from those who were rewarded, others who cherished the "Old Morgan" saw a bank that had become less kind and genteel. Following the Big Bang in the United Kingdom and the US stock market crash in 1987, many old-line bankers found their services were no longer appreciated and they moved on.

However, it is debatable to what extent Warner should shoulder the responsibility. In his 1996 article on Sandy Warner's tenure as Morgan's leader, journalist Robert Teitelman quotes Morgan's vice chairman, Rodney Wagner[11]:

> Lew (Preston) could be rough on people he thought were unprepared or wasting his time. But he could also be kind, smart and witty, particularly with small groups. He listened very carefully. He played a close game, and he was very patient. Dennis (Weatherstone), on the other hand, was very nice, very kind, particularly in personal relationships. He was a little more open than Lew. But don't think that Weatherstone couldn't make decisions very coldly. He's a trader. It is a misreading of him to say he's just a nice guy. He knew where he wanted to go and he got there.
>
> Much of the rap that Warner was tough stems from the late 1980s, when he reorganized corporate finance in the United States. People saw Warner. He was in the middle of it. They didn't see Weatherstone as much. But he was there. And he would make the tough decisions.

The announcement about the changing of the guard at Morgan was well received by the press. The *Wall Street Journal* said that Preston:

---

[9] Ibid., p. 56.
[10] Ibid., p. 56.
[11] Ibid., p.59.

orchestrated a fairly clean departure, leaving Mr. Weatherstone with ample latitude to chart his own course for the years ahead: A new $800 million headquarters on Wall Street is near completion; Morgan has secured approval from the Federal Reserve Board to underwrite and deal in corporate debt, an important strategic goal; and Mr. Preston socked away $2 billion in Morgan's loan loss reserves last month to disarm any threat to Morgan of a default on loan payments by developing countries.

The *New York Times* stated that Preston had developed the strategic plan for Morgan to supplement its traditional bank lending business by moving into deal making and securities ventures: "In a decade when many investment banking and securities firms have foundered, Morgan has expanded into those businesses without sacrificing its reputation as a blue-chip banking firm."

Not all reports, however, were as glowing. A *Euromoney* story, for example, questioned whether Morgan's new management team could achieve an adequate return on equity given its present base of products and its refusal to budge from a blue-chip client base[12]:

> Blue chips are the very clients most able to hammer down fees; yet while other money-centre operations such as Bankers Trust have watered down markets in search of more profitable financings, Morgan remains aloof.

The *Euromoney* article went on to note that Tom Hanley, Salomon Brothers' top-rated bank equity analyst, had downgraded Morgan's shares in April because of Morgan's "narrowly focused and perhaps difficult to implement business strategy." The article concluded with the following quote from a rival investment banker[13]:

> Morgan's blue-chip course is a lonely one. It certainly hasn't been where Bankers Trust or Citi have been, and it's not where Morgan Stanley or Goldman are. It's got to be very careful that it doesn't end up stuck somewhere in the middle.

For Morgan's management team, however, the response to this critique was that Morgan wanted to choose its own direction, rather than become just another securities firm.

---

[12] Ron Cooper, "Wither Weatherstone's Morgan?" *Euromoney*, December 1989, p. 56.
[13] Ibid., p. 58.

Part III

Executing the Plan

13

Taking Stock: Plans for the Early 1990s

By mid-1990, five years had passed since Lew Preston made the commitment to shift the bank into securities and investment banking, and three years since the formal launch of JP Morgan Securities. As the baton was being passed from Preston to Dennis Weatherstone and Sandy Warner, this provided an opportunity for senior management to assess the progress that had been made and the impact their decisions would have on future earnings and Morgan's share price.

In a presentation to the Board of Directors in mid-July, John Olds began by pointing out how dramatically Morgan's business model had changed since the mid-1980s. Specifically, an increasing share of its revenues was from fees it earned providing services to clients, while the share of revenues accruing from net interest margin had declined. He noted that this transformation was consistent with trends in the banking industry, in which the role of banks had changed from one of simply extending credit to one of facilitating transactions.

The backdrop for making these changes was one of ongoing retrenchment in the financial services industry, which still faced considerable excess-capacity. While money-center banks had made provisions to cover losses on developing country loans by the end of the 1980s, Citibank, Chase, Chemical Bank and Manufacturers Hanover had expanded into commercial real estate and leveraged loans. Their predicament was about to worsen, as the US economy slipped into recession when oil prices spiked in August 1990 as Iraq's invasion of Kuwait threatened to disrupt oil supplies. While the recession proved to be

---

The information on Morgan's strategic plan in this chapter is based on internal documents and conversations with senior executives.

© The Author(s) 2020
N. P. Sargen, *JPMorgan's Fall and Revival*, https://doi.org/10.1007/978-3-030-47058-6_13

mild and relatively short, commercial real estate was one of the hardest hit sectors, and most money center banks experienced a significant increase in problem loans.

Morgan stood out by having only modest exposure to commercial real estate and leveraged loans. Nonetheless, Morgan's senior management team was not content to have the bank rest on its laurels. They determined the time was ripe for the Corporate Planning Group (CPG) to map out a strategy to complete Morgan's transformation into securities and investment banking.

The underlying premise was the 1990s would be turbulent for financial institutions, which were still adjusting to regulatory and structural changes. The pace of innovation was likely to be rapid, while capital shortages and poor earnings would stimulate further consolidation. In this environment, success would be achieved by only the best managed institutions.

As the Planning unit members surveyed the scene, they could see how financial institutions that faced pressures on operating margins were responding. First, few at that time would dare to do what Morgan was doing—namely, increase both capital spending and hiring when the economy was weak. Second, financial institutions, especially securities firms, were increasingly conflicted between proprietary trading and client-driven services. Third, predatory practices including acquisitions of competitors, buyouts of entire teams, low-ball pricing and unethical practices such as insider trading and market squeezes were becoming common. This behavior became the subject of high-profile books and movies such as *The Bonfire of the Vanities*, *Barbarians at the Gate* and *Liar's Poker*.

The strategic plan envisioned a market place in the 1990s in which there would be fewer, but larger participants due to ongoing consolidation in the industry. The unit also believed the difficult times in the financial industry created an opportunity for Morgan to capitalize on the disarray and to expand its footprint as regulatory barriers came down. Some of Morgan's inherent advantages included a well-established client base to expand its market share, strong trading and research skills, good execution and distribution along with sophisticated, value-added ideas.

The Planning unit was also fully cognizant Morgan needed to build capabilities in several areas in order to compete globally. One was to develop core processing systems and a globally accessible database from which to derive profit opportunities, management information and data for regulatory reporting, trading systems and analytics. Another consideration was executive compensation might not be sufficient to attract and retain top talent. However, Morgan's management believed its work environment that emphasized teamwork, open communication across geographical boundaries and dedication to client problem-solving were clear pluses.

In setting its goals for the next two to three years, Morgan's management was cognizant that Wall Street analysts had begun to question whether the bank had lost its earnings momentum. The reason: Morgan's overall revenue had peaked in 1987 and then receded in the following two years. This mainly reflected a decline in net interest earnings, partly due to a flattening of the yield curve, which meant there was a narrowing between the yield it earned on long-dated assets and interest it paid to fund its activities. But there were also a series of one-off developments that made it difficult to determine the underlying causes of the decline in net interest income.

For Wall Street analysts, the most important factor in assessing a financial institution was the predictability and stability of its earnings. From this perspective, institutions received greater credit and higher market multiples for generating fee income that was ongoing than trading revenue which was volatile.

Recognizing the importance of this distinction, the Planning unit defined and measured Morgan's core or recurrent earnings the way the markets would, which marked a difference from Morgan's traditional approach. It did so by defining revenue sources from six key areas: (1) Financing, (2) Advisory, (3) Treasury Operations and Securities Sales and Trading (TSST), (4) Securities Trust and Information Services (STIS); (5) Funds Management and (6) Private Banking. In addition, the earnings of the firm's own account were shown separately. Revenue projections were then established for each of these areas and disaggregated into key components.

One of the goals of the exercise was to establish both priorities and the appropriate investment horizon for major commitments for capital expenditures, personnel development and the size and quality of risk assets required to enhance or maintain the profitability of various products and locations. The exercise also entailed analyzing a mix of competitive factors including changes in regulatory environments, capital requirements and the competitive landscape. From this, Morgan's management could formulate both offensive and defensive strategies, while also gaining insights into ways of achieving greater earnings stability.

The Corporate Planning Group began to look at possible acquisitions that would enhance earnings without sacrificing asset quality, the AAA rating or Morgan's culture. CPG viewed its mandate as seeking to augment organic growth in the securities arena with selective acquisitions that would enhance Morgan's core earnings.

Three business lines were identified as areas where an acquisition or joint venture could help build earnings momentum faster and cheaper than organic growth could. They included Securities Trust and Information Services (STIS), JP Morgan Investment Management (JPMIM) and Private Banking (PB). Each of these business lines generated fee income that was fairly predictable and which would help balance Morgan's growing involvement in market-related activities.

Of these targeted areas, CPG flagged STIS offerings as most urgent to review. They predominantly consisted of US and global custody and overseas branch custody, as well as holdings of American depository receipts (ADRs) and commercial paper, and activities linked to Morgan's Euroclear operations. The urgency stemmed from the need to make critical investments to upgrade and consolidate existing systems and to add a capability for managing and reporting various types of pooled investments including mutual funds. This arose, in part, because Morgan had decided not to enter the Master Trust business in the 1970s.

The 1991 plan included technology investments of about $30 million to update and upgrade client reporting capabilities for Morgan to stay competitive in global custody. Further significant expenditures on STIS technology would be required beyond 1991 to expand coverage of investment vehicles, build databases and improve accounting services. When James Flynn, head of Operations, was asked how much it would ultimately cost to transform Morgan's operations into a modern back office in the United States, his estimate was on the order of $350 million.

The gaps in securities support operations had become apparent in each of three business lines—STIS, PB and JPMIM—that CPG was targeting. Because the gaps were related to basic processing and reporting capabilities, rather than cutting-edge technologies, senior management needed to consider whether to close the gaps internally or to join forces with an entity that already had the capability, which would enable Morgan to concentrate its efforts elsewhere, such as analytics. CPG also was cognizant that as competition for custody businesses intensified, margins would come under pressure, which would make it harder to justify new investments.

At the same time, economies could be achieved by ceding processing and reporting functions to a third party. This objective could be accomplished via a merger, joint venturing with another party or simply outsourcing. While the primary goal would be to reduce or eliminate duplicative investment, scale and scope economies could also arise from combining Morgan's processing requirements with another major institution's.

CPG produced a brief analysis of "Acquisition Success Factors" based on academic studies of characteristics common to successful or failed acquisitions and companies with a demonstrated track record as acquirers. The principal findings were that successful acquisitions were the outcome of processes that implemented clear strategic goals, and which gave equal thought to integration plan as to the transaction itself. It was also essential to conduct thorough due diligence to determine the right target, at the right price, with the right plan. The environment for considering an acquisition was deemed favorable then, because Morgan's share price had held up better than most other banks during the industry-wide shakeout in 1990.

CPG's vision was that to be successful in the global custody business required providing institutional clients with a fully integrated platform of information, risk management and analytics-driven services that was complemented by securities lending and fund management capabilities. The typical arrangement at the time was for institutional investors to have a domestic custodian and an international custodian. However, CPG saw market leaders such as Chase and State Street as developing global custody capabilities, in which settlement, safekeeping and other services were performed across markets on a consolidated basis. Among potential candidates, two institutions stood out—State Street and Northern Trust.

State Street Bank and Trust Company was founded in Boston and traced its origins to 1792. In the 1980s, it evolved to become the largest custodian of securities worldwide, providing basic portfolio record keeping required for regulatory and reporting purposes, as well as becoming a pioneer investment management firm in index funds. As a custodian, State Street served mutual funds and other collective investment funds, corporate and public pension funds, insurance companies, foundations and endowments and investment managers globally.

Northern Trust, which was founded in Chicago in 1889, developed into a leading institution in investment management for institutional and high net worth clients in the Chicago area and Florida. It also provided asset and fund administration and fiduciary and banking services.

Both institutions were attractive because they could augment the STIS business lines by bringing Morgan much-needed master trust/master custody capabilities that allow investors to hold a portfolio of managed funds under a single umbrella. In addition, a combination with State Street would help build out JPMIM's business by adding index-fund capabilities to its active management. By comparison, a combination with Northern Trust would increase Morgan's private banking presence in several US markets while also adding to its commercial banking business in the Midwest.

Both State Street and Northern Trust fit Morgan's profile of acquisition candidates. They were both mid-size, well-capitalized holding companies.

Earnings, earnings growth, expense control and asset quality for both institutions were roughly comparable, although State Street's headcount was larger (7600 vs. 5600). Their market capitalizations were also comparable ($1.1 billion for State Street vs. $0.9 billion for Northern), and their market valuations, in terms price/earnings and price/book multiples, were both in the same range as Morgan's.

State Street was the first institution that Morgan's management looked at closely. The circumstances were that John Weinberg, head of Goldman Sachs, informed Dennis Weatherstone that State Street's Chairman and CEO, William Edgerly, was contemplating retiring and wished to explore merger possibilities with Morgan. CPG had looked at State Street and several other specialized banking institutions earlier in 1990, and at that time concluded that the acquisition premium to complete a transaction was too high. In the meantime, however, the shakeout in bank stock prices had created a window of opportunity for Morgan, and it was agreed that it made sense to proceed by meeting with Edgerly and his team.

The initial meeting, which was scheduled for mid-November, would enable Morgan's management to learn about State Street, and it would also help Morgan more accurately define its perceived competitive deficiencies in STIS products. CPG acknowledged that it was difficult to determine what their future revenue potential was, as institutional clients were becoming more sophisticated, self-sufficient and inclined toward a global investment posture.

Both sides found the meeting productive, and it was agreed to hold a second one in late December. In the meantime, CPG produced a product review of custodial services that summarized the options available to Morgan in the global custody business. The key finding was STIS's strategy of progressively building a global capability using existing transactions processing systems in Europe was risky. Morgan should consider other options including acquiring the necessary software from another bank or vendor, or acquire a bank with a significant presence in global custody. The study advocated having a master trust capability as a fundamental building block. It also made more sense to develop a capability first in the United States, rather than starting oversees and then migrating back.

CPG's recommendation was that Morgan should consider putting preliminary feelers out to State Street's management and largest shareholder to ascertain their interest in being acquired. The main advantages it would bring to Morgan included its position as a market leader in global custody, strength in the area of pension funds and mutual funds, and a management that was motivated to consider a merger. At the same time, CPG recommended that Morgan initiate contact with Northern Trust, while it would undertake a more detailed review of US and overseas competitors to understand their strategies and financial and technological commitments.

In the end, both possibilities fell through. The reason Morgan did not pursue Northern Trust is clear: Its management did not want to be acquired, and Morgan did not want to engage in a hostile takeover. However, the reason Morgan's management did not pursue an acquisition of State Street is less evident. James Flynn was not in favor of the merger, and at the time Morgan's management may not have viewed it as a priority, considering it was still enjoying after-tax profits from Euroclear-related activities on the order of $400 million per year. Morgan was also negotiating an extension of its contract as the operator of Euroclear then. (Note: Five years later, the issue of what to do with STIS was revisited, and a decision was made to exit the business in 1995–96.)

The plan for 1990–92 envisioned core earnings growing by roughly 10% per annum over two years. The biggest gains were expected to come from Securities Sales and Trading and Corporate Finance as Morgan expanded into these areas. Upside/downside ranges were also shown to indicate the volatility inherent in each line of business under various scenarios.

Another key component of the plan was cost containment. This was necessitated because the growth of expenses from 1985 to 1990 nearly doubled and was unsustainable, especially with revenue growth having plateaued. Moreover, each of the three main categories—salaries and benefits, occupancy and equipment/furniture and other operating expenses—had experienced comparable growth. The plan called for Morgan to slow the pace of hiring in the next two to three years and to transfer employees from "old" businesses (while maintaining revenues as much as possible) into "new" businesses that would generate the requisite revenue growth being projected.

Senior management was fully apprised that the firm's success in the near term would hinge on its ability to leverage off mature and profitable businesses. They included foreign exchange and swaps; private banking and investment management; and custody and information services. While a good base had been created in advisory activities and capital markets, the firm was still investing in these areas and it was difficult to predict how fast they would take off. Meanwhile, future investments, either to develop new product lines or rejuvenate existing ones, would depend to a large extent on the core earnings generated by existing businesses.

Finally, the plan attempted to assess what the impact would be on Morgan's share price. During the mid-1980s, Morgan's market capitalization nearly tripled to more than $8 billion. Thereafter, its market cap declined to $7 billion as revenue growth slowed after the 1987 stock market crash, while its book value fluctuated around $4 billion.

Throughout the 1980s, Morgan's share price traded at a considerable premium relative to other money center banks on both a price-earnings basis and a price-book basis, reflecting its superior core earnings and strong balance sheet. Morgan's share price also compared favorably relative to leading investment banks, partly because a larger share of their earnings was deriving from trading activity, which is less predictable than bank loans or fee income. One of the key takeaways from this exercise was that although Morgan's share price tripled during the 1980s, it was in line with the overall market.

As of mid-1990, JPM's share price was hovering near the upper end of its historic trading band. Looking ahead, the Planning Group translated what the product managers' forecasts would imply for future earnings. A wide range of outcomes was shown, which ranged from $600 million to $1 billion. The assessment was that the ability to boost the share price through strictly organic growth was constrained, and the best way to add revenue going forward was through acquisitions.

Overall, the outlook was cautiously optimistic about Morgan's future. Thus, despite a precipitous drop in net interest earnings and a dramatic increase in cost structure, the strategic plan anticipated that JPMorgan's after-tax profit should rise moderately over the next three years. The good news in this regard was that Morgan's core earnings were as strong as they were five years prior, and it had a more diversified range of revenue sources and growing experience in the new product areas. At the same time, cost were also beginning to level off, and there was some hope they could actually decline as economies were achieved through regionalization of back office processing.

One objective of the exercise was to demonstrate to Wall Street analysts that the new core earnings were relatively predictable and growing. Together with the firm's fortress balance sheet and unmatched asset quality, senior management was upbeat that JPM's stock would continue to trade at a premium to most other financial institutions, most of whom were in much weaker states. Nonetheless, the key issue that remained to be seen was whether Morgan's management could successfully execute the plan.

14

Risk Management and Derivatives

One area where Morgan had considerable expertise and distinguished itself in the Weatherstone era was the application of risk management procedures and derivative instruments. Both were the outgrowth of heightened financial market volatility that occurred in the 1970s and 1980s.

In previous decades, bankers spent much of their time developing close relationships with their customers so they could understand the credit risks they were taking in extending loans to them. However, there was no systematic attempt to quantify the inherent risks, even as capital markets overtook bank lending as the principal source of finance for corporations. One researcher noted that bankers at many prominent institutions seemed oblivious to business cycle risks. Indeed, many viewed their mission as standing by their customer whenever they needed assistance.

This began to change in the late 1970s, when Bankers Trust, under Charles Sanford, developed a system for measuring the level of credit and market risk the bank was taking. The system was known by the acronym RAROC, which stood for risk-adjusted return on capital. Sanford's main insight was that capital should be allocated along product lines in a way that is consistent with the risks in each activity. The RAROC concept is similar to return on equity (ROE), except the denominator adjusts components of capital according to their riskiness, as measured by the volatility of earnings. It, thereby, allows projects or business lines to be compared on a uniform basis.

© The Author(s) 2020
N. P. Sargen, *JPMorgan's Fall and Revival*, https://doi.org/10.1007/978-3-030-47058-6_14

According to Gene Guill, an economic researcher who went on to work for Bankers Trust, Sanford viewed RAROC as a process, rather than a simple formula with static input parameters:[1]

> The calculation of risk capital is a quest—it presents the challenge of understanding the risks to a business, a transaction, or a position. Our ability to estimate capital improves only as our understanding of risk improves.

Guill contends that Bankers Trust (BT's) pioneering work in risk management transformed it from "a struggling full-service bank into a dynamic, well-capitalized wholesale financial institution." He also notes that "a good idea alone did not ensure the successful transformation of Bankers Trust." In his view, the key to success was that Sanford had a "cadre of senior managers and employees at the bank who were willing to work with him and who fundamentally recognized that he was on the right path."[2]

Whereas BT's efforts to develop a comprehensive risk management framework were driven to improve capital allocation, Dennis Weatherstone's principal motivation was to understand how vulnerable Morgan's positions were to market fluctuations and how much capital the bank should hold. Having spent much of his career in the volatile currency and interest rate markets, he was well aware of how market swings could impact the bank's balance sheet and income statements. This was particularly evident during the events that culminated in the October 1987 stock market crash, when stock, bond and currency markets experienced extraordinary volatility and Morgan and other banks suffered steep losses.

In 1989, Weatherstone adopted a novel practice into JPMorgan that was known as the "4–15 report." Each day, at 4:15 p.m., after the markets closed, he received a report that quantified the amount of risk the bank was running in all of its business lines. The initial report that was prepared was rudimentary and was limited to depict an approximate picture of the bank's trading businesses. Weatherstone, however, wanted more. He asked a team of quantitative specialists in 1988 to develop a technique that could measure how much money the bank stood to lose each day if the markets sold off.

After playing with several ideas, the quants coalesced around the concept of value at risk, which was dubbed VaR. It is a measure of economic capital, which is a function of market risk, credit risk and operational risk. It is also

---

[1] Gene Guill, "Bankers Trust and the Birth of Modern Risk Management," Wharton School, Financial Institutions Center.
[2] Ibid., p. 4.

linked to the RAROC concept in that it is the denominator used to calculate risk-adjusted returns.[3]

The goal of the 4–15 report was to measure how much money Morgan could expect to lose on any given day with a probability of 95%. Management recognized there was a 5% chance the bank could lose a greater amount due to "tail risks." However, Weatherstone and his team determined that if it worried excessively about worst-case scenarios, the bank could wind up taking too little risk. This would jeopardize its ability to compete with other financial institutions. Rather, the aim was to gauge the risk the bank was taking in normal circumstances.

The development of Morgan's risk management framework was quite elaborate. The stated objectives were to identify, record, measure, monitor and control market risks taken by the trading units of the Securities Group and to provide a vehicle for sharing information among key managers.[4] The results served two principle purposes—namely, prudential control and resource allocation. They would enable senior management to evaluate risks and rewards in each of the relevant businesses, and thereby establish a foundation for allocating the bank's capital efficiently: "In short, what we are looking for is a robust 'common currency of risk,' which is readily understood and applied by management to a broad variety of circumstances."[5] VaR ultimately became that "common currency."

The computation of VaR proceeded through five stages that took into account each of the following: (1) movements in ten-year treasury yields; (2) the change in spread between the yield on the underlying instrument and its benchmark; (3) positioning along segments of the yield curve; (4) positioning risks involving shifts within asset classes and maturity bands and costs of liquidating positions; and (5) various options risks measured by the so-called Greek symbols. The requisite analysis included conducting volatility studies of the defined instruments, prices, yields and spreads, as well as judgments about the liquidity of underlying positions. The results were then used to establish limits on trading positions, as well as to render judgments about capital allocation across business units.

---

[3] The relationship between RAROC and VaR is evident from the basic formulae below:

RAROC = Expected Return/Economic Capital, or RAROC = Expected Return/Value at Risk

[4] Internal memorandum, June 23, 1988.
[5] Ibid.

In August 1989, Stephen Thieke was brought in from the New York Federal Reserve Bank to head Morgan's Economic Research Group and to oversee Risk Management. Thieke's hiring was notable in that he was one of a very few senior managers who were hired from outside. He had an extensive background in credit and capital markets, open market operations, banking supervision, securities operations and planning and control functions while at the New York Fed. He served at Morgan for ten years and played a prominent role in shaping its risk management processes.

In a presentation that Thieke made in September of 1994, he spelled out the framework that Morgan used.[6] It began by defining risk as the uncertainty of future economic earnings. This definition was then applied in a systematic way at three different levels. The first was at the micro level—that is, individual risk positions, transactions or credit extension. The second was the macro level—the portfolio of market and credit risks Morgan has within a business unit and across them. The third is strategic and related to capital allocation—that is, the overall business risk represented by the combined activities that comprise JPM.

In the presentation Thieke illustrated how the 4–15 report worked as follows:[7]

> Within our eight market related global products, we have more than 120 risk taking units spread over 14 locations spanning the globe. Our Chairman rather likes the diversification this affords, but has a simple request: "At the end of each day tell me what our risks are and how we did." Our answer is what we call our 4–15 report—creatively named after a daily meeting at that time, which I typically chair, with senior managers from the main market units.

The desirable attributes of the process include the following: (1) transparency about the risks the bank is taking; (2) quantification of those risks, which is the "science" portion of the discipline; (3) timely quality information that management needs to make sound decisions; (4) ensuring proper diversification; (5) independent oversight of the business; and (6) room for sound judgment. With respect to the latter, Thieke observed that while the "science" portion of the discipline continues to improve, the "art" portion lies in management judgments of how best to use the tools and to understand their limitations:[8]

---

[6] Stephen Thieke, "Managing Risk in a Complex and Changing World," September 14, 1994.
[7] Ibid., p. 4.
[8] Ibid., p. 7.

We manage these tools—we are not managed by them. Thus, an extremely important attribute of a good risk management process is the quality and pervasive nature of the risk management culture in the firm—as reflected in its training efforts; its resource allocation process; and its reward structure. Risk adjusted performance evaluation is a must, as is the visibility of saying "no" and "that's too much."

One issue that Thieke addressed was whether Morgan had become more exposed to market risks as its business shifted from bank loans to marketable securities. His answer was that Morgan's overall exposure to market risk was actually less than half the levels of the late 1980s, when measured in value at risk terms, and even more relative to the bank's capital. He also dismissed the perception that new products—specifically derivatives—would be the source of the next major financial crisis. In his view, previous crises occurred "the old-fashioned" way by extending too much credit to the wrong people and taking over-sized market risk bets. He saw the use of risk metrics as a way of lessening these risks.

In 1992, Morgan launched the RiskMetrics methodology to the marketplace, as client demand for its risk management expertise grew over time and exceeded its internal resources. In 1998, in the wake of the Long Term Capital Management fiasco, the Corporate Risk Management Department was spun off from JPMorgan as the RiskMetrics Group. The entity had twenty-five founding employees headed by Ethan Berman.

Prior to the development of its risk metric procedures, Morgan had been involved in the creation of financial derivatives. As the term suggests, they are contracts whose value derives from the performance of an underlying instrument that can be an asset, an index, an interest rate or currency. The purpose for buying them may be to hedge against adverse price movements or to speculate on price movements. The contracts are set for a specified time period and their value is affected by the passage of time.

The origins of modern-day derivatives are typically traced to the 1970s, when the breakdown of the Bretton Woods fixed exchange rate system gave rise to large swings in currencies and interest rates. One way investors could protect themselves from currency gyrations was to purchase forward contracts so they could lock in a price. As a bank that was actively involved in foreign exchange transactions, the use of forward contracts was a key component of Morgan's currency business.

Most forward transactions were for short-to-intermediate periods—typically ninety days—but a liquid market did not exist for longer dated transactions. One way to provide protection for those institutions seeking to hedge currency exposure over longer time periods was via currency swaps that were imbedded in parallel loans. They involved the exchange of cash flows between two companies, each in a different country and having a subsidiary in the other country. Under this type of arrangement, loans were made in equivalent amounts, and each was made in the parent company's national currency. The concept was refined in the early 1970s, when exchange controls were placed on British companies domiciled in the United Kingdom.

After the exchange controls were abolished in 1979, parallel loans continued to be utilized as a way of hedging long-term foreign exchange exposure, and they evolved into a market for currency swaps. They were first introduced to the public in 1981, when Salomon Brothers brokered an agreement between IBM and the World Bank. Interest rate swaps emerged in the Euromarket later that year, when US interest rates were at record highs but beginning to decline.

Morgan and other international banks, which did most of their lending on a floating rate basis, were involved in the first interest rate swaps. They used their ability to borrow on a fixed rate basis to obtain cheaper floating rate financing. Initially the swapping partners were mainly utilities and lower rated industrial companies that preferred fixed-rate financing. During 1982, the first domestic interest rate swap occurred between the Student Loan Marketing Association and the ITT Financial Corporation. Thereafter, the market grew very rapidly, as the number of institutions involved in currency and interest rate swaps proliferated, which made it easier to match counterparties.

The epicenter for growing Morgan's swaps business in the 1980s was Morgan Guaranty Limited (MGL) in London, as Glass-Steagall prohibitions on securities transactions did not apply. The swaps team was headed by Connie Voldstad, who was widely recognized as a pioneer in the derivatives world. Voldstad, however, was reluctant to share information about the swaps desk with Morgan's senior management, which led to a confrontation with Lew Preston over the unit's profitability in 1986. Two years later, Voldstad wound up leaving Morgan along with half a dozen members of his team for Merrill Lynch.[9]

The departure of Voldstad and team left Morgan with a vacuum. In 1990, Dennis Weatherstone called on Peter Hancock, who came from an upper-class British family and earned an Oxford degree, to fill the void. While this was seemingly a tall order considering that Hancock was only thirty-two years

---

[9] According to Gillian Tett, Preston challenged Voldstat that the swaps desk was actually losing $400 million, rather than posting a $400 million profit. See *Fool's Gold*, Free Press, 2009, p. 17.

old then, he had proved to be highly capable working for the derivatives group in New York in the mid-1980s. He attracted the attention of senior management after the 1987 stock market crash, when he was asked to present on what had happened and the role derivatives played in the crash. He was then put in charge of a small group that used derivatives to create "floors" and "caps" on various positions. In the process, Hancock became an expert on derivatives, and he impressed both Dennis Weatherstone and Sandy Warner. He was ultimately rewarded by being placed in charge of fixed income by the mid-1990s.

Hancock and team rode the wave of derivatives in the first half of the 1990s. Morgan was not considered a pioneer in the field then compared with the likes of Salomon Brothers, Merrill Lynch and Bankers Trust, but its people were highly capable, and Morgan had the advantage of having the highest credit rating among financial institutions. This superior rating made it an attractive counterparty. As the derivatives business grew, it produced a steadily increasing share of Morgan's profits, accounting for nearly one half of the bank's trading revenues.[10]

Hancock, however, did not want the derivatives team to become complacent. By 1994, he realized that the derivatives business had reached the stage where its once high profit margins were being eroded by a growing number of entrants. Therefore, he prodded the group to become more innovative and to come up with the next big idea.

Hancock previously approached Bill Demchak, a young banker who was highly regarded, to run a group known as Investor Derivatives Marketing (IDM) in New York. The group marketed derivatives to clients while also serving as an incubator for new ideas. Hancock's instructions to Demchak were that at least half of IDM's revenues each year should come from a product that did not exist before—a challenge that Demchak was happy to accept.[11]

At the same time, Hancock appointed a young banker in the London office, Bill Winters, to run the European side of the derivatives business. The expectation was the "two Bills," as they were known by colleagues, would work closely together about sharing innovative ideas across the Atlantic.

In her book, *Fool's Gold*, Gillian Tett tells the story of how Hancock convened a meeting at the Boca Raton Hotel for a group of young traders from Morgan's offices in New York, London and Tokyo in June of 1994.[12] The offsite began with a raucous party of derivatives traders that was reminiscent

---

[10] Ibid., p. 19.
[11] Ibid., p. 7.
[12] Ibid., Chapter One.

of those I observed at Salomon Brothers, with the attendees (mostly in their twenties) drinking and partying heavily. Both Peter Voicke, the head of global markets, and Bill Winters, the second most senior official, wound up being tossed into the swimming pool with their clothes on.

After the initial frolics, the group met the next day to brainstorm on ideas that could catapult Morgan's derivative business. One that emerged from the meeting was to use derivatives to trade the credit risk that was embedded in corporate bonds and loans. The idea of creating a derivative that enabled institutions to place bets on whether a particular loan or bond might default was particularly appealing to banks. The reason: The possibility of default was their biggest source of risk and they were required to hold considerable reserves—the equivalent of 8% of the loan value—according to the Basel I Accord of 1988.

The idea of credit default swaps per se was not new. Bankers Trust and Connie Voldstad's team at Merrill Lynch had conducted a few deals several years earlier. However, the trades weren't very profitable, and consequently they did not take off.

Hancock and his team were not deterred, partly because they understood how valuable credit default swaps could be to banks and other businesses that took considerable credit risk. Among the questions they asked were whether a derivative product could be created to hedge credit risk that would appeal to these institutions; whether regulators would permit them to be sold; and, if so, how they might transform the financial world.

While the weekend did not provide clear answers to these questions, Tett points out that it motivated the group to delve deeper into these issues about whether banks and other lenders could really gain insurance against default risk that might free up capital into the economy. "I've known people who worked on the Manhattan Project—for those of us on the trip, there was the same kind of feeling as being present at the creation of something incredibly important," Mark Brickell, one of the bankers on the JPMorgan swaps team later recalled.[13]

Working at Morgan, Hancock and his team ultimately could see first-hand how important credit derivatives could be for banks to lay off their credit risk, while still gaining fees from loan origination. Because most of Morgan's loans were directed to high-quality corporate clients and foreign governments, their default rates were very low. Yet Morgan was still required to keep $8 of reserves for every $100 of these loans, which constrained its ability to expand the business. By using credit default swaps, the derivatives team spotted a way for Morgan and other banks to effectively offload their imbedded credit risk to

---

[13] Ibid., pp. 21–22.

other institutions. They were part of an ongoing trend away from traditional bank lending toward a model of originate-to-sell via the use of securitized instruments. (See Box: Growing Importance of Securitization to Financial Institutions.)

According to Tett, one of the first challenges the team faced was to identify institutions that would be willing to assume such credit risk. Blythe Masters, whom Bill Demchak brought on board from Morgan's commodities desk, quickly spotted an opportunity. She contacted the European Bank for Reconstruction and Development (EBRD) to see if it would be interested in assuming the credit risk of Exxon, which was a Morgan client, in the wake of the *Valdez* oil tanker spill that occurred in 1993. The arrangement was that Morgan would pay the EBRD a fee each year in exchange for it assuming the risk of default on Exxon's credit line. If Exxon defaulted it would be on the hook for the loan loss; if not, it would pocket the fee and earn a profit on the transaction. The Exxon deal subsequently became Morgan's first credit default swap (CDS).

Thereafter, the derivatives team became pro-active in growing the CDS business. To do so, it first had to overcome regulatory hurdles and convince the Federal Reserve and the Office of the Comptroller of the Currency (OCC) to lower the 8% reserve requirement on bank loans if banks used CDS to lessen their credit risk. The argument that carried the day was that CDS was an effective way for banks to disperse their credit risk: In August 1996, the Fed issued a statement that banks would be allowed to reduce reserve requirements by using credit default swaps.

Tett observes that a remaining challenge for the derivatives team was to convince Morgan's management and senior lending officers that they needed to overhaul the way they ran the lending business. In doing so, Demchack used a host of supporting data that Morgan factored into its VaR calculations. One of the key findings of this analysis was four-fifths of Morgan's capital was earning less than 10 basis points of return for the bank each year, or effectively 0.1 cent for each dollar that was lent. By comparison, areas of Morgan's business that generated much higher profits—such as derivatives—were typically allocated less capital.

To further expand the use of CDS, Morgan's derivatives team had to figure a way to make credit derivatives easy for clients and investors to buy and sell like other securities. To do so, they expanded the idea of securitization that was the genesis of mortgage-backed securities (MBS). The core concept was to take a pool of loans to various companies and to organize them into tranches according to the credit risk of each pool. Thus, investors who wanted the highest quality pool would buy super senior tranches, which paid relatively low fees, while those investors that wanted to earn higher fees would purchase lower rated tranches.

The key attraction of bundling loans into pools was investors could choose the level of risk they wanted. Also, since investors were willing to pay for the convenience of having the loans bundled by risk category, banks could sell "synthetic collateralized debt obligations" (CDOs) for more than the total value of the individual units.

Tett describes how Morgan's derivatives team would have to convince rating agencies such as Moody's, Standard & Poor's and others to rate the respective instruments as being relatively safe because they were highly diversified by issuers. To convince the ratings agencies, Morgan's derivatives team pointed out that the agencies' own data indicated that the chance of a widespread default on a given pool was exceptionally low. This argument proved effective, and rating agencies wound up granting the coveted AAA tag to a sizable portion of CDOs that were created.

One issue that dogged the derivatives team, however, was what to do with the most senior credits that Morgan held on its books, which came to be known as "super-senior" tranches. One view was that the probability of widespread defaults on such credits was exceptionally low, and if it were to occur it would likely spell trouble for the entire financial system. But European regulators were unconvinced, and Morgan needed to find a counterparty that was willing to assume the risk on these tranches.

Blythe Masters, once again, identified a candidate, this time the American International Group (AIG), which like Morgan carried a coveted AAA rating. Masters succeeded in convincing the head of AIG's Financial Products group, Joseph Cassano, in assuming Morgan's super-senior credit risk for a service fee of 0.02 cent on each dollar per year.[14]

Tett's book goes on to describe how successful Peter Hancock, Bill Winters, Bill Demchack and other members of the team were in building out Morgan's credit derivatives business. By March of 1998, credit derivatives outstanding had soared to $300 billion globally, of which JPMorgan accounted for one-sixth of the total.[15] In the next two years the volume of new deals would increase six-fold, and Morgan alone accounted for half of them. As the derivatives business became an increasing source of Morgan's profits, the team's leaders would each go on to assume greater responsibility within the bank.

In the period immediately leading up to and after the GFC in 2008, Morgan became subject to criticism that its risk management procedures and credit default swaps contributed directly or indirectly to the debacle. One critique was that the VaR metric was a flawed measure of risk and banks had

[14] Tett, op. cit., p. 63.
[15] Ibid., p. 58.

become overly reliant on it. In his book, *The Black Swan*, Nassim Taleb, a statistician and former trader and risk analyst, criticized the use of VaR by financial institutions.[16] In his testimony to the House of Representatives on September 4, 2009, Talib went on to accuse JPMorgan specifically for making financial institutions vulnerable through the application of its risk metric procedures:[17]

> Banks are now more vulnerable to the Black Swan than ever before with "scientists" among their staff taking care of exposures. The giant firm J.P. Morgan put the entire world at risk by introducing in the nineties RiskMetrics, a phony method aimed at managing people's risks. A related method called Value-at-Risk, which relies on the quantitative measurement of risk has been spreading.

One alleged problem was the calculations of VaR were based on historical data, and markets had been unusually calm in the period leading up to the GFC. Another was that VaR calculations assumed probabilities of default risk were normally distributed, and they ignored so-called tail risk, which comes into play during financial crises. A third shortcoming cited by Taleb was that correlations among financial instruments spike during crises.

According to another statistician and derivatives expert, Pablo Triana, the main problem with VaR is that it can be quite easy to get a calculation that's very low if the preceding time period is calm. In his view reliance of the financial community on this metric left the industry highly exposed to the market risks that ensued:[18]

> Simply put, VaR may have been the single most influential metric in the history of finance. No other single number ever impacted, shaped and disturbed market (and this economic activity) as profoundly as it did. VaR's perilously inexact estimations of risk mattered because the model mattered so much.

In 2010 when the RiskMetrics Group was sold to MSCI, a leading provider of risk management products and services, it issued a report that addressed many of the issues critics had raised. The report made clear that the procedures were a process based on a model that had been continually refined since its inception:[19]

---

[16] Nassim Taleb, *The Black Swan: The Impact of the Highly Improbable*, 2007.

[17] Testimony to the US House of Representatives, November 4, 2009.

[18] Pablo Triana, "VaR: The Number That Killed Us," Futures, December 1, 2010.

[19] MSCI, "Return to RiskMetrics: The Evolution of a Standard."

More generally, a risk model does not make a risk management practice. This brings us to a broader definition of RiskMetrics: a commitment to the education of all those who apply the model through clear assumptions and transparency of methods. Only by understanding the foundation of a model, and by knowing which assumptions are driven by practical needs and which by modeling exactitude, can the user know the realm of situations in which the model can be expected to perform well.

The bottom line is that both the developers of Morgan's risk management procedures and Morgan's senior management regarded the quantitative models as analytic tools that could be used to support decisions that were ultimately qualitative. Consequently, they were able to avoid mistakes that other financial institutions made. For example, even though super-senior credit tranches were deemed to have extremely low default probabilities, Morgan's derivatives team understood that correlations could spike during crisis periods. Accordingly, they were pro-active in off-loading this risk, whereas other institutions such as AIG and Citibank were happy to accept this risk to earn small fees. Similarly, Morgan did not become heavily involved in privately issued MBS, because the bank was not a major player in offering mortgages and also because the derivatives team believed the data on mortgage defaults were inadequate to properly assess risks.

Throughout its history, Morgan's inherent conservatism served it well, as it was able to avoid situations that would imperil its capital or require it to seek government assistance. And even as it ventured into the world of quantitative finance, its risk management group did an outstanding job of earning transactions fees for the bank while protecting the bank from both market risk and credit risk. In this respect, superior risk management became a hallmark of the institution.

Box: Growing Importance of Securitization to Financial Institutions

Since the early 1980s, commercial banks shifted their capital investments from traditional lending toward increasing securitization, in which they would earn fees from loan origination and then off-load them to other institutions. Fueling this movement was the standardization of credit risk analysis. Analyses from credit rating agencies on the commercial side and FICO scores on the consumer side became more widespread as the focus of bank loan officers shifted to niche lending markets. Many traditional borrowers subsequently sought lower funding costs through securitization of residential mortgages, commercial real estate, commercial and industrial loans, credit card receivables, auto, home equity and student loans among others.

(continued)

Box (continued)

A key feature of the new financial institution model was the ability to lever-age invested capital, as revenues were now based on transaction volume. A financial institution could originate, package and sell loans, turning over its balance sheet several times a year while generating transactions and underwrit-ing fees. This contrasts with the traditional banking model, where capital was committed to earn an interest spread on a loan over its duration.

As shown in Fig. 14.1, this structural shift along with other beneficial effects from deregulation and consolidation led to tremendous growth in fee-based income, as well as a secular decline in net interest margin (a proxy for the profit-ability of traditional bank lending) from the early 1990s on. The trade-off proved to be lucrative for banks, as aggregate returns on their tangible equity more than doubled over a fifteen-year period.

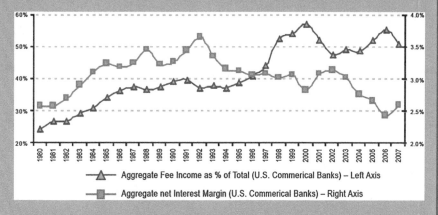

—△— Aggregate Fee Income as % of Total (U.S. Commerical Banks) – Left Axis

—■— Aggregate net Interest Margin (U.S. Commerical Banks) – Right Axis

Fig. 14.1 US bank fee-based income versus net interest margin. (Source: Compustat, Fort Washington (aggregates based on top twenty commercial banks by market capitalization))

15

Strategic Challenges

During mid-1994, shortly before Sandy Warner became Morgan's CEO, senior management assessed the progress that had been made in implementing the firm's strategic plan, and also identified areas that were falling short of plan goals. The overall assessment was mixed. The encouraging news was that Morgan's securities businesses were gaining traction against some competitors since the bank was granted powers to underwrite domestic equities in the fall of 1990. But its securities business lagged its aspirational competitors—Goldman Sachs, Morgan Stanley and Merrill Lynch—by a considerable degree. Consequently, it had its work cut out to become a bulge bracket firm.

The Corporate Planning Group produced a report that showed how Morgan's securities businesses had developed from 1988, the first full year of inception for JP Morgan Securities, through the end of 1993. The relevant time frame, in fact, was much shorter as Morgan did not earn significant global equity revenues until 1992, when it began to earn revenues on US common stock. They totaled $50 billion in 1992 and $82 billion in 1993. The latter represented less than 2% of US market share, compared with 15% or more for each of the market leaders, Merrill Lynch and Goldman Sachs. Morgan made somewhat faster progress on secondary trading in equities, where its revenues more than tripled in 1993 to nearly $165 billion. But its market share in secondary trading was just shy of 1%.

On the resource side, the number of Morgan employees assigned to global equities in 1993 totaled 356 people. By comparison, Goldman Sachs

---

Information in this chapter is based on internal Morgan documents and confidential discussions with executives.

© The Author(s) 2020

N. P. Sargen, *JPMorgan's Fall and Revival*, https://doi.org/10.1007/978-3-030-47058-6_15

employees were more than three times larger. Moreover, the number involved in sales and trading totaled nearly 850 people, almost seven times more than JP Morgan Securities.

Morgan's penetration in the fixed income area was somewhat greater. The principal reason is that the bond area had begun to grow its domestic business in the late 1980s when it was granted underwriting powers by the Federal Reserve. Its growth in revenues, however, did not take off until 1992–93 when its underwriting of corporate debt and private placements expanded significantly.

In 1993, primary revenues from Morgan's fixed income division reached $236 billion. This tally was equal to that of Salomon Brothers, and nearly 60% of Goldman and Morgan Stanley, but it was less than half of Merrill Lynch, the market leader. Morgan's market share on US lead-managed issues surpassed 3% and had risen steadily from 1990 when it was only about 0.5%. While it ranked seventh overall in US market share for lead-managed issues, there was a considerable gap versus the top underwriters.

One area where Morgan was successful was in generating revenues from secondary trading of fixed income globally. Revenues in this area tripled from 1990 to 1993 when they approached $1.6 billion. This tally was second only to Merrill Lynch at just below $2.2 billion, and it exceeded both Morgan Stanley and Salomon Brothers.

Two other areas where Morgan stood out were private placements and loan syndications. In the former, it ranked #1 in 1993, with a 10.7% market share, just ahead of CSFB and Merrill Lynch. On the loan syndication side, it tied for second place with Citi at 11%, with Chemical Bank the top arranger of loans globally, capturing a 12% market share.

One of the factors behind Morgan's success in penetrating fixed income was it dedicated considerable resources to this area. The total number of fixed-income professionals in 1993, for example, was 852, or roughly 2.5 times the number in equities. It also compared with about 460 fixed income professionals at Goldman.

A further sign of progress was the surge in Morgan's investment banking revenues that occurred in 1992–93 amid the buildout of its debt and equity businesses. As of 1993, JPM's investment banking revenues approached $550 billion, or more than twice the amount two years earlier. Moreover, the breakdown of revenues was encouraging, with debt and equity financing representing 43% and 20% of the total, respectively, and the advisory business accounting for the remainder.

At the same time, Morgan's management realized it faced stiff competition from its aspirational competitors. The top players—Merrill Lynch, Goldman

Sachs and Morgan Stanley—saw their investment banking revenues double over the 1990–93 period from a base that was considerably higher than Morgan's. Furthermore, the number of professionals these institutions assigned to investment banking was roughly comparable with Morgan, which meant they were more successful at leveraging their people.

One reason for their success was the investment banks deployed far more junior analysts to support their MDs or partners than Morgan did. The ratio of top professionals to analysts at Goldman, for example, was 7:1, whereas it was just over 1:1 at Morgan. This was a clear signal that Morgan was top-heavy in investment banking compared with its competitors.

In sum, the comparative study revealed several findings about Morgan's ability to penetrate the world of securities and investment banking. First, it had made reasonable progress in underwriting corporate bonds and stocks in the domestic market, considering that it had only been granted these powers five years and three years, respectively. It had also been successful penetrating the business for secondary trading, especially on the fixed income side, and it had established itself in private placements and loan syndication.

The main challenge it faced was the competition that stood atop the world of securities and investment banking was stiff. The bulge bracket of Goldman Sachs, Merrill Lynch and Morgan Stanley were well established and successful in growing their businesses, and they did not show signs of faltering. In this context, the realistic opportunity for Morgan was to take market share away from securities firms and banks that had gone out of business or been absorbed—such as Drexel Burnham and Frist Boston—or from those that had faltered for reputational reasons—such as Salomon Brothers and Bankers Trust.

Another challenge was internal. In 1990, Ramon de Oliveira was put in charge of a small equity team in New York after he formed a fledgling high yield group in London that included convertible debt. As he built out the high yield and equity platforms from scratch, he often encountered resistance from bankers who were involved in extending credit to corporate clients. He illustrated this by noting a conflict with bankers in 1989, when the junk bond market blew up. Morgan's research unit issued a buy report on Macy's bonds, but Morgan's bankers were worried about its credit risk. At a meeting to discuss the matter, de Oliveira explained that whereas bankers viewed a loan as "good" or "bad," investors assessed whether its bonds were rich (expensive) or cheap.

Morgan was ultimately successful in building its business in high yield and convertibles. The need to hedge converts, in turn, created need to develop equity capabilities, and the Fed granted Morgan powers in 1990. De

Oliveira was fortunate to recruit Jes Staley to head the syndicate desk and Clayton Rose to head research and sales. The timing was propitious, as the resolution of the Gulf War in the spring of 1991 marked the beginning of a ten-year bull market in equities.

As regards Morgan's overall profit and loss (P&L), the encouraging news was the firm was able to offset declines in its net interest income from increased revenues from securities transactions. It was also gaining traction on its derivatives business and risk management, as is discussed in the previous chapter.

The main disappointment was that Morgan had not made the desired progress building out businesses that drove core earnings—namely, global custody, investment management and private banking. Yet, these areas were the ones that Wall Street analysts assigned the highest multiples in valuing the firm, because their earnings streams were more predictable and diversified than those obtained from securities and derivatives transactions.

Three years after the corporate plan identified gaps in securities support operations, little progress had been made in closing them. The premise then was that JPM could develop a competitive securities processing business for outside clients (institutional and high net worth) by consolidating support activities conducted in Securities Trust and Information Services (STIS) and JPMorgan Investment Management (JPMIM). However, to do so successfully, the respective services needed to be upgraded to meet the requirements of buy-side clients (i.e. institutional investors) that were significantly more complex than traditional sell-side clients (i.e. broker-dealers).

Morgan's management decision to refrain from acquiring State Street in 1991–92 meant that the ability to acquire such capabilities globally had passed. Consequently, by the mid-1990s it needed to decide whether to upgrade its STIS platform or to pursue a different course.

The assessment of the planning group was there were important challenges to make the STIS platform meet client needs. They included (1) upgrading technology to handle the real-time needs of its clients whose businesses involved multiple currencies and entities, (2) covering more markets to catch up with its primary competitors and (3) standardizing its processes along the lines of Euro clear, which was a market leader.

To be successful, Morgan would have to streamline its cost structure by eliminating duplication, automating both routine and complex tasks, while also leveraging experienced staff and progressively outsourcing commoditized market segments. It would also have to develop a pipeline of younger people and train them. It was also recognized that the operations teams in both STIS and JPMIM would have to be upgraded, but one of the principal uncertainties was how effective they would be in collaborating with each other.

Ultimately, the size of assets under management and the volume of transactions processed argued for the establishment of a subsidiary that was separate from both JPMIM and JPM Securities Inc.

By 1995, it had become clear that to meet its objectives for clients Morgan would have to make significant investments in JPM's securities services businesses or exit them. The principal concern was that revenue growth from 1992 to 1994 was modest, plateauing at just under $500 million annually, while the contribution to Morgan's P&L had been flat for the three years at just over $70 million annually.

A close look into the revenue components revealed that the US and global custody business was not making money. Furthermore, there was consolidation in the industry, which resulted in pressure on margins. Success in the global custody business required having a growing asset base and value-added products for clients. Yet, when STIS was compared with the industry leaders—Mellon, State Street, Bankers Trust, Chase and BoNY—it ranked poorly. Nor was it well positioned to become a top provider.

Consequently, the recommendation was made to sell STIS' third-party business, while retaining selected segments for central banks, private banking clients and Euroclear deposits. The proceeds from the sale were estimated to be somewhere between $415 million to $540 million. This meant it would have only a minor impact on Morgan's net income in the vicinity of 4%.

Progress on the asset management front also left much to be desired. Although there was no question that JPMIM was critical to Morgan's success, its business had not grown to the extent that was envisioned in the 1991 planning document. From JPMIM management's perspective, its "incremental approach" to building its resources—both human and technological—had left it unprepared to expand from its reliance on the defined benefit marketplace to the defined contribution space in the United States and to increase its presence overseas.

Morgan's management, however, was unsure whether JPMIM had the proper incentives to grow its business over the long term. JPMIM's comp structure was based on its return on equity. This formulaic approach created incentives for its management to under-invest in the business. Thus, it could earn a higher ROE in the short run by refraining from investing in technology to support growth, but this would penalize its long-run growth. Morgan's management, in effect, faced a Hobson's choice that also hindered cooperation between JPMIM and STIS and with the Private Bank, as the respective areas sought to enhance their own earnings.

As part of the Strategic Plan for 1995–97, JPMIM's management committed to grow its business to $800 million by the end of the period, implying an annual compound rate of 13% over the 1994 estimate of about $550 million. To meet this target, JPMIM calculated that it would need to grow its head-count by 8% annually, to just under 1800 employees. It would also have to build and institutionalize a training program, as there was no existing person-nel pipeline to meet the growth objective.

To reach its target, JPMIM was banking on increasing its market share in the Defined Benefits (DB) space, while also gaining a foothold in the Defined Contribution (DC) marketplace through expansion of its Pierpont mutual fund offering. One of the uncertainties it faced was whether participants in DC plans sought an unbundled product, which JPMIM was well positioned to serve, or a family of funds to provide "one-stop shopping," where it trailed the competition. The plan also called for JPMIM to expand its capabilities in its overseas offices in Tokyo, Melbourne and Frankfurt, as well as in Private Banking investment offices in Geneva, Paris, Madrid, Milan and Hong Kong.

Another way that JPMIM sought to expand its business involved placing investment activities that had been in the Private Bank within its umbrella. In a memo to Private Banking, Nicholas Potter, the outgoing head of JPMIM, commented on the changes as follows:[1]

> This realignment is a continuation, and a logical conclusion, of our efforts to converge the investment management processes of PBIM with those of JPMIM in order to ensure that all PBIM products reflect the best attributes of both groups...These changes are designed to further enhance our ability to attain this vision by creating an investment management group that clearly focuses on the quality, cost effectiveness and innovative nature of our investment management products, while SDI (self-directed investors) meets our clients' brokerage needs and Private Banking client managers continue to focus on the marketing, sales and client servicing of our "integrated investment services approach" to the private market.

Within Private Banking, however, the changes were interpreted as a way for JPMIM to capture revenues that were being generated within the Private Bank. If so, it meant that some of the revenue growth JPMIM would report in the future would detract from revenues that had been reported by the Private Bank. Consequently, there was need for JPMIM and PB to develop fee-sharing arrangements, just as the Private Bank did with JP Morgan Securities.

One concern within the Private Bank was these changes were occurring at a time when it was confronting considerable obstacles, both internal and

---

[1] Memo from C. Nicholas Potter to Private Banking, June 22, 1994.

external, toward attaining the objectives spelled out in the plan that was formulated in mid-1991. One of the biggest challenges was that PB was transitioning away from reliance on customer deposit-taking and lending to become more investment oriented. In the process a lot of mid-to-senior people were transitioned out of the bank, and many junior people were opting out, because compensation was below market and morale was low. At the same time, competitors were building their businesses and offering more lucrative compensation.

Another concern was the reorganization would leave the Private Bank virtually stranded from the investment process, and it would be increasingly reliant on the brokerage business which was nascent. JPMIM had a rigorous investment process that met the needs of its institutional customer base—predominantly US pension plans and their consultants. However, high net worth clients tended to be less process driven, and those in Europe were driven more by absolute returns rather than by performance relative to a stated benchmark.

Private Banking, even at Morgan's minimum $5 million level and up, was largely a retail business, which required a significant commitment to marketing and sales. Moreover, to capture liquid wealth the Private Bank had to take it away from another financial institution. Consequently, product innovation was a vital tool; yet JPMIM was reluctant to stray from its core offerings.

One of the biggest challenges Morgan faced in allocating resources and awarding compensation is its management information system was not fully transparent in assigning costs and revenues to the respective business units. And, individual P&L statements for dealers, currencies, securities and swap positions were even farther into the future.

Each of these management initiatives would eventually supplant older practices. However, Dennis Weatherstone at times would find it difficult to change habits he learned from his time in London, when the Bank of England still countenanced "hidden" or "inner reserves." Essentially, excess profits in good years were folded into undisclosed reserves for a rainy day and practitioners, large and small, took full advantage of this flexibility.

During the 1970s and 1980s, when Weatherstone had responsibility for Morgan's dealing areas, he would provide a cushion for them by instructing Jack Ruffle, Morgan's Comptroller, to reallocate the revenues generated by other business units to Morgan's treasury division. Thus, part of the spread the Private Bank earned on clients' deposits were re-allocated to the treasury division. Under normal circumstances, this would have led to a second set of internal books in which the Private Bank would be allocated the full spread to avoid distortions to its profitability. However, this did not happen. In 1992, David Hopkins, who was responsible for its management, was instructed to close all accounts with assets of less than \$2.5 million, because they were unprofitable!

Similarly, when JPMIM went through a series of challenging market environments in the early 1990s that might have caused a brain drain, Rod Lindsay was persuaded that the way its profits were counted had to bow to external market pressures. Some of this made eminent sense. For example, star research analysts had to be compensated based on their recommendations, rather than whether the portfolio managers followed their advice. And, the people who helped invent portfolio protection techniques had to be recognized in both good and bad times.

In the process, however, the expenses were borne by other areas of the bank, and over time, the distortions grew. This, in turn, led to a lack of willingness by JPMIM to fund new investments, extend its mutual fund product line or open offices outside the United States. These distortions finally came to an end, when Kim Schappert became the head of JPMIM in 1994 and showed the door to a person who had been altering the books to enlarge JPMIM's bonus pool.

Over time, it was increasingly evident that business units were competing with one another for increased headcount, capital allocation and the size of the year-end bonus pool. Nearly all business units were gaming the system. Separate accounting records were created by the different profit centers. In the process, costs shifted and revenues were contested. In the end, senior management had to decide who to believe—the risk takers or the bean counters—and who was most valuable to the enterprise.

The simple fact was the bank's products had become too diverse and its activities too broadly dispersed. Meanwhile, senior management was overstretched and largely unacquainted with the new markets and instruments their direct reports oversaw. While there were ways of controlling both people and risk, they went against the grain.

The root cause of the problems was that as Morgan grew in size and function, it became increasingly complex and more difficult to manage. Compounding the problems was the centralization of all major decisions being funneled to Preston and Weatherstone. Yet, they were unfamiliar with many of the complexities of securities markets (both front and back offices) and were also reluctant to delegate responsibility down through the ranks. In short, it was becoming increasingly difficult to govern Morgan effectively.

16

A Chance Encounter

While Morgan confronted strategic challenges in the early mid-1990s, they were not readily apparent to those outside the firm at the time. While I was at Salomon Brothers, I routinely followed Morgan's research on economies and markets and compared Morgan's assessments with ours. I subsequently become a client of Morgan when I joined Prudential Insurance to become the chief investment officer for its global bond and currency unit in the autumn of 1991.

The circumstances for my leaving Salomon Brothers were the head of government bond trading, Paul Moser, violated a US Treasury Department rule by bidding for more than 35% of a Treasury refunding. Even worse, he submitted bids using names of customer accounts that were unauthorized. What made Salomon vulnerable was that its leadership—John Gutfreund, Tom Strauss and John Meriwether—was aware of what had occurred but failed to report it to the authorities. When this was disclosed to the public in early August, rumors were rife that the regulators could force Salomon's closure. Like others at the firm, I was shocked and saddened by what happened. I had been approached by Prudential in the summer, when the head of its global bond and currency group left the firm, and I decided to accept the post, as I was skeptical Solly could fully recover from the indiscretion.

My first task at Prudential was to decide on a strategy for managing $6 billion of global bonds and currencies. Given the context in which inflation rates around the world were converging and Europe was pressing forward with plans to have a common currency, I favored investing in higher yielding government bonds. The rationale was they were likely to outperform lower

© The Author(s) 2020
N. P. Sargen, *JPMorgan's Fall and Revival*, https://doi.org/10.1007/978-3-030-47058-6_16

yielding instruments not only because of their higher coupons, but also because yield differentials were likely to narrow in a falling interest rate environment.

Things started to go awry, in May of 1992, however, when Danish voters rejected the Maastricht Treaty to become part of the euro-zone by the narrowest of margins. This provoked a flight out of higher yielding bonds into safer instruments such as German, Dutch and Swiss government bonds, as investors began to question Europe's commitment to a common currency.

While I disagreed with the markets' assessment, I closed out positions and went neutral relative to our benchmark until the outcome was clearer. This proved to be fortuitous when George Soros and other prominent hedge fund managers shorted the British pound, Italian lira and other high-yielding currencies in the fall of 1992 and forced them outside the ranges policymakers had set for them.

One of the lessons I learned from this experience was the importance of being flexible when you are not sure what is happening in markets. Another lesson was that markets often overreact to events, which can create buying opportunities. This was the case at the beginning of 1993 when our unit reinstated positions to take advantage of much higher bond yields and cheap currencies.

We were rewarded with truly extraordinary performance throughout the year. The international bond fund that we managed for Prudential's own account exceeded its benchmark by ten percentage points, which meant we added $100 million of outperformance to its bottom line.

Despite this, I found there was rarely time to enjoy the moment. The reason: Competition was stiff and markets could change on a dime. I had to monitor our flagship global bond fund carefully during the final week of 1993 to make sure it would rank in the top quartile of its peers. This was the case even though it was ahead of its stated benchmark by five percentage points. It also made me envious of US bond managers. The reason: Domestic bond market volatility was considerably lower due to the absence of currency swings, trading did not occur around the clock and performance was measured in basis points not percentage points.

I felt even stronger about this in 1994 when bond markets and currencies behaved contrary to what most global managers expected. The circumstances were that the United States' growth had re-accelerated after a lackluster recovery from the 1990 recession, and Alan Greenspan worried inflation could accelerate. The Federal Reserve, in turn, raised interest rates by 25 basis points at every meeting of the Federal Open Market Committee (FOMC), for a cumulative increase of 250 basis points. It then made two additional rate hikes in 1995 that lifted the funds rate to 6.0% from 3.0% at the start of 1994.

The strategy most global bond managers pursued was to favor non-dollar bonds relative to US bonds for defensive reasons, but also to hedge the currency exposure back into dollars. However, the exact opposite occurred. European bond yields rose more than US bond yields, while the dollar weakened.

As I agonized over how to position portfolios, I realized that many hedge funds that invested in European bonds were not dedicated to international bonds, as we were. Consequently, they unloaded their holdings of European bonds when they sold off.

What I could not fathom, however, was why the dollar should weaken when the Fed was raising interest rates aggressively. The only reason I could think of was Treasury Secretary Lloyd Bentsen talked the dollar down at times, because he thought the bilateral trade deficit with Japan was too large. But this made no sense to me, as a stronger yen also undermined Japan's economy and contributed to deflationary pressures there. I wondered why he would think yen appreciation would lessen the US trade deficit materially when it had little impact over the prior decade.

This made me question whether I was in the right job. I was able to thrive at Salomon Brothers working with traders, because I could help them filter incoming data and separate the real news from the noise in the markets. However, I did not relish the pressure of managing positions, especially when markets moved against me.

Beyond this, I questioned whether Prudential was the place where I should spend the rest of my career. Ironically, a training session on diversity in the workplace got me thinking about it, when the instructor asked the attendees whether they were "inside the house" or "outside the house." I realized that even though Morgan and Salomon had very different corporate cultures, I always knew I belonged. By comparison, I felt more like an outsider at Prudential, because I managed a boutique operation that was not integral to the firm. This made me wonder whether I was better suited for Wall Street after all.

These issues were weighing on me on a business trip to London in August. Fate intervened as I was about to check out of the Hyde Park Hotel in Knightsbridge to return to the United States. When the elevator door opened I was surprised to find John Olds, who I had not seen in eleven years. We both looked at one another incredulously and then proceeded to catch up on what had happened in the interim.

John explained that he had just completed an assignment running the Euroclear operations out of Brussels. Sandy Warner, who was about to replace Dennis Weatherstone as chairman and CEO, had asked him to serve as the head of the Private Bank, and he was on his way to New York.

When Olds asked me what I was up to, I told him about Prudential and mentioned that I was contemplating returning to Wall Street. He seized on this to indicate he was seeking a candidate for the position of the global markets strategist for the Private Bank. I told him I would be delighted to interview for the job, and we agreed to get together after Labor Day.

In the interim I reflected on what it would be like to return to Morgan. After all the years away, I was out of touch with what was happening internally. However, I had the opportunity to observe Morgan as a competitor while I was at Salomon. It had done an excellent job building its credentials in global and international bonds on the research side. Victor Filatov, who I had worked with in the International Economics Department, had been given the assignment of developing the JPMorgan World Government Bond Index and other metrics that were used as benchmarks to judge investment performance of global bond funds. They received a following among global bond managers and investment consultants soon after, and Morgan's indexes were the primary alternative to the metrics that Salomon pioneered.

Morgan also used its team of international economists to monitor what was happening in overseas economies and markets. I would occasionally exchange views with my former colleagues to see where we agreed or disagreed on assessments. The quality of Morgan's research continued to be excellent on the economics side. However, Morgan did not produce path-breaking fixed income research, where Salomon and Lehman Brothers were the acknowledged industry leaders. One area where Morgan did stand out was its research on emerging markets, which included the construction of an index for emerging market bonds that became the industry standard.

When Rimmer de Vries stepped down as the head of the International Economics Department, it was merged with the US Economics Department and was headed by Will Brown, who became Morgan's chief economist. Under his tenure, both *World Financial Markets* and the *Morgan Guaranty Survey* were merged into a new publication, *Global Data Watch*. It provided up to date information on both developed and emerging economies and their financial markets. The main difference from the prior publications was the format included an upfront summary of major developments rather than lengthy essays. It was mainly targeted at traders and investment professionals rather than policymakers.

When I moved to Prudential, I was able to observe Morgan as a customer. As one of the largest global bond and currency managers in the United States, our business was widely sought by financial institutions that had global fixed income and currency capabilities. While we had an extensive list of counterparties, we conducted the lion's share of our business with a handful of firms. Morgan consistently ranked in the top five in both international bonds and currencies. It competed on the securities side with the likes of Goldman Sachs, Lehman Brothers, Merrill Lynch, Morgan Stanley and Salomon Brothers, and it provided excellent sales and trading and research. On the currency side, Morgan's capabilities were generally superior to the securities firms and its main competition was from global banks.

As I reflected on the relationships our firm had with Morgan, what stood out was Morgan's people were consummate professionals who conducted themselves with high integrity at all times. I did not recall ever having to resolve a dispute over a transaction, and I typically received positive feedback from my colleagues who conducted business with Morgan.

Another issue I thought about was what it would be like working at Morgan's Private Bank. I had spent my entire career on Wall Street working with institutional investors who were highly sophisticated. I enjoyed the challenge of advising them, as it meant I would have to be at the top of my game. When I met with clients of Salomon Brothers, the routine was the same most of the time. I would begin by sharing our views on the global markets and conclude by discussing our strategy for beating the Salomon World Government Bond Market Index. That, after all, was how they were compensated. I would then take their questions and hone in on what they were thinking.

The world of private banking, by comparison, was a mystery to me as I little or no contact with the Private Bank during my tenure at Morgan. All that I knew was its office was located in midtown. But my visits there were entirely with personnel from JPMIM.

The impression I gathered from Morgan's bankers who covered institutional clients was not flattering. One of the jokes was that the main responsibility of private bankers was to walk the dogs of wealthy heiresses in Central Park. The other was that the Private Bank was the burial ground for bankers who had failed in their assignments.

I dismissed these stories, however, when I traveled to Switzerland and met with representatives from Swiss banks and other private banking boutiques such as Pictet, Julius Baer and Vontobel. The bankers I met were very sophisticated and also very knowledgeable about alternative investments such as hedge funds and private equity. It made me realize Morgan's private bankers had to be equally qualified to compete with them.

When I got together with John Olds my first question was why he was willing to leave Euroclear, where he had been successful in boosting its profitability. He explained that Morgan had a five-year contract to run it, which was about to expire, and that its chairman, who was from Deutsche Bank, wanted it to be led by European institutions going forward.

Olds also indicated he enjoyed the challenge of running businesses that were new or undergoing transformation. He was excited about the opportunity to run the Private Bank at a time when the market for wealthy investors was large globally—with more than 7 million people controlling more than $10 trillion of investable assets. It was also a rapidly growing market thanks to stellar performance of financial markets since the early 1980s and the growth of entrepreneurs that received funding from private equity and venture capital.

Olds mentioned a study by Sanford Bernstein that concluded the prospects for the high-net-worth market appeared brighter than for those for either the pension or mutual fund markets.[1] It showed that in the 1990s, assets controlled directly by individuals accounted for two-thirds of the growth of assets under management, which was up from one-half in 1975–84.

To capitalize on this opportunity, Olds indicated Morgan's Private Bank would have to re-orient itself. Previously, it focused on discretionary asset management (via JPMIM) and fiduciary trusts that served the needs of those with "old" money. Going forward, it would have to offer a broad array of integrated financial services that were easily accessed, suitable for wealthy individuals (as opposed to institutions) and all placed in a context where the client would receive objective advice.

Olds favored a client-centric—rather than a product-centric—strategy to grow the business. He was also cognizant that wealthy investors had been conditioned to expect considerable choice in the products they purchased and also solid investment performance. He acknowledged that Morgan faced gaps on both these scores, but he was committed to address them to achieve the goals for the Private Bank. The task ahead was formidable, as it would require the commitment by Morgan's management to invest in the people, the technology infrastructure and the product array to meet the competitive challenge.

Olds mentioned that he and his management team were mapping out a strategy to convince Sandy Warner and other members of senior management of the importance of the undertaking. In his view, the payoff for Morgan would extend well beyond the Private Bank's P&L and the higher

---

[1] Sanford C. Bernstein & Co, Inc., "*The Future of Money Management in America*," 1994 edition.

price-earnings (P/E) multiple that it commanded in comparison with the securities business. He cited numerous linkages among private clients and other clients and businesses of Morgan especially in underwriting of equities, IPOs, secondary offerings and derivatives to defray downside interest rate or price risk and foreign exchange exposure. The bottom line was he believed Morgan's senior management was committed to the transformation of the Private Bank he was contemplating.

After sharing his views with me, he asked what I would be seeking. I told him I was excited by the opportunity of returning to Morgan and being part of a business that was being transformed. I also welcomed the challenge of expanding my expertise into areas such as public and private equity and hedge funds. Most of all, advising Morgan's private clients would broaden me. In the institutional business, I would give the same advice to each client about how to beat their benchmark. However, in the private client arena, the advice could be different for different individuals because their risk tolerances, sophistication and level of wealth varied. I likened it to the world of medicine, where there were specialists and general practitioners, and I would in effect be making that change.

When I was given the formal offer to become the global markets strategist for the Private Bank several months later, I was quick to accept. For once, the decision to make a job change was a no brainer. It felt like I was going home again.

Part IV

Playing Defense

17

9 W 57

When I returned to Morgan at the beginning of 1995, I was excited to be back and wondered how much it had changed since I left eleven years ago. Like other newly hired employees, I was scheduled for an orientation session at the old headquarters at 23 Wall Street. This time, however, the entrance was on 15 Broad Street, as the front entrance was blocked. Much to my surprise, the magnificent lobby was gone. There was no chandelier, no roll-top desks and no bankers wearing pinstripe suits. Instead, the lobby had been converted into an ill-designed conference center that did not fit the contours of the once majestic space.

Inside the conference room, the attendees were greeted by a representative from Human Resources, who welcomed everyone and told them what a special place Morgan was. Shortly after, a video was shown depicting the history of Morgan dating back to the mid-nineteenth century. The spokesperson then went on to discuss the importance of Morgan's core values and the pride its people felt in doing first class business in a first class way.

Once the meeting concluded, I headed over to the new headquarters at 60 Wall Street to see what it was like, as well as to visit former colleagues. The first thing that struck me was how tall and modern the building was, with the number of employees having doubled from the early 1980s. Sales and trading was housed on the eighth floor and occupied the entire level. It was readily apparent that Morgan was fully ensconced in the world of trading with separate areas designated for equities, fixed income, emerging markets, derivatives, foreign exchange and commodities.

The Economics Department was located on a floor that also housed other research departments including fixed income and equities. When I met with Will Brown, he told me how the primary mission of the department was to

© The Author(s) 2020
N. P. Sargen, *JPMorgan's Fall and Revival*, https://doi.org/10.1007/978-3-030-47058-6_17

keep sales and trading and Morgan's institutional clients abreast of economic news around the world and the multitude of data releases.

I explained to Will and my former colleagues that one of my responsibilities was to ensure the Private Bank and its clients were aware of Morgan's views on the global economy and world financial markets. I would brief members of the Private Bank at weekly meetings and would also publish commentaries that distilled the views of JP Morgan Securities for its clients.

Upon leaving Morgan's headquarters, I came away impressed by what had been achieved in the years I was away. I was also struck by the physical similarities between the new Morgan and Salomon Brothers. The principal difference was Solly's trading floor at One New York Plaza was more impressive. It was two stories high and offered a commanding view of New York harbor. Otherwise, there was little to differentiate them physically, and the days when Morgan's officers could dine in the private dining room were long gone. Instead, those who worked on the trading and research floors went to the cafeteria and brought back meals to their desks just like at other securities firms.

As I headed to the offices of the Private Bank at 9 West 57th Street, I looked forward to working in midtown for the first time in my career. Like many New Yorkers, I knew the building well by its distinctive architecture. It was named after Sheldon Solow, the real estate developer whose company built it in 1974. It had a concave vertical slope on the south and north facades, facing 57th and 58th Streets, and offered a panoramic view of Central Park above the 23rd floor. Outside the front entrance was a red sculpture with a giant nine symbol, and just behind it was Brasserie 8½, the restaurant that was featured in the trendy television series *Sex and the City*.

The building also brought back fond memories when I would make periodic presentations at JP Morgan Investment Management, which was located in it in the 1980s. Since then, JPMIM relocated its offices to a building on Fifth Avenue and 44th Street, and the Private Bank took over its space. Once inside I was taken to my office on the mezzanine level between the first and second floors, which had an area where one could look down on the bankers who occupied the first floor.

My boss, Susan Bell, who headed the unit called SDI, which stood for Self-Directed Investors, hosted a lunch for me. She also invited her chief lieutenant, Liz Patrick, and Rick Zimmerman, who headed the salesforce, to join us. They explained how SDI was the newcomer to the Private Bank, and it offered brokerage services via JP Morgan Securities. Previously all client money was managed on a discretionary basis by portfolio managers who were affiliated with JPMIM. Clients could now decide whether to have their funds managed on a discretionary basis, to do it on their own via SDI, or to utilize a combination of discretionary and brokerage services.

Even though I worked for the Private Bank, my legal affiliation was actually with JP Morgan Securities, as I was representing the research it provided. Jean Brunel, whom I knew from my first tour at Morgan, was the chief spokesman for JPMIM, and he was responsible for representing its views, which were completely independent from the securities side. I soon realized this could pose a challenge for Morgan's bankers and clients, as the two views would not necessarily be the same.

When I asked why Morgan didn't call the SDI unit a brokerage operation like other securities firms, Susan explained there were sensitivities within Morgan's Private Bank about the term. Brokerage carried the connotation of being a sleazy business, in which salespeople could take advantage of clients by churning their accounts and offering them products that were inappropriate.

The heart of the problem was the industry's prevailing compensation practices, in which brokers were paid by the transaction revenues they generated. This created a conflict of interest between brokers and their clients. To lessen this risk, SDI salespeople were paid a salary and bonus based on broad performance criteria, rather than on the transactions they generated.

Another potential problem was the poor experience private clients of brokerage firms had in purchasing complex and potentially illiquid securities. An example was the decision by NationsBank to end its joint venture with Dean Witter at the end of 1994. The breakup followed a string of lawsuits and accusations about misleading and improper sales practices by Dean Witter brokers. To lessen this risk Morgan's Private Bank beefed up its training, compliance and supervision areas.

In a memorandum to the officers of the Private Bank, John Olds shared the strategy paper that had been developed by its senior management and which was presented to Sandy Warner. It articulated the value proposition of the Private Bank as follows:[1]

Investors face a bewildering array of choices in handling their assets. Morgan can optimize wealth for clients by advising on and managing the integration of their investment, structuring, and liquidity needs. *This is our value proposition* (italics included). It is anchored in the needs of the market and capitalizes on the firm's traditional strengths of objectivity and teamwork across disciplines. Our

---

[1] Private Banking Strategy Paper, August 16, 1995, p. 11.

value proposition has a natural strategic parallel in that optimizing wealth for clients can and should be managed to maximize private client contribution to the firm.

This approach dictated the type of organization that was necessary to pursue the high-net-worth market successfully. It emphasized that Morgan needed an integrated approach to serve their needs as distinct from a product-centric approach that most firms followed. Together, the client manager, product specialist and service specialist would form a unified client team that was aimed at integrating the needs of each client. The strategy paper pointed out how uniquely qualified Morgan was to act in this way:[2]

> A private client-focused strategy that draws products and services together to serve the high-net-worth market is sought by many but achievable by few—perhaps only by a true universal bank. JPM may be the only firm that is well positioned to capture this opportunity at this moment.

Another unique aspect of the strategy was the vision of the Private Bank embracing a "buy-side" perspective to managing clients' money:[3]

> Our challenge as an organization becomes how best to align the interests of private clients with JPM's internal product capabilities to maximize long-term shareholder value. We believe this means treating SDI as a buy-side, client-service group under the Private Banking umbrella and taking the same approach when investment responsibility is delegated to us. The client views his wealth as a single pool and we must respond accordingly.

Morgan's private banking approach to dealing with its client base was founded on the same principles that historically had guided all of its businesses: focus on clients' needs and engage them only in activities that met their objectives. The strategic plan included safeguards to make sure that this was the case. One of the first steps was to be sure that a client's risk profile was vetted thoroughly, so a determination could be made about the appropriate asset allocation and products for the client. In addition there was need for proper vetting of products, especially structured products in which derivatives were embedded, to make sure clients understood the risks that were entailed in them.

---

[2] Ibid., p. 12.
[3] Ibid., p. 22.

With this mandate, John Olds helped get me started by recruiting Shom Bhattacharya, a Rhodes scholar who had worked for Chemical Bank, to head credit risk and product development. Shom had been introduced to John Olds years earlier by Scott Nycum, who knew him from their days at Oxford. When I met Shom I realized how knowledgeable he was in areas where I had no background, and how valuable he was to the Private Bank. Equally important, he was a wonderful colleague who had a great sense of humor. Within a short period of time, Shom was able to develop guidelines for vetting risks entailed in lending to private clients, and he created a unique "heat map" for vetting new products.

Another safeguard was management did not want individual salespeople to have the latitude to sell any stock they liked. Therefore, it was important to have a recommended list of stocks that could be sold to clients. One of the responsibilities of the strategy group would be to cull the list of stocks recommended by the Morgan's equity research department to provide an added level of protection. Like most securities firms, the list of recommended names was extensive and there were few sell or hold recommendations.

Olds subsequently introduced me to Brian Seidman, who had worked for him in Morgan's corporate planning group before going on to become an equity research analyst. I was happy to bring Brian on board, as he was familiar with Morgan's equity research and personnel. We complemented one another, as he would conduct "bottom-up" stock research with my "top-down" global markets assessment.

As I formulated the outlook for global financial markets in 1995, I was cognizant of how grueling the previous year was for most investors. The Federal Reserve's aggressive tightening of monetary policy resulted in both the bond market and stock market generating negative returns for 1994.

As 1995 began, it had become apparent that the spike in interest rates was also taking a toll on emerging economies, most notably Mexico. A flight from capital caused the Mexican government to devalue the peso against the dollar by 15% in December 1994, and it ignited the first financial crisis since developing countries were able to tap international financial markets. Mexico's central bank responded by raising short-term interest rates to help maintain investor confidence. However, the peso weakened further, as investors worried about the toll higher interest rates and a weaker currency would take on Mexico's economy and banks.

Mexico's central bank was ultimately forced to allow the peso to float freely, and it eventually fell by 50% versus the dollar at the low, while inflation soared. Foreign investors responded by liquidating positions in Mexico and other emerging markets that had been popular in the early 1990s.

Policymakers in the United States worried that the situation might lead to contagion, in which capital flight could spread to Argentina, Brazil and other leading emerging economies. To stave off this threat President Clinton met with newly confirmed Treasury Secretary Robert Rubin, Under Secretary Larry Summers and Fed Chairman Alan Greenspan to formulate a response that would stabilize the situation. In January 1995, they proposed a $50 billion bailout package for Mexico that would be administered by the International Monetary Fund (IMF) with support from the Group of Seven (G-7) industrial nations and the Bank for International Settlements (BIS).

Amid this, US bank stocks also came under pressure as investors tried to assess the fallout. Morgan's stock price was also impacted, because it held positions in Mexican securities and those of other Latin American countries. Morgan and other US exposure also had exposure to Mexican banks, although not to the same extent as in the previous decade.

Shortly after I joined the bank, Ramon De Oliveira, the head of the Morgan's Equity Division, made a startling announcement on the public address system that the division would be laying off a large number of employees. The reason was that Morgan was facing challenges from the sell-off in the financial markets. He went on to discuss whether this unprecedented decision might be construed as a change in Morgan's corporate culture. He indicated it was an issue that Morgan's senior management weighed, but that management ultimately decided it had no choice but to bring expenses under control by reducing its headcount. He concluded that while market environment was challenging, he was confident Morgan would come through as a stronger firm.

As I heard this, I was incredulous that Morgan once again could face a developing country crisis, this time when the problems originated in the capital markets. But there was little time for me to ponder about the future of Morgan.

My responsibility was to brief the Private Bank and its clients on what this development meant for the global economy and financial markets. The easy part was to convey the view of Morgan's Economics Department that the US economy was headed for a "soft landing." This meant that the pace of US economic growth and inflation were both likely to moderate, which would pave the way for the Federal Reserve to ease monetary policy. The house view was also reassuring that the US-led stabilization plan for the Mexican economy was likely to succeed and stave off the risk of contagion. Fortunately, these views were consistent with those of JPMIM, so that our private clients would be hearing the same message whether they had a discretionary relationship or brokerage account.

The more difficult part was formulating Morgan's view on the US and global equity markets. Because Morgan's equity department had not hired a strategist to cover these markets, I was on my own. My take was the prospects were favorable for US stocks, because the economy and profits were holding up well and the Fed had latitude to ease policy if the economy stumbled. The critical uncertainty was whether the Mexican crisis could be contained. I made what I considered to be a "safe" call by stating that a reasonable expectation was for the US stock market to generate a return in the vicinity of 10%, which was the long-term trend at the time.

As I was preparing a presentation on the outlook for global financial markets, I was contacted by Jim Glasgall of *Business Week*, who was writing a feature story on the topic. He asked if I could be quoted, and I told him I needed to check with Susan Restler, who headed our marketing department. She thought it was fine, and checked with Joe Evangelisti, who headed media relations for the bank, to keep him in the loop. He told her that it was okay for me to be quoted, but I should make sure my title was global strategist for the Private Bank (but not Morgan), which I relayed to Glasgall.

When the article appeared the following week, it was the feature story and I was the first person quoted. The good news was the quote was accurate and sensible. The bad news was the article identified me as JPMorgan's global strategist. When Evangelisti called to complain, I explained what happened, but he made it clear it shouldn't happen again.

When I shared what happened with my colleagues, they told me how much Morgan had changed since I left the bank in the mid-1980s. At that time, Morgan was a commercial bank that did not seek publicity, because clients valued its discretion and professionalism. As it entered the world of securities, however, publicity and the media were critical to grow the business, but the securities unit had not hired a strategist for whatever reason.

One of the best aspects of my job was interacting with the various teams in the Private Bank and their clients. Within the United States teams were organized into ten geographic regions, each with a dominant metropolitan area. The five largest areas—Los Angeles, New York, Chicago, San Francisco and Washington, D.C. —each had more than 100,000 wealthy investors and made up 25% of the market in the United States.

Being from New Jersey, I quickly bonded with the SDI team headed by Phil DiIorio. In the spring I was invited to a client outing at Baltusrol, the premier golf club located in Springfield, New Jersey. The event began with a lunch in the clubhouse at noon, followed by a round of golf, cocktails and dinner. I was slated to speak for 15–20 minutes at the conclusion of the event around 9 p.m.

When I asked what was expected, word came back to "keep it light," as most of the attendees would be wined, dined and exhausted at the end. I realized I needed a gimmick to keep peoples' attention, and came up with idea of using the O.J. Simpson trial as a pretext for discussing the market outlook. I told the assembled that they were the jury that would have to judge which market was most mispriced—the stock market, the bond market or the US dollar. I would play the role of a trial lawyer, presenting the case for and against each market, and the clients would then have to submit their forecasts for the respective markets when we reconvened in 1996. The gimmick worked. The clients and bankers had a good time, and I was able to engage them in how challenging the market environment was.

Another memorable event was a dinner hosted by the team covering the Washington, D.C., area, which was headed by Scott Nycum. I had known Scott in the 1980s, when he was located in Sydney, Australia, and he had seen me make several television appearances on business trips there while I was at Salomon Brothers. The D.C. office was able to recruit Alan Greenspan to speak at the dinner based on his prior relationship with JPMorgan. My assignment was to ask Greenspan questions, which in typical fashion he managed to answer without giving away any secrets. After the event, the D.C. team was excited with how well it was received and Scott announced I had become an honorary member.

My first overseas trip was a visit to the Private Bank's office in Geneva, the hub for European and Middle Eastern operations. Shom Bhattacharya accompanied me, as we were slated to meet the SDI team there as well as with the bankers. When we entered the office building, in addition to signing in at the front desk, we were also required to sign a pledge that we would not violate Swiss secrecy laws. While I was aware Swiss-domiciled banks would accept money from anonymous sources, I had not appreciated the extent to which the laws were enforced.

John Gent, who headed the SDI team, came across both as very intelligent and knowledgeable about the private client business. He explained some of the principal differences in the way money was managed in Europe to us. One of the most important was that investors outside the United States were primarily interested in absolute returns, rather than returns relative to a benchmark, which was the US custom in asset management. Second, clients in Europe and the Middle East did not equate the risk of an asset class with its standard deviation, because this was a measure of how much returns could deviate from the norm, both to the upside and to the downside. From their perspective, the relevant measure was downside risk.

For these reasons, hedge funds were popular investment vehicles for private clients and Gent's team had developed analytic capabilities to advise clients on them. Gent also brought on board a Swiss-trained mathematician, Pascal Roduit, who developed an analytic framework to assess downside risk. It was called RADAR (for risk-adjusted absolute returns) and was used to make tactical calls on global markets and currencies. Gent explained that this approach was quite different from the process that JPMIM used which deployed highly diversified holdings of stocks to dampen volatility and to control tracking error relative to a benchmark.

At the end of our visit, we concluded it had been productive for both sides. Shom and I committed to travel regularly to Geneva, and to visit other Morgan offices in Europe including London, Paris, Rome and Madrid and to make periodic trips to see key Morgan clients in the Middle East.

In making these visits I was struck by the importance overseas clients attached to views on the US dollar. This was similar to my experience when I toured overseas offices while I was at Salomon Brothers. I was delighted, as I had covered the dollar throughout my career and had very strong views on it—namely, it was very cheap and should appreciate against other currencies.

By mid-year, the economic backdrop had turned favorable, as inflation concerns had lessened and the Fed was poised to ease monetary policy, which helped alleviate the Mexican peso crisis. This fueled large rallies in both stocks and bonds. The dollar also surged against most currencies, in part because Treasury Secretary Rubin favored a strong dollar, whereas his predecessor, Lloyd Bentsen, favored a weaker dollar as a way to reduce the US trade deficit with Japan. In my view, Rubin's stance was sensible, because the US economy was strong while Japan's had not recovered from the bursting of the stock market and real estate bubble at the beginning of the 1990s.

The year ended on a positive note with the dollar surging, bond yields declining and the US stock market generating a return of 37%, its strongest showing since 1958. While bank share prices did exceptionally well, Morgan's lagged during the first half of the year before rallying in the secod half. Accordingly, spirits at the firm had improved considerably from the start of the year and everyone was in a festive mood at the Christmas party for SDI. While it was held at a midtown bar that lacked the grandeur of the good old days, I recall feeling comforted that I had made the right career decision to return to Morgan.

18

Technology and the New Economy

Investor optimism continued into 1996 amid signs the US economy had achieved a soft landing despite aggressive Fed tightening during 1994. By the second half of 1995, a lessening of inflation pressures paved the way for the Fed to begin lowering interest rates gradually. This contributed to further stock market gains, especially for the tech-heavy NASDAQ index which posted a return of 40% in 1995.

This was the backdrop for the annual meeting of Morgan's managing directors (MDs) that was to be held at the Millennium Broadway Hotel conference center in late January. Sandy Warner would be addressing some 420 MDs—the largest such gathering in Morgan's history. Roughly one-third of the attendees had flown in from overseas. I was looking forward to the session, as it would be my first opportunity to hear Warner and other members of the senior management team provide their assessment of how Morgan was doing and what priorities were going forth.

I had only a vague idea of what was happening at upper echelons of the firm. Based on what my colleagues told me, it wasn't a bad thing to be detached from the head office. Many of them considered the Private Bank to be the last vestige of Morgan's true culture, while "downtown" had become just another securities firm. Some felt the less interaction with headquarters, the better.

My own view was it was important to understand Morgan's overall strategy and where the firm was headed. Because Warner did not speak publicly very

© The Author(s) 2020   **179**
N. P. Sargen, *JPMorgan's Fall and Revival*, https://doi.org/10.1007/978-3-030-47058-6_18

often or send firm-wide memos, I had little inkling what he would say. Warner had created a conclave of senior managers called the House Arrest Group to discuss issues that affected the entire firm. It met once a month in the credit policy committee room on the 20th floor of 60 Wall Street, and attendance was mandatory for the members. That's why the name was derived.

The members who held prominent positions during my first tenure included Kurt Viermetz, Peter Smith, Roberto Mendoza, Walter Gubert, Peter Woicke and Tom Ketchum. Others including Peter Hancock, Ramon de Oliveira, Nick Rohatyn and Joe McHale were either not at the bank then or were in areas that did not overlap with my responsibilities. What stood out, however, was there had been a generational shift in senior management since I left the firm in 1984.

The principal difference from the way Preston and Weatherstone managed the firm was Warner sought to strip out management layers, flatten hierarchy and drive responsibility down to business heads. The goal was to keep pace with increasingly specialized, fast-changing businesses. Warner had eleven business heads report to him directly including John Olds and Kim Schappert, and Pilar Conde and Mike Corey, the co-heads for proprietary trading. Another difference from the past was Warner did not name a president. However, he surrounded himself with senior advisors including Viermetz and Mendoza, CFO Tony Mayer, Chief Counsel Ned Kelly, Stephen Thieke and former Chief Counsel Michael Patterson (son of the former chairman) who also served as chief administrative officer.

There was uncertainty at the time how the decision-making process would work. For some, Warner had embraced matrix management, in which employees report to more than one supervisor, typically to both a functional manager and a product manager. To be effective, this required a global communications network that was becoming feasible with the growing use of personal computers and e-mails.

Warner began the MDs meeting by reviewing the business results for the previous year. He noted that for much of 1995 Morgan was still coping with the fallout from the Fed-induced bond market selloff the previous year, the Mexican peso crisis and the collapse of Banco Nacional de Credito, a Spanish bank that Morgan had invested in for the Corsair Fund, a well-publicized private equity offering.

The good news was the firm's profitability increased as the year progressed. Net income for the full year rose to $6.42 a share, up from $6.02 the previous year. Some of the improvement was due to a cost-control program that was launched in 1994: As of end 1995, Morgan's head count was down to 15,600 people from just over 17,000 at the end of 1994, and the pace of layoffs accelerated as the year progressed. At the same time, Morgan had sold its custody and processing businesses and pared back its mortgage unit which incurred sizable trading losses.

One of the decisions the House Arrest Group discussed at its meeting two days prior was how to control the soaring cost of technology. Morgan had shelled out about $1 billion on it in 1995, and the firm was struggling with the usual problems of incompatibility across its numerous platforms. The issue under consideration was whether it made sense for Morgan to outsource its technology requirements.

Warner spent the remainder of his remarks launching into his "New Paradigm" motivational speech. The thrust was the task of transforming Morgan from a commercial bank into a global financial services provider that had been launched by Lew Preston was all but complete. Going forward the focus of management would be to execute on the plan while serving the needs of Morgan's clients globally.

Warner's message was that to succeed, Morgan's organizational structure needed to be less hierarchical. He stressed he couldn't constantly be settling disputes or micromanaging people. Business heads would have to be mature, apolitical, team-oriented, "Morganesque." They also needed to pass those traits down the line.

Warner's remarks were well received, and he seemed at ease leading the firm. An *Institutional Investor* article on his leadership of Morgan cited Peter Woicke saying, "its tremendous how this guy has grown," and Walter Gubert observing, "He seems like he's really enjoying it."[1] The article went on to mention how much Warner had changed from the days when he joined the firm. John McCoy, his neighbor in Ohio at the time who also became chairman of Bank One, recalled that Warner would arrive at his town so wound up that he would kid Warner that no one wanted him in a foursome. McCoy's take years later when Warner was Morgan's CEO was "Now he seems a lot more relaxed, more comfortable."[2]

I came away from the meeting encouraged that Morgan had capable leadership. However, I was struck by a remark Warner made about Morgan's business heads when he said, "They don't have to like one another—some don't—but they do have to deal with each other professionally as colleagues. They can't be consumed by politics."[3] This was a very different message from ones I heard from Walter Page and Lew Preston that embraced the firm's

---

[1] Robert Teitelman, "Morgan Enters the Warner Era," *Institutional Investor*, March 1996, p. 62.
[2] Ibid., p. 61.
[3] Ibid., p. 61.

collegiality. I didn't know what to make of it at the time, but wondered if this is what my colleagues were warning me about the new rules of the game at headquarters.

Meanwhile, I went back to my job of deciphering the global economy and markets. The environment for US markets was clearly favorable with growth accelerating, inflation and inflation expectations declining, and the Fed poised to lower interest rates—the so-called Goldilocks scenario. What also stood out was corporate profits were rising as a share of GDP amid moderate wage increases and improved productivity growth. I referred to this development in my presentations as the "US profits revolution."

It was difficult to assess at the time whether the improvement in productivity was a new secular trend or a temporary phenomenon. Economists, after all, had a poor track record in this area. Throughout the post-war era up to the mid-1990s, real economic growth had averaged about 3.5% per annum with two distinct periods. The first was the post-war recovery from 1948 to 1973, in which real GDP growth average 4% per annum boosted by labor productivity growth of nearly 3% per annum. The second was the period following the first oil-shock until the mid-1990s, when the pace of economic growth moderated to 3% per annum as labor productivity growth fell by half to 1.5%.

One issue economists debated in the mid-1990s was whether the groundwork for a revival of US productivity growth was being laid based on advances in computer technology. They included the development of smaller and faster micro-processors, sophisticated software and fiber optic networks. All of these, in turn, gave rise to widespread use of the internet that transformed telecommunications.

As would be evident several years later, these developments spawned a boom in capital spending. The growth rate of business investment in high-tech equipment and software, for example, averaged nearly 24% per annum in the second half of the decade.[4] Consequently, by the end of the 1990s investment in information-processing equipment and software exceeded 3% of GDP compared with 1% at the beginning of the decade. At the same time, business equipment and software spending rose from 7% of GDP at the beginning of the 1990s to 10% at the end of the decade.

The investment boom in this period is widely regarded as a key factor that boosted labor productivity growth to a 2.5% annual rate in the second half of

---

[4] Nicholas Sargen, *Global Shocks*, Palgrave Macmillan, 2016, pp. 122–123.

the 1990s. In turn, it helped restore overall US economic growth to 4% per annum.[5]

As these developments unfolded the term "The New Economy" became increasingly popular. It originally appeared in a 1983 cover article in *Time* magazine that described the transition from heavy industry to a new technology-based economy.[6] By the second half of the 1990s the term became widespread, especially as NASDAQ emerged as a rival to the New York Stock Exchange and tech stocks outpaced the broad market. A wide divergence also opened up between growth stocks that were linked to technology and value stocks that were associated with the "Old Economy."

The primary beneficiaries in the financial services arena were securities firms such as Goldman Sachs, Merrill Lynch and Morgan Stanley that constituted the bulge bracket for underwriting and distributing equities. They also benefited from a high volume of initial public offerings (IPOs) and dot-com stocks that outperformed more traditional companies. Investment boutiques such as Hambrecht and Quist (H&Q) and Robertson Stevens in the Bay Area also benefited from a surge in IPOs by internet companies and dot-coms.

IPOs were especially attractive to high-net-worth clients, because their share prices often surged on the first day of trading. For example, a study by Professor Jay Ritter of the University of Florida showed that the mean first-day return of IPOs issued from 1995 to 1998 ranged from 14% to 22%, and it subsequently soared to more than 70% in 1999.[7]

However, prices of many IPOs plummeted shortly after if the company's performance fell short of expectations, and they typically lagged the broader market's performance. An article by Nelson Schwartz of *Fortune* observed: "The fact is, the typical IPO of the last decade proved to be at best a mediocre investment—and at worst an outright wealth destroyer."[8] The article noted that of the nearly 3500 companies that went public from 1994 to 1998, more than half were below their offering price and one-third were down by over 50%.

This made me wonder why so many high net investors liked to play the game. One reason I presumed was they viewed it like a lottery, hoping they would find the next Cisco, Microsoft or AOL, even though the odds were slim to none. Another reason was that some figured out the name of the game was to gain access to the initial offering, hold the stock for a day and then flip

---

[5] Economist Robert Gordon, an acknowledged expert on productivity, disputes this interpretation. He contends the increased use of computers was one of five positive shocks.

[6] "The New Economy," by Charles Alexander, *Time* magazine, May 30, 1983.

[7] Jay R. Ritter, "Initial Public Offerings: Updated Statistics," University of Florida, March 8, 2016.

[8] Nelson D. Schwartz, "The Ugly Truth about IPOs," Fortune, November 23, 1998.

it after making a sizable gain. This was frowned upon by the underwriters, and most brokerage firms penalized their salesforce if it happened. The only way they could enforce it with clients, however, was to let the client know they would be excluded from future offerings. This generally worked as a deterrent for retail customers; but it was rarely enforced with institutional clients.

The appeal to the underwriters was obvious: They typically earned a share of 5–7% of the IPO proceeds, with roughly half of that going to the lead underwriter. The underwriter could also garner brokerage commissions when founders of companies cashed out, and its investment arms were at an advantage in running the portfolios of the executives.

If the investment banker's job was to sell the company on the idea of going public, the research analyst's job was to sell the company to investors. During the IPO boom, the role of equity analysts was broadened on Wall Street to turn them into marketers. They were no longer judged by how well they followed an industry, but increasingly by how many deals they brought in the door. This created an inherent conflict for analysts between the desire to attract big deals that would boost their compensation and the need to make accurate earnings forecasts.

True to its colors, Morgan did not want to play the game the way the rest of Wall Street did. The equity research department was an outgrowth of the former Financial Analyst Department (FAD) that did in-depth research of companies. Consequently, many of Morgan's company reports read as detailed tomes in contrast to the typical four-page summary reports of the brokerage houses. Morgan's analysts' compensation was also not tied as closely to deals they helped bring in.

That said, Morgan's analysts followed the industry custom of launching coverage of a company with a "Buy" rating, and they were slow to lower ratings on companies due to the fallout it could create with clients of the firm. Consequently, the strategy team at the Private Bank would cull Morgan's recommended list to provide an extra layer of protection for our clients.

For the most part, Morgan was somewhat of a bystander during the IPO boom. The firm had some excellent analysts such as Bill Rabin, who covered networking companies such as Cisco and 3-Com and Greg Guiling, who covered telecommunications. However, Morgan lacked a high-profile presence in the tech space in investment banking.

This was very evident when I made trips to our offices in San Francisco and Los Angeles. Being born and raised in the Bay Area, I always enjoyed visiting the San Francisco office, and I quickly bonded with many of the bankers and the salesforce from the area. However, I was struck by the lack of name recognition Morgan had on the West Coast, presumably because it didn't have any branches there and Bank of America and Wells Fargo were so dominant. On the brokerage side, firms such as Merrill Lynch, Goldman Sachs and Morgan Stanley had much greater client penetration.

Equally surprising, Morgan did not have a representative office in Silicon Valley in the mid-1990s, even though it was booming and had the fastest wealth accumulation of any region in the United States. One of the goals of the San Francisco office was to establish a presence there, and I would make presentations to clients and prospects both in San Francisco and in Palo Alto.

When I traveled to Los Angeles, the office seemed more vibrant and connected with various segments of the community. My luncheon talks, for example, would typically have an audience that was two to three times larger than the events in the Bay Area. Owen Harper, who was (and still is) a senior banker covering both Northern and Southern California, recently told me the challenges the Los Angeles (LA) office faced in attracting customers initially. At one of the first events for prospects, management was worried about a low turnout and it hired unemployed actors to show up for the event!

The boom of technology also gave rise to a revival of private equity, both in venture capital and leveraged buyouts. After declining from 1990 to 1992, the volume of investor commitments to private equity rose from $21 billion in 1992 to more than $300 billion by 2000, which outpaced the growth of other asset classes.[9] In the process the volume of LBOs also increased.

One of the main differences from the experience of the late 1980s was that private equity firms focused on making buyouts attractive for both management and shareholders. According to *The Economist*, companies that would have previously turned up their noses at an approach from a private equity firm were now pleased to do so.[10] Also, private equity investors became more focused on the long-term development of companies they acquired and deployed less leverage than in the 1980s.

During this period, capital markets also opened up for private equity and venture capital transactions. Whereas the industry leaders in LBO financings in the mid-1980s included Manufacturers Hanover, Citicorp, Chase and Bankers Trust, by the 1990s Chemical Bank became the dominant player under Jimmy Lee. He established a syndicated leveraged finance business and related advisory businesses. It included the first dedicated financial sponsor coverage group, which covered private equity firms in much the same way that investment banks traditionally covered various industry sectors. Chemical

---

[9] Wikipedia, "Private Equity in the 1990s."
[10] Ibid.

also gained market share through its acquisition of Manufacturers Hanover in 1992.

Chemical added to its lending prowess by acquiring Chase Manhattan in August 1995 in a deal valued at nearly $10 billion. The combined bank would take the better-known Chase name. However, Chemical was the dominant partner in the merger and its Chairman and Chief Executive, Walter Shipley, kept those titles at the new company. The deal, which became effective in March 1996, created the biggest bank in the United States, overtaking Citicorp with combined assets totaling nearly $300 billion. The combined bank also became the nation's largest lender to large corporations, the largest in trading revenues and the leader in securities processing.

Chemical's acquisition of Chase occurred amid a flurry of merger activity in financial services, as many executives decided the surge in stock prices created a favorable environment to sell. A *New York Times* article quoted Thomas Labrecque, who had been the head of Chase and would become the #2 in the merger, as saying he might have waited until the next year to do a deal, but the pace of bank mergers in 1995 influenced his timing.[11] Previously, he had been in discussions with Bank of America, which offered the allure of building a coast-to-coast institution. However, the negotiations stalled as Chase executives felt BoA would have too much control of the combined institution. Walter Shipley's take was upbeat. He said he expected to integrate the banks in three years rather the four years it took for Chemical and Manufacturers: "We've got the book now. Last time we were writing the book."[12]

David Rockefeller, who retired as Chase's chairman in 1980, was cautiously optimistic, offering the following assessment:[13]

> In view of recent developments in the banking industry, such a move seemed inevitable. I'm pleased, of course, that the Chase name will continue to stand among the great banks of the world. The sad aspect of such a combination, in order to realize the necessary economies of scale, is that jobs of many employees apparently will be affected.

The press release accompanying the merger announced that Chase and Chemical expected to cut expenses by $1.5 billion a year eliminating 12,000 of the combined 75,000 jobs and closing 100 overlapping branches. About a third of the job cuts would be in metropolitan New York.

[11] Saul Hansell, "Banking's New Giant: The Deal," *The New York Times*, August 29, 1995.
[12] Ibid.
[13] Ibid.

The flurry of bank merger activity would continue throughout 1996, as both the broad market measured by the S&P 500 index and the NASDAQ posted returns of 20% or more for the year. This boosted their cumulative gains for 1995–96 to 56% and 68%, respectively, raising questions about the sustainability of the markets' rise. Professor Robert Shiller of Yale University, who was a leading critic of the efficient markets hypothesis, argued that stock market valuations had become extremely stretched in the mid-1990s and reflected irrational behavior on the part of investors.

In a speech in early December, Fed Chair Alan Greenspan offered the following assessment about market valuations:[14]

> Clearly, sustained low inflation implies less uncertainty about the future, and lower risk premiums imply higher prices of stocks and other earning assets. We can see that in the inverse relationship exhibited by price/earnings ratios and the rate of inflation in the past. But how do we know when **irrational exuberance** (bold included) has unduly escalated asset values, which then become subject to unexpected and prolonged contractions as they have in Japan over the past decade?

While markets around the world immediately sold off, it didn't last for very long as the stock markets quickly renewed their ascent amid favorable earnings reports. Not long after, Greenspan tempered his remarks when he asked how an individual could question the judgment of millions of investors. Meanwhile, the market beat went on at a rapid pace.

---

[14] Alan Greenspan, "The Challenge of Central Banking in a Democratic Society," December 5, 1996.

19

Three Ring Circus

The stock market continued its ascent in early 1997, but the mood within the Private Bank had turned somewhat negative. The catalyst was an exodus of several highly regarded MBAs who had been recruited from leading business schools. It would prove to be an omen for a series of surprise developments that unfolded over the next two years.

The Private Bank had launched a training program run by David Kelso in January of 1995. David previously served in that capacity at Goldman Sachs, and the program was run in a way that allowed the MBAs to gain on-the-job experience during the day followed by sessions that began in the late afternoon. He was a master at engaging the trainees, and he kept them on their toes by presenting various hypothetical situations and then peppering them with questions about how they would react. Watching David in action reminded me of Professor Charles W. Kingsfield in the film *The Paper Chase*. The main difference was he lacked John Houseman's dignified English accent.

Senior members of the Private Bank would also give presentations on their areas at the sessions and then take Q&A. In this way, the trainees could gain a broad overview of how the Private Bank was run. I spoke on various occasions about markets and then questioned them about the key factors that were driving the stock, bond and currency markets. I enjoyed the experience which was similar to what I had done at Salomon Brothers, and it allowed me to get to know many of the MBAs fairly well.

The exodus began shortly after the MBAs received their bonuses for 1996. During the previous year, bonuses for MBAs were kept in a narrow range because management felt it was too early to differentiate them. By the second year, the range of bonuses was broadened based on the respective performance

N. P. Sargen, *JPMorgan's Fall and Revival*, https://doi.org/10.1007/978-3-030-47058-6_19

appraisals. However, some of the top-rated recruits believed their bonuses were considerably below what they could earn at firms such as Goldman, Morgan Stanley and Merrill Lynch.

Compensation was especially relevant for those seeking careers in sales and trading, because brokerage houses paid their employees on the basis of sales commissions rather than on salary and bonus. It posed a serious challenge for Morgan's Private Bank, because its business model was built on the concept that SDI personnel were part of a team that served clients. Moreover, paying commissions would create incentives for them to sell products that might not be in the client's interest.

When I asked a top-rated MBA why he was leaving, he indicated family considerations were involved. He would be joining a firm run by his father-in-law. However, he also mentioned that he was troubled by the lack of transparency in the way bonuses were paid. He received his degree from the University of Chicago's business school, and he said the first thing he was taught was that people respond to incentives. In his view, Morgan's process for awarding bonuses was opaque and difficult for employees to reconcile what they were paid with how they performed. I found his points to be well reasoned and I passed them along to Human Resources.

It became increasingly clear that the mindset of younger people was very different from my generation. Those who were joining Wall Street in the go-go 1990s came with the expectation it was the place to make your fortune early on and they were not interested in climbing the corporate ladder like their parents did. A conversation I had with a bright Wharton undergrad drove this home to me, as I knew her father. She was upset with her compensation, because she had put in long hours and wasn't being rewarded for her "sweat equity capital." I was dumbfounded by this and wondered what the proper return on sweat equity should be!

These departures were a precursor of even bigger news in the spring when we learned that both John Olds and Susan Bell would be leaving the Private Bank. Shom Bhattacharya and I were saddened by the news, considering that John Olds had recruited us and Susan Bell was a wonderful boss. Because there were no formal announcements about their departures, we could only speculate about the reasons.

Shom and I understood full well the implications of losing John Olds. He was both a visionary and a master strategist who understood how individual investors were becoming a dominant force in finance. As household wealth ballooned in the 1980s and 1990s, he observed the mass affluent—that is, households with less than a million dollars of financial assets—increasingly placed their money with mutual funds and brokerage houses. Higher-end clients invested with asset managers, private banks, private equity firms and hedge funds. Olds also realized how fragmented the market was for serving private clients and how Morgan had the potential to become a dominant player.

Shom and I suspected that Olds may not have been able to convince Sandy Warner of the potential. The Private Bank, after all, had long been considered as being outside Morgan's main line of business, and both Lew Preston and Dennis Weatherstone had been reluctant to invest in it or to acquire outside providers. Consequently, we wondered whether plans for the Private Bank would be scaled back.

One consolation was that Jamie Higgins would succeed Olds as head of the Private Bank. He worked closely with Olds when they were in Asia in the 1980s and Olds asked him to head private banking for the United States. The good news was that Higgins shared Olds' vision and was committed to execute his plan. However, he would report to Ramon de Oliveira, who became the head of JPMIM in 1996. In this respect, the role appeared to be downgraded.

Susan Bell's departure was also a major loss as she had built SDI from scratch beginning in 1991. Three years later, when John Olds arrived on the scene, he told her to think of SDI as a laboratory for conducting brokerage in a way that was unique on Wall Street. By 1996, the unit achieved a milestone in which it generated more than $100 million in revenues.

Consequently, many of us wondered why Susan would retire when she was relatively young. She had a very successful career at Morgan, and it was reasonable she wanted to leave the stress of Wall Street to explore her passions. One of them was writing. She would now have time to take courses at Sarah Lawrence and eventually write a novel.

But many of us also suspected Susan might have been worn down having to negotiate with her counterparts in JP Morgan Securities, as well as with bankers who did not embrace SDI. The main challenge she faced was the securities unit viewed SDI as its distribution arm, but her primary responsibility was to ensure that whatever was sold to clients was in their interests. Liz Patrick, who succeeded Susan, was very capable, but we were unsure how much clout she had with downtown.

I told Shom that one of the consequences of Susan's departure was we would be more exposed to "product push." Throughout my tenure at Salomon Brothers, I was never required to pitch a product I did not believe in. I wanted the same to be true at Morgan. But I could detect subtle pressures from the derivatives area when our strategy unit was asked to formulate investment ideas that could be imbedded in options and sold to clients.

The ideas typically consisted of a basket of stocks our group recommended that were sold either as a call option or as a market participation deposit (MPD), which was a deposit that made periodic payments based on how the option performed. We established a solid track record in 1996, in part because the bull market in stocks boosted the values of the options we were creating. Nonetheless, we were also well aware that the options would expire worthless if the basket sold off.

During the spring of 1997, I saw an opportunity to buy a basket of equity markets in Southeast Asia. They had underperformed other markets considerably because export growth in the region had slowed, and some observers were heralding an end to the "Asia miracle." Having been a long-time believer in the "Asia Tigers," I recommended creating a basket consisting of equity markets in Indonesia, Malaysia, the Philippines, Singapore and Thailand which was launched in June.

Unfortunately, it would prove to be one of the worst calls of my career. Shortly after the basket was created, I spoke with Bob Aliber, who had just returned from a trip to Southeast Asia. Much to my surprise, he told me there was a speculative boom in commercial real estate that he thought would turn into a bust. Bob's call proved prescient. A few weeks later, Thailand's currency came under attack and the authorities were forced to devalue the Thai baht.

I held out hope for a while that the IMF would be able to stabilize the situation. Its support program called for the Thai central bank to raise interest rates to attract foreign capital. Instead, the program back-fired when Thai banks faced a financial squeeze. Their loans to real estate developers plummeted in value while their effective borrowing costs rose because they had borrowed in US dollars.

Before long, the other Southeast Asian economies came under attack, as capital flowed out of the region. This was reminiscent of what occurred in Latin America in 1995 after the Mexican peso was devalued. The main difference was the US government arranged a $30 billion rescue package for Mexico, whereas it remained on the sidelines during the crisis in Southeast Asia. I subsequently contacted Jeff Shafer, the second in command on international policy at the US Treasury, to find out whether assistance would be forthcoming. He indicated there was little support in Congress because it viewed the region as less essential to American interests.

I did not relish having to explain what went wrong to our clients when the call option on the basket expired worthless. The consolation for those who purchased the MPD was that while they lost the interest they would have earned on the deposit, their principal was protected. My message to them was that the financial systems in many Asian countries were more vulnerable to currency and interest rates swings than I realized. I was also worried the contagion could spread to much larger economies in North Asia such as Japan, South Korea, Taiwan and China. If so, it could have global repercussions.

In late October, I was invited to appear as a guest on Louis Rukeyser's *Wall Street Week* program, the oldest and most highly rated business program on television. When Rukeyser asked me how bad the situation was, I told him that it was the worst crisis in Asia in the post-World War II era. My assessment was that if the contagion did not stop, it could eventually spread to the United States.

I was worried because the crisis in Asia marked the first time that problems in financial systems were spreading globally. Yet policymakers in the Group of Seven (G-7) industrial countries were reluctant to act to stabilize the situation. By early 1998, the contagion was beginning to spread to Latin America and other emerging economies.

The US stock market, nonetheless, was largely unfazed by these developments. It posted an annual return of more than 20% in 1997 for the third consecutive year. One reason was economic growth advanced at more than a 4% annual rate while inflation remained close to the 2% rate the Fed was targeting. Investors were enamored that this "Goldilocks scenario" could continue indefinitely.

The earnings story, however, was less clear. Whereas profits based on S&P 500 operating earnings showed healthy growth, those reported in the national income accounts indicated the share of company profits had begun to decline relative to GDP. I pointed this out in my commentaries as I believed the latter measure was a better representation of what was happening. The reason: It covered all companies that filed income tax returns and, therefore, was less subject to accounting distortions. I considered it a possible red flag that corporate America was beginning to feel the fallout of the Asian crisis.

These developments occurred as the wave of consolidations in financial services that began in the late 1980s continued unabated and which culminated in a buying frenzy in the late 1990s (Table 19.1). The most significant was the merger between Citibank and Travelers Group in April 1998. It created the world's biggest financial-services company with banking, insurance and investment operations in 100 countries. The new company, which was called Citigroup, had combined assets totaling nearly $700 billion and a market capitalization of about $135 billion.

The deal was well received on Wall Street, as the share prices for Citi and Travelers rose by 26% and 18% respectively. It was heralded as creating a universal bank that could provide customers with "one stop shopping." At the press conference announcing the mega-merger, Citi's Chairman John Reed

Table 19.1   Number of large US bank mergers 1980–98

Year	Large mergers	Large interstate mergers
1980	0	0
1981	1	0
1982	2	0
1983	5	0
1984	7	0
1985	12	7
1986	9	5
1987	19	11
1988	14	8
1989	2	0
1990	6	1
1991	16	12
1992	22	15
1993	17	11
1994	15	10
1995	14	11
1996	28	21
1997	25	24
1998	34	32
Total	248	168

Note: The acquiring firm and target bank have more than $1 billion in assets. Year is based on consummation date
Source: Federal Reserve

said one of the goals was to make investment products such as stocks and bonds available to middle-class customers around the world.[1] Citi had built a global retail franchise alongside its corporate banking business, while Travelers was an insurance and investment conglomerate run by Sandy Weill. He had previously purchased Salomon Brothers in 1997 to add to its Smith Barney brokerage operations.

The merger received considerable attention because it effectively rendered Glass-Steagall obsolete. Some observers considered it either an act or a courage or hubris because Congress had not yet repealed the law separating commercial and investment banking. However, Weill and Reed had previously alerted the Federal Reserve, US Treasury, President Clinton and key members of Congress to gain their support. Subsequently, Travelers applied to the Federal Reserve Board to become a bank holding company. The deal was approved by the Fed without Travelers having to divest itself of its nonbank holdings.

[1] "Citicorp and Travelers Plan to Merge in Record $70 Billion Deal," by Mitchell Martin, *The New York Times*, April 7, 1998.

The Citi-Travelers pairing occurred against a backdrop in which several leading investment banks were seeking to expand their footprint in anticipation that Glass-Steagall barriers would be coming down. During 1997, Morgan Stanley merged with Dean Witter, a major retail stockbroker with widespread distribution, and Merrill Lynch acquired Mercury Asset Management, the largest investment manager in the United Kingdom. In Europe, UBS acquired S.G. Warburg, and Deutsche Bank made a series of tactical acquisitions to acquire senior talent and expand aggressively into investment banking and securities operations. As Charles Ellis observed:[2]

> Global banks were moving with their huge balance sheets into the investment banking and securities business, and regulatory restraints were coming down everywhere. Competition's center of gravity was moving inexorably toward permanent capital and big balance sheets.

What took place marked a break with the previous pattern of bank megamergers. The combinations entailed institutions with assets over $100 billion each, which some called "supermegamergers."[3] The stated motivation was to increase shareholder value by achieving "economies of scope" by capturing opportunities to cross sell products across an enlarged client base.

Some observers, however, noted that another managerial objective may have been empire building as executive compensation was correlated with firm size. In an article published in 2000, Charles Calomiris and Jason Karceski asked:

> Is the current merger wave in American banking helping to promote efficiency by increasing the size and scope of banks, or is the bank merger wave driven by darker aspirations: the search for monopoly rents or the job security and personal perquisites of bank managers?

Indeed, years later both John Reed and Sandy Weill would concede the Citi-Travelers merger had been founded on faulty principles and was a mistake.[4]

---

[2] Charles D. Ellis, *The Partnership: The Making of Goldman Sachs*, Penguin Books, 2009.

[3] Alan N. Berger et al. "The consolidation of the financial services industry: Causes, consequences, and implications for the future," *Journal of Banking and Finance* 23, 1999.

[4] Reed conducted numerous interviews with the financial press and media during and after the 2008 financial crisis in which he stated the concept of "one stop shopping" for financial services was flawed. Sandy Weill also acknowledged this in his final annual meeting as chairman of Citigroup. See "Citi's Creator, Alone with His Regrets," *New York Times*, Jan 2, 2010.

Amid these gargantuan deals, Goldman Sachs remained one of the last Wall Street partnerships. However, Jon Corzine, who became the senior partner in 1994, actively sought to take it public. He believed Goldman required an infusion of permanent capital to keep it competitive in global markets, but he needed to convince other members of senior management. During 1997, Goldman's profits exceeded $3 billion, representing a return on equity in excess of 50%. It played key roles in the privatizations of Deutsche Telekom and China Telecom, as well as being the lead manager of Chrysler with Daimler Benz, the largest industrial merger at the time.[5]

Corzine's dream was to make Goldman a dominant provider of financial services. He initiated talks with several investment management firms including Robeco, Wellington and Grantham Mayo Van Otterloo. At the same time, he initiated talks with Sandy Warner, Bill Harrison and the CEOs of US Trust and Mellon Bank.[6]

Meanwhile, global markets took another turn for the worse in the summer when the financial contagion that originated in Asia swept through Latin America and Russia.

For the first time since the onset of the crisis, the US stock market began to sell off. I wrote a commentary that the bull market in equities that began in 1991 could be coming to an end if policymakers did not stop the contagion. My conviction grew in mid-August, when the Russian government shocked investors by devaluing the ruble and declaring a 90-day moratorium on repayment of foreign debt.

Amid this, rumors swirled in the markets that a prominent hedge fund was in trouble. Before long word was out on the Street that it was Long Term Capital Management (LTCM), which was run by John Meriwether and proprietary traders that he brought with him from Salomon Brothers.

My initial reaction was to dismiss this as idle speculation, because Meriwether's team was highly sophisticated and included two Nobel laureates, Myron Scholes and Robert Merton, who were acknowledged experts in risk management. Furthermore, LTCM had enjoyed remarkable success since it was founded in 1994 with annualized returns of more than 40%. The core investment strategy involved convergence trading, in which quantitative models were deployed to exploit arbitrage opportunities between liquid securities globally and asset classes.

What I did not realize at the time was how highly leveraged LTCM was. According to Roger Lowenstein, LTCM had equity of $4.7 billion at the

[5] Ibid., p. 578.
[6] Ibid., p. 580.

beginning of 1998. It had borrowed nearly $125 billion for a debt-to-equity ratio of more than 25 to 1.[7] It also had off-balance sheet derivative positions with a notional value of $1.25 trillion, most of which were interest rate and currency swaps.

As 1998 progressed, LTCM had been positioned for spreads to narrow between higher yielding and lower yielding instruments. However, as the Asia crisis spread to other regions, there was a flight to quality worldwide and LTCM had to de-lever its portfolio. It had to do so, moreover, when many of its competitors were selling instruments that LTCM was holding. From May through July, the fund posted three consecutive months of negative returns that cumulated to more than 25%, and its positions were further at risk by Citigroup's decision to exit Salomon Brothers' arbitrage business in July.

The situation grew worse in early September when Russia's central bank abandoned its "floating peg" exchange rate policy and allowed the ruble to float freely. This resulted in the Russian currency losing two-thirds of its value from the level one month earlier, and the flight to quality intensified around the world.

With most of LTCM's positions increasingly under water, John Meriwether contacted his principal banker, Jon Corzine, to ask Goldman for additional funding.[8] He also considered possibilities ranging from a major capital infusion to selling LTCM to a "white knight," and he approached both Warren Buffet and George Soros. The challenge that Meriwether faced, however, was the amount of capital required to keep the fund solvent kept rising as the onslaught in financial markets continued.

By mid-September, it was apparent that a consortium of financial institutions was needed to stop the hemorrhaging. John Corzine called the Treasury Department on September 20 to alert Robert Rubin about the situation. Two days later, the New York Fed hosted a breakfast for Jon Corzine and John Thain of Goldman, Roberto Mendoza representing Morgan and David Kamansky and Herb Allison of Merrill Lynch to discuss a rescue package.

Bill McDonough, president of the New York Fed, chaired the session and told the assembled that the Fed would not bail out the institutions that lent to LTCM. He indicated the institutions involved should be prepared to absorb losses of roughly $300 million each. In the end, the group agreed on a proposal put forth by Herb Allison. It called for sixteen institutions to each invest $250 million to reach a total of $4 billion that John Thain specified was

[7] Roger Lowenstein, *When Genius Failed: The Rise and Fall of Long Term Capital Management*, Random House, October 2000.
[8] Ellis, op. cit., p. 590.

necessary.[9] The final deal was modified to up the ante to $300 million for eleven institutions when Bear Stearns and Credit Agricole declined to participate.

What was not fully appreciated then was the crisis surrounding LTCM marked the first time in which Morgan and/or Citi were not leading the effort to find a solution.[10] Rather, the torch for arranging the meeting had been passed to Goldman Sachs, while Merrill Lynch played a key role in putting forth the proposal that was accepted. This was an indication of the growing importance investment banks were playing in arranging financing for hedge funds.

The issue that remained unresolved was whether this capital infusion into LTCM would stabilize financial markets. When it did not, the Federal Reserve sprang into action by cutting the federal funds rate by a quarter of a point to 5.25% in late September. The Fed then lowered the funds rate another 25 basis points in October, and in November it cut both the funds rate and the discount rate by that amount.

It marked the third time in the Greenspan era that the Fed came to the rescue of the financial system. Thereafter, investors became convinced that the Fed would do whatever was needed to halt the slide in financial markets—the so-called Greenspan put. The stock market ended the year with a powerful rally, which boosted the return for 1998 to nearly 27%, the fourth consecutive year of supra-normal returns.

---

[9] Ibid., p. 592.

[10] Roberto Mendoza crafted a plan that would have separated LTCM's positions into two baskets—one for debt instruments and the other for equities—and then sell the securities back to issuing entities at a discount. But it was not accepted.

20

Market Frenzy

What ensued over the eighteen months following the rescue of LTCM made the market moves of previous three-plus years look tame by comparison: From October 1998 to the peak of the market in March 2000, the S&P 500 index increased by about 50% while the NASDAQ composite rose by more than 270% surpassing the 5000 level.[1]

Investor optimism was fueled by developments in the technology sector that were linked to the turn of the millennium, which was commonly referred to as Y2K. The idea that investors latched on to was the need for businesses to replace software systems that might fail on January 1, 2000, because existing systems were not programmed to handle dates beginning with the year 2000.

Many businesses moved forward capital spending plans to develop and purchase new, more sophisticated systems rather than incur unknown costs repairing existing systems. Accelerated software investments also spilled over to hardware spending, and they contributed to a surge in overall business investment. The mistake many investors made was to project strong investment demand throughout the next decade.

As economic growth reaccelerated from a brief slowdown in mid-1998, economists and Wall Street analysts revised their projections for the economy and corporate profits steadily upward. At the stock market's peak in March 2000, Wall Street analysts were projecting earnings growth for S&P 500 companies would increase at compound annual rate of 14% per annum over the long term. This pace was nearly three times faster than the trend growth rate of the US economy. Meanwhile, the price-earnings multiple for the S&P 500

---

[1] For a more complete discussion, see Sargen, *Global Shocks,* op. cit., Chapter 9.

© The Author(s) 2020
N. P. Sargen, *JPMorgan's Fall and Revival,* https://doi.org/10.1007/978-3-030-47058-6_20

index climbed to twenty-four times one-year forward earnings, while valuations for the NASDAQ index reached levels that were substantially higher. Prices of so-called dot-coms skyrocketed even though they didn't generate positive profits.

In addition to technology, one of the sectors that led the stock rally was financials which was highly levered to the economy. While the sector was hit hard during the sell-off in mid-1998, it subsequently rebounded when the stock market renewed its ascent. Morgan's share price, however, lagged its peers. Its earnings were impacted by a sell-off in emerging markets and it was not as involved in financing technology companies and start-ups as its competitors.

Meanwhile, Morgan's Private Bank continued to experience a drain in talent, as securities firms offered higher compensation packages to top producers in SDI. One of the most shocking departures was the New Jersey team headed by Phil DiIorio to join Merrill Lynch. Phil and his colleagues had consistently been the top performing team since the inception of SDI, and he was considered extremely loyal.

While some viewed the departure as being compensation related, I was close to Phil and his team and knew that other factors weighed on their decision. One of the most important considerations was the head of the US Private Bank was seeking to convert SDI personnel into financial advisors who no longer would sell securities to Morgan's private clients.

Shortly after their departure, I received a call at my house from Ramon de Oliveira. He knew I was close to Phil and his team and asked me if there was a chance the team would consider returning. I mentioned that Phil had hinted that Merrill conducted its private client business very differently from what he was accustomed to at Morgan. Therefore, I thought it made sense for Ramon to reach out and speak with him directly. The good news was that Ramon was able to bring Phil and his team back in the fold.

About at the same time, Ramon decided to put Jes Staley, who headed the equity division, in charge of the Private Bank when Jamie Higgins had to step down for personal reasons. The clear message Ramon and Jes conveyed was the Private Bank needed to improve profitability by bringing in more business and doing so without increasing costs. Jes was proactive in replacing the head of the US Private Bank with a person who understood the urgency of expanding business. He also promoted Mary Erdoes to lead the sales effort. One of her challenges was to convince the personnel of the need to grow revenues by being pro-active with clients in offering services Morgan provided.

Amid all of this, my colleagues began to wonder about Morgan's long-run viability and whether it could be acquired by a competitor if results did not improve quickly. While the 1980s were known as a period of merger mania, the volume of M&A activity paled with what occurred in the 1990s. For example, in 1998 alone, more than 12,000 deals involving US companies were announced for a total value in excess of $1.6 trillion.[2] This volume was more than four times greater than in 1988, which was the height of the 1980s merger boom.

As Alfred Rappaport and Mark Sirower note, the most striking feature of the acquisitions in the 1990s was the way they were being paid.[3] In 1988, nearly 60% of the value of large deals over $100 million was paid for entirely in cash, and less than 2% was paid for in stock. By 1998, the profile had completely reversed: 50% of the value of large deals was paid for entirely with stock versus only 17% that was paid in cash.

This shift had important ramifications because companies whose share prices were appreciating could use their appreciated shares effectively as a currency to pay for acquisitions of companies whose share process lagged.[4] In the case of Morgan, its share price lagged the composite for bank stocks for several years, which meant that it was becoming increasingly vulnerable.

Consequently, my colleagues and I would speculate at times about which institution would make an ideal partner for Morgan. During the Preston era, Morgan's senior management at times reflected on the possibility of combining with Morgan Stanley once Glass-Steagall barriers came down. Part of the appeal was that both institutions shared a common heritage and values. In addition, Preston and Weatherstone had high regard for Morgan Stanley's management team headed by Richard Fisher, Parker Gilbert and Lewis Bernard. The trio had done an excellent job expanding the firm's capabilities while keeping its culture intact.

By 1997, however, there was a complete turnover of Morgan Stanley's management team when Morgan Stanley was acquired by Dean Witter and Phillip Purcell became chairman and CEO of the merged firm. At Dean Witter, Purcell saw the potential of the asset management well ahead of most other firms, and its assets under management expanded ten-fold from 1982 to more than $100 billion in 1997. His record of building shareholder value continued following the acquisition of Morgan Stanley, and it would go on to achieve significant gains in league table rankings during his eight-year tenure.

---

[2] Alfred Rappaport and Mark L. Sirower, "Stock of Cash?: The Trade-Offs for Buyers and Sellers in Mergers and Acquisitions," *Harvard Business Review.*

[3] Ibid.

[4] Rappaport and Sirower also point out that in an exchange of shares, it can become less clear who is the buyer and who is the seller, depending on how the shares perform when the merger is consummated.

The problem was that Purcell was also highly controversial and not well liked by Morgan Stanley executives. This effectively ruled out any possibility of JPMorgan being reunited with Morgan Stanley, even though it was performing very well at the time.

The institution that was the most highly regarded by my colleagues and other executives at Morgan was Goldman Sachs. It had established itself as the premier investment bank in the world. Its reputation for excellence was well deserved. The firm transformed itself over a sixty-year period from a US commercial paper dealer into a full-scale investment bank with a global presence. In his tribute, Charles Ellis attributes Goldman's success to the following attributes:[5]

It has recruited better people than any other financial firm, adapted to or created change faster and more forcefully, attracted more important clients, developed leadership in more businesses, spawned more centimillionaires, and set the standard of excellence on Wall Street and around the world. Goldman Sachs today is the most powerful and most dynamic organization in the history of finance.

While Morgan might take exception to the last statement, considering the role it had played for 150 years, there was no denying that Goldman Sachs had overtaken Morgan's prowess during the 1990s. Goldman also had a unique corporate culture that was revered by its employees. It was enunciated by the firm's managing partner, John Whitehead, in a memo he wrote in the late 1970s titled "Our Business Principles."[6] They have also been featured in every subsequent annual review published by Goldman Sachs, which lists its core values as teamwork, integrity, placing clients' interest first and the other core values expressed in the fourteen principles.

What was unknown at the time was Jon Corzine and Hank Paulson had approached Sandy Warner about a possible merger between the two institutions shortly after Goldman went public in May of 1999. This occurred after the Citi-Travelers merger made it apparent that Glass-Steagall was about to be repealed.

While the initial discussions did not lead anywhere, follow-up meetings in the summer proved more fruitful. Goldman Sachs was represented by Paulson, John Thain and John Thornton, while the Morgan team consisted of Warner, Roberto Mendoza and Walter Gubert.[7] According to Charles Ellis, Warner

[5] Charles D. Ellis, *The Partnership: The Making of Goldman Sachs*, Penguin Books, 2009 edition.
[6] Ibid., Chapter 11.
[7] Ibid., p. 638.

was enthusiastic that both sides found greater combined strength than they had expected, and he reported to the senior management team that both Thain and Thornton considered a merger of the two entities to be a "home run."[8] Goldman seemed particularly interested in Morgan's derivatives capabilities, its global presence with both corporations and governments, its strength in Latin America and its prestigious investment management business.

As the discussions progressed, Warner wanted to reach an agreement with Paulson whereby they would be co-chairmen of the combined firm. However, Paulson made it clear that he would be the CEO and would pick the management team. Warner countered with the suggestion that they could become co-non-executive chairman, and Thain and Thornton would be co-CEOs. They would address the tough issues involving implementation and reorganization of the combined institution.[9]

One of the major hurdles that would have to be confronted involved redundancy and potentially sizable layoffs, which Paulson was reluctant to consider. In the end, he opted to go against the recommendation of Thain and Thornton, and he called Warner to indicate the deal was off. Another key consideration for Paulson was that Morgan was spending about the same amount on M&A and the securities business as Goldman. However, Morgan could not generate even half of the revenues Goldman earned.

While Paulson was gracious in telling Warner his conclusion, Warner was frustrated that the negotiations had gone on for several months without a successful outcome. When Paulson backed out at the last moment before he was scheduled to brief Goldman's Board of Directors, Warner could only wonder whether he had been acting in good faith. Warner was also under increasing pressure to strike a deal from Lee Raymond, chairman and CEO of Exxon, who was the chair for Morgan's Board of Directors.

According to Ellis, Paulson realized that most of Goldman's management committee were bullish on Morgan at the time. However, as the years passed and Morgan was acquired by Chase, those involved in the discussions—including Warner—came around to the view that Paulson had made the correct decision for Goldman even though the combined balance sheet assets would have been formidable:[10]

---

[8] Ibid.
[9] Ibid., 539.
[10] Ibid., 641.

But the real strength of a modern-day financial intermediary is not balance-sheet capital nearly so much as it is reliable, ready, large-volume access to the capital markets. And that depends on the creativity and connectedness of people with superior talent, drive, and strategic dynamism. These assets were far greater at Goldman Sachs and were increasing.

Shortly after Goldman's Board of Directors meeting in September, a story appeared in the *Wall Street Journal* that Goldman Sachs had agreed to a merger with Morgan but then reneged. When Warner was asked to comment on the story, he indicated that Paulson had spun it to suggest that Morgan sought out Goldman whereas the opposite was the case. Paulson denied this and stated that the leak had come from Morgan. Once the word was out, my colleagues and I realized a merger with a major investment bank was unlikely. However, we were uncertain if a commercial bank would be interested.

What we did not know at the time was Walter Shipley, who engineered the merger of Chase and Chemical Bank in 1995, approached Warner in 1998 about merging the two firms. A series of meetings were held at Morgan's complex in the Galleria Condominium on 57th Street.[11] In addition to Shipley and Warner, Chase was represented by Bill Harrison and Jimmy Lee while Morgan's team included Walter Gubert, Peter Hancock and Ramon de Oliveira. During the negotiations, Shipley at one point proposed Warner would become the CEO of the combined entity. However, Warner ultimately declined because he did not believe the proposed price was in the interests of Morgan's shareholders.

Meanwhile, the stock market continued its steady ascent, as investors chased companies whose stock prices were rising the most. There was an extensive debate between those who maintained the stock market was efficient and those who believed valuations were too high and the market was mispriced.

One argument that was used to justify an increase in valuations was that both inflation and interest rates had fallen to low levels, which helped to justify higher price-earnings (P/E) multiples. The model the Federal Reserve used to assess the stock market lent credibility to this argument, as it compared the earnings yield on the stock market (the inverse of the P/E multiple) to the yield on the ten-year treasury. Using this metric, the stock market did not appear to be significantly mispriced in the 1995–97 period, although valuations were considerably higher by 1999.

Further justification for the stock market's relentless surge came from commentators who contended the equity risk premium—or excess return for

---

[11] Source is not named to preserve confidentiality.

stocks over bonds—was too high. In a book titled *Dow 36,000: The New Strategy for Profiting from the Coming Rise in the Stock Market*, James K. Glassman and Kevin Hassett argued that the historic risk premium for stocks versus bonds was too high, considering that over long investment horizons, returns for stocks were consistently higher than for bonds.[12] They contended that if the equity risk premium was set at zero, there would be a four-fold market increase rising to 36,000 by 2002–04. As would become clear soon after, the principal shortcoming of their argument is that investors may think they have a long-term orientation until the market sells off, at which point they become short-term focused and run for the door.

A leading proponent of the camp that believed the market was a bubble was Professor Robert Shiller of Yale University. He contended that investors were subject to irrational exuberance. I accepted this characterization was an accurate description of many retail investors who were trend followers. However, I was also cognizant that several prominent value investors such as Julian Robertson, Grantham, Mayo, van Otterloo (GMO) and others bucked the trend either by shorting tech stocks or by investing in stocks that were out of favor. The problem they incurred was the tech surge was too powerful and lasted too long for them to retain assets under management.

In my own case, my call for a bear market in 1998 turned out to be premature. Consequently, I was reluctant to stick my neck out again until there was clearer indication the bubble was about to burst. By late 1999, I concluded the market was experiencing an all-out buying frenzy, and it was only a matter of time before it rolled over. One illustration was that Merrill Lynch issued a research report on Qualcomm calling for it to triple in value over the next five years. The market's response was a doubling in the share price in the next three months!

At the same time, Wall Street analysts were publishing reports recommending dot-com companies that had no meaningful earnings, and they developed new metrics for valuing companies based on the number of "hits" for their websites. These developments were especially favorable for financial services companies that were extensively involved in financing technology companies and in underwriting start-ups.

Morgan, however, was largely a bystander in the process. While the companies that were its most important clients were those with the largest market capitalizations, the list of names had changed considerably during the 1990s to include rapid growing companies in technology and telecommunications.

---

[12] Crown Publishing Group, October 1999.

The big unknown for Morgan was how long the mania would last and whether there was still time for it to become more actively involved in the sector. One warning signal was that the Federal Reserve had taken note of the economy's strength and was becoming concerned that it could over-heat. Consequently, it began to tighten monetary policy by mid-1999. Normally, this would have caused investors to turn more cautious about the outlook. However, one view that gained adherence was that the Fed's efforts to supply excess reserves to the banking system ahead of Y2K would find its way to the stock market. The fallacy with this argument was the excess reserves were simply held by banks as a precaution against possible technical disruptions, rather than being used to back new loans. Therefore, any impact on the stock market was likely to be fleeting, but many investors failed to grasp this as 1999 wound down.

21

The Managing Directors' 2000 Convocation

The annual gathering of managing directors (MDs) at the start of each year was an event attendees always welcomed. It provided a venue for senior management to brief Morgan's executives on how the firm was performing and the plans for the coming year. The MDs, in turn, were expected to disseminate the information to their subordinates so that management and employees would all be on the same page.

The venue also provided an opportunity for the attendees to be briefed on key developments that were influencing the financial services industry and Morgan's businesses. One presentation that stood out a few years earlier was by Greg Geiling, Morgan's top-ranked analyst in telecommunications equipment. He discussed how the rapid deployment of the internet was disrupting traditional forms of communication and was influencing businesses and consumers alike. He illustrated this theme by showing a screen of a newspaper sports article that contained a video clip of a baseball player hitting a home run. All of us marveled at how rapidly internet usage was transforming our lives and we wondered what the next application might be.

As the MDs gathered for the January 2000 convocation in the auditorium of the Millennium Hotel, the attendees anticipated it would have special importance. The reason: Morgan's stock price had lagged rival banks and prominent investment banks since the mid-1990s. At the MDs' gathering Sandy Warner and other members of senior management would provide their assessment of what was required to get Morgan back on track. The agenda also included sessions on "Technology: The Wave of the Future" and on "Attracting and Retaining Talent."

© The Author(s) 2020
N. P. Sargen, *JPMorgan's Fall and Revival*, https://doi.org/10.1007/978-3-030-47058-6_21

Warner opened the meeting by highlighting the challenges Morgan faced in becoming a leader in the securities industry. He reviewed the progress that had been achieved on several fronts including derivatives, foreign exchange and commodities, and emerging markets. He mentioned the main shortfall was Morgan had not attained the status of becoming a "bulge bracket" firm in the lucrative area of equities. Consequently, competitors such as Goldman Sachs, Merrill Lynch and Morgan Stanley earned a disproportionate share of industry profits. He used a football analogy to explain what Morgan was confronting: It had done well advancing the ball into the "red zone," but a final push was needed to get into the end-zone and score a "pay dirt."

Warner went on to explain that senior management had been working on a strategic plan to overcome the competitive challenges Morgan faced. The goal of the meeting was to present the plan to the MDs and to convince them that it would be successful.

The essence of the plan was that Morgan needed to expand its customer base in wealth management to include high net worth (HNW) individuals, as well as the mass affluent. The latter was defined as households whose liquid net worth was below $1 million but which had the potential to become millionaires over time.

The opportunity of serving this market was readily apparent. During the 1990s, assets controlled by individuals accounted for two-thirds of the growth of assets under management compared with only one-half in the prior decade. The number of individuals in the United States with investable assets of $1 million or more was estimated to be 3.5 million households. Moreover, new millionaires were being created at a rapid rate as a result of host of market innovations—such as the spread of information technology, industrial consolidations, leveraged buyouts and growth of venture capital. One benefit of being able to serve the new millionaires was that many made their money by building tech businesses, and wealth management could provide an entrée for taking them public.

The opportunity for Morgan was that the HNW market was highly fragmented and underpenetrated, with no provider accounting for more than 5% of total assets under management. Merrill Lynch was the acknowledged leader with a full array of offerings that included brokerage activity, asset management, trust and fiduciary and liquidity management. These were areas where JPMorgan also was a leading provider.

While Morgan was a late entrant into the retail market, Morgan's senior management believed its impeccable reputation and in-depth research would enable it to close the gap. In order to get word out to the public about Morgan's new offering, it would advertise its retail capability in the media for the first time.

Warner called on Peter Hancock, who had become the firm's chief financial officer, to go over the financial implications. He explained the offering would contain three client segments: (1) households with liquid assets of $10 million or more; (2) those with assets of $1 million to $10 million; and (3) those with liquid assets of less than $1million. The first segment would have access to Morgan's private bankers, whereas the next two segments would be covered via access to customer service representatives (on-call) and via internet access (online), respectively. Hancock indicated the undertaking would cost Morgan in the vicinity of $250–$300 billion over three years to build out the platform.

Hancock then asked the attendees to register their initial reaction to the plan by using remote controls they had been given, with scores ranging from 5 (best) to 1 (worst). Upon hearing the plan, I recall thinking "Does management fully understand the difficulty of producing results in a relatively short time span?" While Morgan had a long history serving the ultra-wealthy, it seemed like a "Hail Mary" play to suddenly embrace the mass affluent after years of ignoring the opportunity.

The vast majority of responses were 3s and 4s, and my assessment was in line with others. Hancock closed the session by mentioning that the attendees would be given a second chance to vote at the end of the proceedings once they had an opportunity to fully absorb the strategic plan.

Thereafter, the focus of the meeting shifted to the growing importance of technology and the application of the internet in social media. The featured speaker was Todd Krizelman, who co-founded TheGlobe.com as a twenty-year-old student at Cornell in 1995. His firm allowed users to post their own web pages, chat and play games with one another. It would precede the launch of Facebook by several years. When it went public in November 1998, its share price soared from $9 to $97 before closing at $63.50 on the first day of trading. This earned it notoriety as the most successful IPO at the time.

As I listened to Krizelman, I thought how odd it was to have a twenty-some-year-old in a tie-dyed T-shirt and jeans address a convocation of senior Morgan executives. It would have been one thing to explain how he and his co-founder, Stephan Paternot, concocted the idea for their firm and acquired the funding to bring it public. Instead, he explained how he ran his start-up business, which had 400 employees, as if Morgan's management could learn from his experience.

It was befuddling to many why Morgan had selected a dot-com representative to address the forum considering there were increasing signs of a tech bubble. The NASDAQ Composite index, for example, had risen four-fold from 1995 and its price-earnings ratio of 200 dwarfed that of Japan's stock market ratio of 80 when Japan's bubble burst in 1989.

In fact, the US tech bubble burst just a few weeks after the MDs' meeting. The company's share price plummeted to zero, and Krizelman's stake in the company went from being in excess of $100 million to practically nothing. He and his partner were subsequently forced out of it later in 2000 and the firm was dissolved the next year. More telling was how out of touch Morgan appeared: The firm embraced technology just as it was about to roll over.

The afternoon session on "Winning the War for Talent" proved even more bizarre. The spokesman was a representative from a recruiting firm who specialized in placing MBAs and undergrads with Wall Street firms. His principal message was that young people coming out of college were different from their parents and predecessors, and firms had to adapt to their expectations. Little of what he said was memorable except for one observation: Namely, in lieu of the long hours they put in, newly minted recruits to Wall Street expected firms to provide them concierge services such as laundry and dry cleaning as well as after-hours meals and limousines. My reaction to all of this was "What did my generation do wrong?"

The meeting culminated the next morning with Hancock summarizing the strategic plan and what the MDs had been presented. When he asked them to register their votes on the plan, both he and Warner were stunned to find that the scores had actually gone down. Warner was visibly upset and scolded the audience for their lack of support. Some of my colleagues recall him calling the assembled group "a bunch of losers."

After the meeting concluded, I huddled with colleagues to get their take on what had transpired. Most were trying to collect their thoughts and were still in a state of shock. What was clear is many of us had misgivings about how Morgan was faring for several years, but prior to the meeting we had kept our thoughts to ourselves. Now, for the first time, we felt free to share our views about the direction of the firm with one another. I recall one colleague saying that glasnost and perestroika had come to Morgan at last!

Morgan's senior management was very talented and had a good grasp of the financial services industry. Yet, we were puzzled by how out of touch they were about expanding Morgan's capabilities in wealth and asset management. The discussion of the opportunities in both areas reminded us of what John Olds had been preaching for the past decade. But the approach that was presented left us scratching our heads about why the mass affluent would suddenly want to embrace JPMorgan. It had completely ignored them previously.

Nonetheless, the presentations were filled with bravado about overtaking Merrill Lynch in short order. We were unsure what the problem was, but suspected the House Arrest Group had become very insular and subject to Groupthink. In the process, Morgan had become a hierarchy. The top of the organization issued orders that were expected to be followed without question from subordinates. The rank and file were not asked what they thought as was the case in the firm's glory years.

Those of us in the Private Bank could at least take comfort that the importance of our business unit was finally being recognized. And whatever personal misgivings we might have about the new offering, we realized it was our responsibility to carry it out.

One of the senior management's requests was that MDs should sign up to become the first clients. I was willing to do so for two reasons. First, I could observe the pluses and minuses of the offering as a client. Second, the investment advice would be provided by the Private Bank and the strategy team that I headed. In this respect, I felt we were eating our own cooking.

When the launch began several months later, we could quickly see how prospects reacted to the offering. The marketing tactic was to screen potential prospects and invite them to events where the Private Bank would sponsor breakfast, luncheons and dinners. After the meal, a representative from Morgan would describe the offering to the assembled, and I would conclude with a presentation about our views on the economy and markets.

The Private Bank rolled out the red carpet for the premier event in Manhattan in the spring. Prospects received invitations to have lunch at the Russian Tea Room. In addition, they could bring two guests to hear Morgan's pitch. Based on the RSVPs we were expecting a large group. However, the attendance was much larger than we had expected, and it was standing room only for Morgan representatives.

After lunch was served, I gave an update on our views for the balance of the year. It seemed to be well received, and I asked if there were any questions. One gentleman asked why Morgan was recommending the pharmaceutical sector when drug manufacturers were gouging patients. I explained that our job was to figure which sectors would outperform the stock market, as measured by the S&P 500 index, and our decision to over-weight pharma was that it was one of the more defensive sectors. Unfortunately, the gentleman did not like the answer, and he proceeded to recite everything that he thought was wrong with pharmaceutical companies. The host rescued me after several minutes and concluded the event by thanking everyone for coming and asking the attendees to fill out a card where they could rate the event and proposal.

When I returned to the office, I visited the group that had hosted the event and asked for their impressions. They were very excited, as they received about a dozen responses from people who indicated they were interested in learning more about Morgan's offering. I did not want to discourage them, but couldn't help but think we had just held a very expensive event in a top restaurant and were only able to elicit interest from a dozen or so people.

Thereafter, I toured several of Morgan's offices for similar events. However, most were held in our offices rather than at expensive restaurants. The reaction we received was generally the same: People wanted to know who their representative would be and who would be managing their money. Our answer was the determination would be made once they became a client, and that if they opted for less expensive platform, all transactions would be conducted on-line. After hearing this, most people were uninterested.

By mid-2000, we were only able to add only a few hundred new clients—a far cry from the ambitious goals that were set at the MDs' meeting. While it was soon apparent to those of us at the Private Bank that Morgan's foray into the mass affluent marketplace was Dead on Arrival (D.O.A.), senior management held out hope that prospects would come around once they fully understood the offering.

Meanwhile, management was beset by a bigger issue—namely, its share price was being dragged down by a sell-off in technology stocks. As discussed in the previous chapter, the unprecedented surge in tech stocks during 1999 was fueled by the perception the Fed was being highly accommodative as it flooded the banking system with excess reserves to guard against a possible run on the banks if there was a Y2K glitch. Investors responded by driving tech stocks to unsustainable levels, especially great for dot-com names.

When it became apparent in early 2000 that Y2K was over-blown, the Fed began to drain excess reserves from the banking system. Alan Greenspan subsequently signaled to the markets in February that the Fed was prepared to raise interest rates further to keep the economy from over-heating.

The tech sell-off began in mid-March amid news that Japan had once again slipped into recession. It triggered a global sell-off in equities that mainly impacted tech stocks. On March 20, *Barron's* featured a cover article titled "Burning Up Warning: Internet companies are running out of cash—fast," which predicted the failure of many internet companies. Thereafter, share prices of many dot-coms plummeted when the Federal Reserve raised interest rates and the yield curve inverted, which many interpreted as a leading indicator of a recession.

Most large cap tech stocks held up against the onslaught for a while. And Morgan's tech analysts, who had been strong advocates for names such as Cisco, Intel, Oracle, Sun Microsystems, Qualcomm and JDS Uniphase, urged investors not to panic on grounds that they had produced solid earnings. However, the sell-off broadened when Cisco, considered to be the bellwether for internet stocks, announced that it would not meet analysts' earnings expectations for the first time in its history. This dealt a blow to the idea that the rapid expansion of the internet was unstoppable, and the entire tech sector began to swoon.

By the middle of 2000, the NASDAQ index had fallen by roughly one half from its peak level and share prices of Wall Street firms were adversely impacted. Consequently, many securities firms including Morgan wound up rescinding offers they had made to MBAs. No need for concierge services after all! Guess they'll still have to do their own laundry.

By summer, word was out on the Street that Morgan was in play. My colleagues and I did not know which firm the acquirer would be, but rumors were rife that Deutsche Bank and Chase Manhattan were the leading contenders. The Deutsche Bank connection seemed logical because Kurt Viermetz had close ties to the German bank and there was a mutual respect between the two institutions. That said, I could not fathom what it would be like working for a foreign institution. From a personal perspective, I was relieved that Morgan's new partner would be Chase, because the added benefit to me was John Lipsky was its chief economist and we could resume our collaboration.

When it was announced on September 14, 2000, that Chase Manhattan would acquire Morgan for an all-stock deal valued at $30.9 billion, my initial reaction was it seemed like a good fit.[1] Chase had been striving to transform itself into a global financial powerhouse, and adding Morgan would catapult it into the ranks of investment banking. In prior months, there had been several high-priced acquisitions of mid-size financial companies, including the acquisitions of PaineWebber by UBS and of Donaldson, Lufkin & Jenrette by Credit Suisse. The rush of deals meant that only three middle-tier securities firms remained—Morgan, Lehman and Bear Stearns.

Together, Chase and Morgan would have combined assets of $650 billion, making it second to Citigroup's $800 billion. The combined entity would have just shy of 100,000 employees including 16,000 from Morgan. Morgan's brand would be maintained for wholesale business, while Chase would be the brand for retail banking. Bill Harrison would serve as CEO of the combined institution, while Sandy Warner would be its chairman.

In a town hall meeting to announce the merger to the rank and file, both Harrison and Warner sounded upbeat about the potential synergies. They also downplayed the number of job losses that would be entailed.

After the meeting, there was considerable grumbling from colleagues who felt Warner and his top lieutenants made out like bandits. Warner alone saw

---

[1] Patrick McGeehan and Andrew Ross Sorkin, "Chase Manhattan to Acquire J.P. Morgan for $30.9 billion," *New York Times*, September 14, 2009.

the value of his stock in the company soar to $289 million.[2] They blamed him for pursuing a strategy that left Morgan vulnerable and also for ruining a once great culture. They also noted that Peter Hancock had resigned shortly before the merger was announced. Rumors circulated that both Hancock and Roberto Mendoza had approached Morgan's Board of Directors about replacing Warner as chairman and CEO but were rebuffed. As noted in the previous chapter, what was not disclosed to the public were the prior merger conversations between Morgan and Chase in 1998, in which Warner declined the opportunity to become CEO because he believed the price tendered then was not in Morgan's shareholders' interests.

While Morgan's rank and file were unhappy the firm was acquired, one saving grace was it was sold at a substantial premium over the market price. This meant it was a good deal for Morgan's shareholders. Some executives I interviewed believe Warner was pressured by the chairman of Morgan's board, Lee Raymond of Exxon, to complete a deal. A former Morgan executive mentioned that when Exxon acquired Mobil in 1998, Raymond dramatically shrunk the size of Exxon's board, and he asked Walter Shipley and Jamie Houghton (a Morgan director) to become members of the new board.[3]

What ensued after the merger was not pretty. Employees of both Morgan and Chase were unhappy. Many managing directors from Morgan felt the firm had been sold to a less prestigious institution and one that was much larger and more bureaucratic. For their part, Chase employees were upset that Chase's share price fell by 9% upon announcement of the merger. Also, many felt that their new colleagues from Morgan were arrogant and treated them condescendingly. I recall one occasion when I met a Morgan banker covering the New York City region and asked him how things were going. His response: "Terribly—both sides hate each other!"

For Bill Harrison, this was a much different experience than Chemical Bank's acquisitions of Manufacturers Hanover and Chase Manhattan, which both went smoothly. Moreover, the problems of integration with Morgan were further compounded by the appointment of co-heads for various business units. This often meant they were pre-occupied with who would get the nod eventually rather than on how their subordinates were faring.

By 2001, the mood at the combined firm remained grim as the stock market continued to plummet and the United States faced the tragedy of 9/11. Morale continued to sink the following year, when a series of accounting

[2] Paul Tharp, "J.P. Morgan Execs Score in Big Payday," *New York Post*, September 14, 2000.
[3] Name withheld for confidentiality.

scandals led to the unraveling of corporations such as Enron, WorldCom, Global Crossing and Tyco that JPMorgan Chase had helped finance.[4]

Amid this I was contacted by a former Morgan colleague to see if I would be interested in becoming the head of investments for the Western & Southern Financial Group, a financial services company in Cincinnati, Ohio, that dated back to 1888. When I met John Barrett, the chairman and CEO, he explained that he had been a great admirer of Morgan's culture, and he was striving to establish a similar culture. Much to my surprise, he convinced me that my wife and I should leave the New York area. After twenty-five years on Wall Street, I felt saddened by what had occurred, but also grateful that I could once again be part of a culture that made me proud. It turned out to be the right decision, as John Barrett delivered on his promise to make my time at the firm one of the best experiences of my career.

---

[4] Jake Ulich, "Year of the Scandal," CNN Money, December 17, 2002.

22

Why Morgan Matters

In the Preface, I describe this book as a story of how an iconic firm battled market forces to preserve its heritage but ultimately lost when it was acquired by a rival institution.

To be clear, Morgan is not a story of a failed institution. Throughout its history, Morgan routinely played the role of rescuer of other financial institutions. It also lent support to the US government and those abroad on several occasions. And it never asked for federal assistance, as many of the leading financial institutions did during the 2008 Global Financial Crisis (GFC). However, Morgan was required to take it so as not to taint other banks.

What happened to Morgan over the past forty years is truly remarkable in the annals of financial history: It went from being a pre-eminent wholesale bank to being acquired by a rival that was primarily retail oriented in 2000; it has since evolved into a financial power-house with capabilities in wholesale, retail and investment banking.

My thesis is the building blocks for Morgan's revival were laid during the mid-1980s to mid-1990s, when Lew Preston and Dennis Weatherstone transformed Morgan to encompass investment banking and securities. The main obstacle that hindered its success was their reluctance to make targeted acquisitions in areas where Morgan had existing expertise that could have funded the expansion into securities. Jamie Dimon deserves credit for reviving Morgan's legacy: He pulled off what his predecessors were unable to achieve and built on the foundation that had been laid, while integrating diverse cultures into a cohesive whole.

The fact that Morgan was acquired is not noteworthy by itself—the same can be said of most of its rivals. At the beginning of the 1980s, for example,

© The Author(s) 2020
N. P. Sargen, *JPMorgan's Fall and Revival*, https://doi.org/10.1007/978-3-030-47058-6_22

there were ten US money-center banks. Twenty years later, only three names were left—JPMorgan Chase, Bank of America and Citicorp—and each of them was the product of mergers. A fourth name was later added to the list—Wells Fargo, which also expanded as a result of mega-mergers.

As regards investment banks, only two organizations of significant size are still independent—Goldman Sachs and Morgan Stanley.[1] They became part of the Fed's umbrella during the financial crisis, as they were restructured to become bank holding companies.

Today, JPMorgan Chase heads the roster of US financial institutions in terms of asset size and market capitalization (Table 22.1). It is also the most profitable bank, and its share price has exceeded that of other large banks substantially since the onset of the GFC.

Looking ahead, Morgan is on solid footing with talented people, a strong balance sheet and excellent risk management, and will likely remain a premier financial institution. That said, it remains to be seen whether Dimon's successors will be equally adept in overseeing a large and highly complex organization.

Table 22.1 Assets and market capitalization of ten largest US bank holding companies, December 31, 2019

Rank	Bank name	Total assets (billions of $)	Market capitalization (billions of $)	Branches
1	JPM Chase	$2687	$426	5000
2	BoA	2434	300	4300
3	Citibank	1951	161	2400
4	Wells Fargo	1928	197	5500
5	Goldman Sachs	993	83	0
6	Morgan Stanley	895	85	0
7	U.S. Bancorp	495	83	3000
8	PNC	410	67	2300
9	TD Bank N.A.	394	67	1200
10	Capital One	379	58	750

Source: Federal Reserve, ADVs

[1] The list of key financial institutions that either have merged or no longer exist includes a remarkable roster of securities firms: E.F. Hutton, Kidder Peabody, Paine Webber, Dean Witter and Merrill Lynch, Salomon Brothers, First Boston, Shearson Lehman, Drexel Burnham, Bache & Co. and Bear Stearns.

Could Morgan Have Stayed Independent?

One issue that has weighed on Morgan alums over the years is whether the bank could have remained independent. Many viewed the merger with Chase as a defeat for a storied firm that had been pre-eminent throughout the twentieth century. They were saddened by the loss of a culture they cherished and faulted the firm's leadership. Many were disappointed that Sandy Warner was unable to unite the various business units into a common cause. Yet, the course Morgan pursued was formulated by Lew Preston and Dennis Weatherstone when they opted to serve the bank's existing customer base rather than expand it.

By comparison, the perspective of Wall Street analysts was Morgan was similar to a host of banks that struggled to stay independent in an era of mega-bank mergers. They viewed its strategy of building investment banking and securities businesses from scratch as a tough slog which was both time consuming and expensive. Viewed from their vantage point, Morgan's customer base of top-tier US corporations and ultra-wealthy individuals was insufficient to generate the revenues needed to finance the build-out.

What is missing from these perspectives is an understanding of the strategic game plan that was discussed in Part II of this book. The plan was very sophisticated and extremely thorough. It called for Morgan to make targeted acquisitions in areas where Morgan had existing capabilities such as global custody, investment management and private banking. These areas had more predictable earnings streams that could have been used to finance the expansion into investment banking and securities.

Instead, Preston and Weatherstone wound up passing on every opportunity. They made the correct decision in not taking a stake in Citibank in the early 1990s, because Morgan and Citi were inherently polar institutions and it would have been a huge distraction. But they missed a golden opportunity to acquire States Street for $2 billion when its share price was less than $3 in the late 1980s. It would subsequently rise nearly twenty-fold to $55 by 2000, when Morgan was acquired by Chase (Fig. 22.1).

Beyond the pure investment gain, the acquisition of State Street could have transformed Morgan. According to a former senior executive, it would have provided the means for Morgan to build or acquire a mutual fund complex that would have broadened its asset management capabilities into the defined contributions space. At the same time, it would have compensated for the eventual loss of Euroclear's contribution, while providing one of the most competitive and comprehensive international securities clearing and

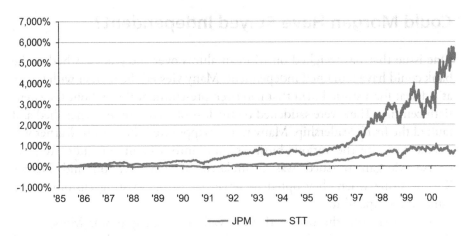

Fig. 22.1 Share price of State Street Bank versus JPM, cumulative returns from 1985 to 2000. (Source: Bloomberg, Fort Washington)

settlements infrastructures for global investors. By making the acquisition, Morgan would have led the pack in most securities-related activities from investment management to investment banking and prime brokerage.

The bottom line is that by passing on State Street and other targeted acquisitions, Morgan failed to capitalize on the tremendous expansion of wealth that occurred in the 1990s and beyond.[2] Instead, management chose to build out Morgan's trading capabilities in currencies, gold, securities and financial derivatives. While Morgan had core competencies in these areas, the market values assigned to them are considerably lower because trading revenues are more volatile than fee-generating businesses. By the time Morgan's management realized the tremendous opportunity in wealth management in the late 1990s, it was "too little, too late."

Impact of Bank Consolidation

To understand what happened to Morgan one also needs to consider the broader context of the wave of US bank consolidation that occurred from the 1980s onward. During the first three decades following World War II, the US banking system was highly fragmented and tightly regulated. Even the largest

---

[2] Note: Had Morgan acquired Northern Trust around the same time, its share price also increased twenty-fold, and it would have added to Morgan's Private Banking.

institutions individually possessed no more than about 3% of US bank assets in the 1960s.[3]

Beginning in the 1980s, the banking system was transformed as barriers to interstate and intrastate banking came down and technology impacted banking. Thereafter, a wave of mega-mergers resulted in a marked increase in the share of banking assets by the largest institutions.

According to a Federal Reserve study, the ten-year stretch from 1988 through 1997 involved more than 140 mega-mergers between institutions with assets of more than $1 billion each.[4] Subsequently, nine of the ten largest M&A transactions in US history occurred in 1998, and four of them— Citicorp-Travelers, Bank America-NationsBank, Bank One-First Chicago and Norwest-Wells Fargo—were in banking.[5]

One of the main findings of a study by the FDIC was that forces driving the wave of mergers had changed over time.[6] The first wave of industry consolidation occurred in the mid-1980s and early 1990s when banks' profits were hit by problem loans to developing countries, LBOs and commercial real estate. As restrictions on interstate banking were relaxed, banks expanded their geographical footprint to capture more customers. This was tantamount to horizontal integration and was designed to achieve economies of scale.

By comparison, the second wave of M&A occurred in the mid-to-late 1990s when bank profitability was restored. It entailed vertical integration, as financial institutions sought to expand the scope of their businesses and commercial and investment banking converged. As Glass-Steagall prohibitions were relaxed, banks sought to acquire investment banking capabilities, and much of the bank M&A that occurred was financed by the leading banks using their rising share prices to pay for the acquisitions.

By the early 2000s, the top four banks accounted for about one-third of total banking sector assets. Moreover, that tally would rise above 50% during and immediately after the 2008 Financial Crisis, when JPMorgan Chase and Bank of America were encouraged by regulators to acquire institutions that were financially troubled.[7]

Prior to the crisis, there was an extensive debate among economists and policymakers about whether the growing concentration of assets by the largest

---

[3] Richard Sylla, "United States Banks and Europe: Strategy and Attitudes", p. 54.

[4] Allen N. Berger et al., "The Consolidation of the Financial Services Industry: Causes, Consequences, and Implications for the Future," *Journal of Banking Finance* 23, 1999, pp. 135–194.

[5] Ibid.

[6] Kenneth D. Jones and Tim Critchfield, "Consolidation in the U.S. Banking Industry: Is the 'Long, Strange trip' about to End?" FDIC, February 2005.

[7] See Baily et al., "The Big Four Banks: The Evolution of the Financial Sector," Brookings, May 2015.

institutions was desirable. The prevailing view was that the US banking system was too fragmented and inefficient, and consolidation would produce a more efficient system. But the debate was far from settled.

In the wake of the financial crisis, the main issue that has arisen in the public arena is whether bank consolidation has affected the safety and soundness of the US financial system, and what can be done to protect it.

One of the goals of the Dodd-Frank Act enacted in 2010 was to lessen the risk of another financial crisis and to alleviate the need for taxpayer funding of bank bailouts. While capital and liquidity requirements for major institutions were increased, some experts believe the financial system is still at risk, because the banking industry became even more concentrated after the GFC. Moreover, some including Professor Charles Calomiris of Columbia University contend the provision to provide for orderly liquidation of failed institutions is unworkable, and the path of least resistance remains bailouts.[8]

These concerns have spawned a number of proposals to force major changes in the structure of the financial industry. They include (1) forcing a break-up or downsizing of the largest banks and (2) limiting the functions of banks via the Volcker Rule or re-instatement of Glass-Steagall. This has led to calls from politicians such as Elizabeth Warren and Bernie Sanders that the biggest banks need to be broken up.

Before one can meaningfully talk about reforming the US financial system, however, one must first understand the forces that gave rise to the so-called shadow banking system. This term refers to credit intermediation that occurs outside the formal banking system.[9] It is comprised of mutual funds, finance companies, Real Estate Investment Trusts (REITS), holding companies, hedge funds, private equity funds and similar entities.

The importance of banks and thrifts as providers of credit has shrunk steadily relative to non-banks over the past five decades (Table 22.2). During the 1960s, for example, banks and thrifts provided just over 50% of all credit that was extended in the United States compared with only 6% by

Table 22.2 Share of credit to US borrowers, banks versus non-banks

	1960–69	2000–07	2008–12
Traditional channels (banks and thrifts)	51%	20%	8%
"Shadow banks"	6%	28%	80%

Source: FESDUD, Studies in Financial Systems No.10 (US), Federal Reserve Flow of Funds

---

[8] Charles W. Calomiris, "Four Principles for Replacing Dodd-Frank," The *Wall Street Journal*, June 16, 2017.

[9] The creation of the term is attributed to Paul McCauley of PIMCO.

non-banks.[10] By comparison, during the period from 2008 to 2012, the share of overall credit provided by traditional banks was down to only 8%, while the share provided by so-called shadow banks had spiked to nearly 80% of all loans extended.[11]

Viewed from this perspective, attempts to rein in the largest banks could backfire if they promote faster growth in non-bank credit intermediation (NBCI). Indeed, as one study by the IMF observed: "the global financial crisis and ensuing aftershocks have also brought into sharp focus the risks to financial stability associated with NBCI."[12] Accordingly, if reform of the financial system is to be successful, it must deal with issues relating to banks and to non-banks alike.

Pros and Cons of Downsizing Large Banks

My former boss, Henry Kaufman, has been a leading advocate for reducing bank concentration dating back well before the financial crisis. One of his main concerns is that concentration is a growing problem throughout the US economy, with many sectors moving in the direction of becoming oligopolies. He sees this problem as being especially acute in the financial sector, which impacts virtually every part of the economy. And he warns that financial conglomerates are difficult to manage effectively, contain inherent conflicts of interest between client activity and proprietary trading and also may contribute to heightened market volatility due to the volume of their trading activities and the size of the assets they control.

In his book *Tectonic Shifts in Financial Markets*, Kaufman presents his case for reining in the activities of the largest financial organizations.[13] He argues they have not been an anchor of stability and required enormous support from the federal government during the 2008 crisis. The top firms were also at the forefront of securitization and risk management techniques that helped spawn the crisis. As regards universal banking, Kaufman observes:[14] "The giants claim that vertical integration offers economies of scale and allows them to serve customers better through one-stop shopping. There is little or no

---

[10] See FESSUD, Studies in Financial Systems No. 10 (US), by Robert Polin and James Heintz, Chapter 1.

[11] Some of the reduction in the bank share in the post-crisis period is due to an overall net decline in lending by government sponsored entities in 2008–12.

[12] Tobias Adrian and Bradley Jones, "Shadow Banking and Market-Based Finance," IMF, 2018.

[13] Kaufman, op. cit., Chapter 8.

[14] Ibid., p. 77.

evidence of the former, and while the latter may be true, the cost of convenience for financial markets is diminished competitiveness."

The alternative view has been articulated by researchers at Brookings. In a report titled "The Role of Finance in the Economy: Implications for Structural Reform of the Financial Sector," Martin Baily and Douglas Elliott begin by observing that it is extremely hard to determine the right size of the financial system or any industry based on well-grounded economic theories.[15]

The core of their argument against breaking up large banks or downsizing them is summarized as follows:[16]

> We believe that the best analysis indicates considerable economic benefits to size and scope and that these advantages are likely to grow further with increasing globalization, complexity, and improved management systems. America should have at least a few financial institutions with global scale, capable of providing a wide range of related commercial and investment banking services, operating on a scale in individual product lines that produces real efficiency.

Rather than break up large banks, Baily and Elliott favor continuing to designate them as systemically important financial institutions (SIFIs). As such, they are required to operate with higher safety margins and are also subject to closer regulatory oversight than non-designated institutions.

The Future of US Banking

So, where does this leave us today and what does the future hold for US banking?

In light of all that has happened one should appreciate how difficult it is to answer this question. Forty years ago, no one could have foreseen "the long, strange trip" described in the seminal Brookings study, the proliferation of shadow banking or the 2008 Global Financial Crisis. Since then, the recapitalization of US banks and stress tests conducted by the Federal Reserve have restored the public's confidence in the banking system, which is now at the forefront globally.[17] This is clearly a positive development.

As regards bank M&A, there has been a discernable slowdown over the past decade for two reasons. First, the asset holdings of the largest financial

---

[15] Baily, op. cit.

[16] Ibid., p. 2.

[17] See Matthew De Silva interview of Robert Engle, "How do you predict the next financial crisis," August 28, 2017.

institutions are near regulatory ceilings. Second, in light of the concerns about Too Big to Fail, regulators are reluctant to raise the current limits. Therefore, should the largest banks seek to enter new business lines in the future, they most likely will be required to divest other lines of business.

Beyond financial stability, another important consideration for regulators is that as banks have become larger and more complex, they have also become more difficult to govern. Henry Kaufman contends there is a direct correlation between institutional size and rule breaking, and he cites the finding of the CCP Research Foundation in the United Kingdom that reports more than $300 billion in fines, settlements and provisions related to financial wrongdoing in a five-year period beginning in 2010.[18] Moreover, the tally for the six largest US institutions over the past two decades exceeds $180 billion, with two-thirds related to mortgages and toxic securities (Table 22.3). This has caused critics to argue that, even if they are financially sound today, they have become "Too Big to Manage."

One consequence is that all banks, large and small, are subject to greater regulatory scrutiny. According to a study by Rice University's Baker Institute for Public Policy, passage of the Dodd-Frank Act roughly doubled the number of regulations applied to US banks, and it hiked their compliance costs by $50 billion annually.[19] US banks now collectively spend about $220 billion annually on compliance, representing 10% or more of most bank operating costs.[20] Moreover, some estimates call for them to double by 2022.

An unintended consequence of Dodd-Frank is that it may reinforce the trend of bank consolidation by making the plight of small banks more

Table 22.3 Violations of six leading US financial institutions since 2000

(Billions of dollars)			
	Total violations		
Firm	Number	Volume	Mortgage/toxic securities
Bank of America	182	$82.6	$63.2
JPMorgan Chase	135	34.5	18.8
Citigroup	97	25.0	15.5
Wells Fargo	136	17.3	9.3
Goldman Sachs	37	13.1	9.2
Morgan Stanley	79	9.7	5.4

Source: Good Jobs First, Violation Tracker

[18] Ibid., p. 77.

[19] The study was conducted by Thomas Hogan and Scott Burns. See article by Jeff Falk, Rice University News and Media Relations, September 13, 2019.

[20] Stuart Brock, "The Cost of Compliance," *International Banker*, November 7, 2018.

challenging. The researchers at Rice University found that since its passage, legal costs of small banks have increased by $1 billion annually, and their annual spend on data processing, auditing and consulting has risen by nearly $500 million.[21] The report notes that "Compared to large banks, increases in small banks' non-salary expenses were bigger and more likely to be statistically significant." The main reason is they lack the scale to absorb the increased regulatory costs that larger financial institutions enjoy.

The Future of JPMorgan Chase

As history attests, it is inherently difficult to predict which institutions will be industry leaders. Morgan was able to stay pre-eminent throughout the twentieth century, because it benefited from several positive attributes—sound management and talented professionals, an ethical culture, a fortress balance sheet and superior risk management. Yet, even these attributes were not sufficient to keep it independent during the era of bank consolidation.

A key consideration that weighed on both Preston and Weatherstone was their desire to preserve Morgan's heritage and culture. The bank's motto of "doing only first-class business, and that in a first class way" enunciated by J.P. Morgan, Jr., was not something to which the rank and file merely paid lip service. It guided them when they dealt with clients and also made them proud to be with the bank.

Morgan's culture, however, could be a hindrance at times. For example, because most officers began their careers at the bank, they only knew how to do things the Morgan way; consequently, they had difficulty assimilating people from outside and resisted new approaches that were necessary for Morgan to adapt to a rapidly changing financial landscape. Morgan was also predominantly a blue-blood organization in the 1970s and 1980s with few female or minority officers, although that would change over time.

When Preston and Weatherstone set out to build a securities capability, they were well aware of the conflicts between bankers and traders. They worried that by mixing the two, they could create a variant of Gresham's Law in which bad ethics drive good ethics away.[22] They hoped to minimize these risks by training internal hires and turning bankers into market-savvy advisors to corporations. Yet, the loyalty employees felt was eroded when bankers who

---

[21] Rice study, op. cit.

[22] Gresham's law is a monetary principle stating that "bad money drives out good" when there are two forms of money in circulation—for example, gold and silver.

could not make the transition to become financial advisers were either let go or encouraged to retire.

The spirit of teamwork also began to fade when differentials in compensation widened considerably, as bonuses were awarded in addition to base salary. As David Fisher, the first president of JP Morgan Securities, observed, teamwork was much easier to maintain when the pay differential for people in similar jobs was within $10,000 than when it became multiples of that figure. Strains between business units also increased over time, especially as profits lagged and there was pressure to produce better results.

It was not until Jamie Dimon came on board in mid-2004 that Morgan had a leader who could succeed in running a highly complex financial services conglomerate.[23] One of his crowning accomplishments is his ability to combine both wholesale and retail banking with investment banking, while also overseeing about 255,000 employees worldwide. Morgan is now the largest US bank and sixth largest in the world, and its balance sheet, earnings and share price are the envy of its peers (Fig. 22.2).

One of the keys to Dimon's success is his ability to combine a strategic vision of global finance with detailed knowledge of each of JPMorgan's six main business lines: They consist of investment banking, commercial banking, retail financial services, card services, asset and wealth management, and treasury and securities services. He is also adept at the so-called plumbing of banking that includes technology and operations, and he has a strong grasp of

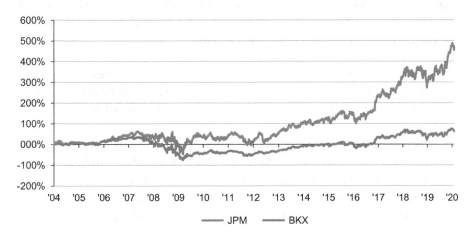

Fig. 22.2 Share price of JPM versus KBW NASDAQ Bank Index, cumulative return from 2004 to 2020. (Source: Bloomberg, Fort Washington)

---

[23] JPMorgan Chase now includes four former NYC money center banks (Morgan, Chase, Chemical and Manufacturers Hanover), Bank One, Bear Stearns and Washington Mutual.

management information systems to assess performance of individual business lines.

One former Morgan executive contends Dimon is the first Morgan leader who is both a business manager and keen observer of financial services. Another believes Dimon was well prepared to assume the helm of a complex financial organization having served a full apprenticeship under Sandy Weill: "He arrived with a full deck of cards in terms of the range of experiences; he saw good and bad leadership; he had strong natural skills and knows b.s. when he sees it; he stands on the shoulders of (Morgan) predecessors; and he arrived at the right time."[24]

When Dimon succeeded Bill Harrison as CEO in mid-2005, he spelled out his vision in the company's 2005 Annual Report.[25] He began by asking whether JPMorgan Chase was in the right businesses. He concluded it was well positioned in each of the areas, but he also noted they all competed in consolidating industries. Therefore, he was prepared to invest in technology and innovation to reap economies of scale in systems, operations, distribution, brand and R&D, among others. At the same time, Dimon stressed the need for the firm to become more efficient. He spelled out steps that would be taken to remedy the situation, including the need to improve accountability and decision making.

Dimon then went on to assess various risks the firm faced including commercial and wholesale credit risk, market and trading risk, interest rate and liquidity risk, reputation and legal risk, and operational and catastrophic risk. He observed the first three types of risk are cyclical, which requires the firm to be prepared for inevitable cycles, and he wrote:[26]

> A company that properly manages itself in bad times is often the winner. For us, sustaining our strength is a strategic imperative. If we are strong during tough times –when others are weak—then opportunities can be limitless.

This assessment would prove prescient when the collapse of Lehman Brothers sent shock waves throughout the global financial system in September of 2008. Leading up to the crisis, Dimon had maintained a "fortress balance" sheet, with Tier I capital at 8.5% and total capital at 12%. Beyond this, the bank had previously taken steps to lower risks including (1) limiting the

---

[24] Source withheld for confidentiality reasons.
[25] Letter from Jamie Dimon, JPMorgan Chase Annual Report 2005.
[26] Ibid., p. 9.

amount of low-prime and sub-prime credit it issued in credit card and other businesses and (2) not offering higher risk, less-tested loan products.[27] Consequently, while JPMorgan Chase sustained a loss in investment banking and took hits to earnings in retail and card services, it was much better positioned overall than other leading financial institutions.

JPMorgan Chase, in turn, benefitted as it attracted assets of individuals and corporations that sought a safe haven refuge. During 2008, its assets under management rose by more than $600 billion to $2.175 trillion, with the acquisitions of Bear Sterns and WAMU accounting for more than one half of the increase. Since 2008, customer and wholesale deposits rose by nearly 50% to stand at $1.5 trillion at the end of 2018, while assets under custody (which includes Assets Under Management (AUM) and custody, brokerage, administrative holdings and deposit accounts) rose by $10 trillion to $23.2 trillion as of end 2018. The bottom line is that Jamie Dimon deserves credit for the revival of JPMorgan as the world's pre-eminent financial institution.

One blemish on JPMorgan Chase's record is the $34.5 billion in violations it has paid since it was acquired in 2000.[28] Of this total, more than one half were inherited and relate to toxic security and mortgage abuses that originated with Bear Stearns and Washington Mutual. But the firm has also been involved in a series of high-profile trading violations relating to manipulation of foreign exchange, precious metals and energy as well as an ongoing investigation of alleged rigging of the European Interbank Offered Rate.[29] These infractions along with publicity over a $6 billion trading loss by the "London Whale" in 2012 concerned Morgan alums that the firm was not living up to its heritage.

Because of JPM's stellar performance throughout his tenure, Dimon has maintained the confidence of Morgan's board and its shareholders. However, the big unknown is how the firm will fare once he steps down as CEO. His successors will face the daunting challenge of managing a highly complex institution that is unrivaled in financial history. Moreover, new challenges lie ahead including the risk of cybersecurity, which Dimon has called the biggest threat in the financial services industry, as well as the rise of "fintech" that seeks to displace traditional banking models through the application of financial technology. The coronavirus pandemic is yet another example of unforseen shocks that affect the economy and financial instituions.

---

[27] Ibid.

[28] See Goods Jobs First, Violation Tracker.

[29] They relate to manipulation of the European Offered Rate and precious metals trading. Morgan also took a large loss in 2012 with a trader known as the London Whale.

Based on how Morgan has performed over the past fifteen years, my take is the underpinnings of the firm—talented management and people, fortress balance sheet and sophisticated risk management—are sound. They will likely keep it at or near the top of global financial institutions for years to come. This achievement would extend the legacy of J.P. Morgan, although the current institution is vastly different from the one he founded and was pre-eminent throughout the twentieth century.

Index[1]

---

[1] Note: Page numbers followed by 'n' refer to notes.

© The Author(s) 2020
N. P. Sargen, *JPMorgan's Fall and Revival*, https://doi.org/10.1007/978-3-030-47058-6

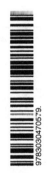